Personnel Policy
in the City

This volume is sponsored by the
OAKLAND PROJECT
University of California, Berkeley

Personnel Policy
in the City

The Politics of Jobs in Oakland

FRANK J. THOMPSON

UNIVERSITY OF CALIFORNIA PRESS
Berkeley • Los Angeles • London

University of California Press
Berkeley and Los Angeles, California
University of California Press, Ltd.
London, England
Copyright ©1975, by
The Regents of the University of California
First Paperback Edition, 1978
ISBN: 0-520-03509-7
Library of Congress Catalog Card Number: 74-79774

2 3 4 5 6 7 8 9 0

For
BENNA, SAM, *and* **ALIZA**

The Oakland Project

At a time when much is said but little is done about the university's relationship to urban problems, it may be useful for those who are looking for ways of relating the university to the city to take a brief look at the Oakland Project of the University of California, which combined policy analysis, service to city officials and community groups, action in implementing proposals, training of graduate students, teaching new undergraduate courses, and scholarly studies of urban politics. The "university" is an abstraction, and as such it exists only for direct educational functions, not for the purpose of doing work within cities. Yet there are faculty members and students who are willing to devote large portions of their time and energy to investigating urban problems and to making small contributions toward resolving them. Our cities, however, do not need an invasion of unskilled students and professors. There is no point in hurtling into the urban crisis unless one has some special talent to contribute. After all, there are many people in city government—and even more on street corners—who are less inept than untrained academics. University people must offer the cities the talent and resources which they need and which they could not get otherwise.

In 1956 a group of graduate students and faculty members

at the University of California at Berkeley became involved in a program of policy research and action in the neighboring city of Oakland. As members of the Oakland Project, they tried to meet some of the city's most pressing analytical needs and also to make suggestions that could be implemented.

Members of the project made substantial time commitments (usually about two years) to working in a particular Oakland city agency. Normal working time was two days a week, although special crisis situations in the city sometimes necessitated much larger blocks of time. Since project members worked with city officials and remained in the city to help implement the suggestions they made, they avoided the "hit-and-run" stigma that members of city agencies often attach to outsiders. By attempting first to deal with problems as city officials understand them, project members developed the necessary confidence to be asked to undertake studies with broader implications.

The Oakland Project became a point of communication for individuals and groups in the city of Oakland and throughout the University of California. Its focus expanded from a concentration on city budgeting to a wide range of substantive policies and questions of political process; for example, revenue, police, personnel, federal aid, education, libraries, and the institutionalization of policy analysis. The Project provided assistance to governmental (mayor, city manager, chief of police, head of civil service, superintendent of schools) and nongovernmental (community group) actors. In order to transmit the knowledge gained, Oakland Project members taught courses—open to both undergraduate and graduate students—dealing with urban problems and policies. The Project's scholarly objective is to improve policy analysis by providing new ways of understanding decisions and outcomes that affect cities. Its members have based numerous research essays on their experience in the city.

It is hoped that the books in this series will be another means of transmitting what they have learned to a wider audience.

AARON WILDAVSKY

Contents

x   *Contents*

Tables and Charts

Tables

Charts

Acknowledgments

Aaron Wildavsky hired me as a research assistant on the Oakland Project in the fall of 1968. Since then, he has been an energetic, insightful, persistent and, above all, patient critic of my work. His help has been priceless. Others also provided highly perceptive commentary. Bob Biller contributed the kind of creative thinking that seems to come naturally to him. William Muir's unfailing ability to ask questions which I could not answer undoubtedly saved me from many errors. Then, too, members of the Oakland Project helped. Bill Lunch, Jesse McCorry, Judith May, Arnold Meltsner, Jeff Pressman, Jay Starling, and David Wentworth offered useful suggestions, social support, and good humor. Professor Meltsner in particular gave me detailed criticism of initial chapters. Later in my work on this manuscript, George Goerl, Robert Golembiewski, Karen Johnson, William McClung, Robert Miewald, and Lloyd Musolf provided insightful comments. I am particularly indebted to Professor Johnson who went over the many pages with special care. Though he was not involved in my research efforts, I am grateful to Andrew McFarland who provided crucial assistance early in my graduate career.

Thanks must also go to Oakland officials, particularly Personnel Director James Newman and City Manager Jerome

Keithley, in whose offices I interned. My acquaintances in City Hall gave generously of their time and information. They taught me much.

Financially, grants from the National Aeronautics and Space Administration, the Urban Institute, and the National Science Foundation kept food on my table and the rent paid. The Public Personnel Association provided supplementary support during my final year in graduate school.

Finally, I want to thank my wife, Benna. Cataloguing her contribution would require a separate volume in itself.

All these people and institutions deserve credit for improving this work. Its present defects are, of course, my own doing.

1

The Lost World of Urban Personnel Policy

> Analysis of the sources from which power is derived
> and the limitations they impose is as much a dictate
> of prudent administration as sound budgeting proce-
> dure. The bankruptcy that comes from an unbal-
> anced power budget has consequences far more di-
> sastrous than the necessity of seeking a deficiency
> appropriation.
>
> Norton Long[1]

"Oakland police need help" read the sign brandished by the off-duty police officer. In July 1969 he and more than 150 other policemen picketed for higher fringe benefits in front of City Hall during the city council's regular Tuesday evening session.

Year after year the head of Oakland's building and housing department urgently requests more inspectors so that the city's codes can be enforced more thoroughly. Invariably the budget analyst denies him those additional posts.

In an open letter to the mayor and city council a minority leader from the East Oakland-Fruitvale Planning Council argues that Oakland's new museum should remain shut until its staff reflects the racial composition of the city's population.

In November 1970 Oakland's police chief fired a jailer on the grounds that he had severely beaten a prisoner. In January 1971, the Civil Service Commission reinstated him.

[1] Norton Long, "Power and Administration," *Bureaucratic Power in National Poli-tics,* ed. Francis Rourke (Boston: Little, Brown, 1965), p. 15.

Since all these events illustrate important aspects of personnel politics, they are not as disconnected as they may seem
at first glance. Almost everyone knows that city officials face
enormously complex problems—high taxes, poor housing, inadequate schools, crime, poverty, polluted air, and more. Many
realize that local officials feel impotent to comprehend and
control the forces that produce these complex and continuing
urban crises. Concern therefore arises that city governments
will fail to cope and that the legitimacy of local political
institutions will ebb. Studies of urban politics multiply and
proposals for rescuing cities abound. Some call for revenue
sharing, others for community control, and still others for
improved police technology. Clearly, problems of urban governance are no longer a "lost world' to social scientists.[2]

Yet substantial gaps in our understanding of urban politics
persist. One major area of neglect is the process by which
officials design and implement personnel policy.[3] Despite our
intense interest in urban government, we possess minimal
knowledge of such personnel processes as *manpower*—city hall's
method of establishing the number, type, and location of
occupational roles it will contain; *recruitment*—the finding and
screening of people to fill jobs; *incentives*—the providing of
rewards and resources to motivate and enable employees to
perform in certain ways; and *removal*—the displacing of employees from organizational roles. In short we know surprisingly
little about the politics of jobs.

This ignorance is lamentable because such politics markedly
influences how city governments allocate important benefits.
Personnel processes, for instance, help shape the quality, quantity, type, and regularity of city services. A manpower decision
to add 150 patrolmen to the police department while simultaneously slicing the library staff by one-third reveals much about
what government intends to do for citizens. Relationships
between city officials and employee leaders often determine
how well the departments will function. New Yorkers who saw

[2] Lawrence Herson, "The Lost World of Municipal Government," *American Political
Science Review* 51 (June 1957): 330-345.
[3] I define policy "as a hypothesis containing initial conditions and predicted consequences." See Jeffrey L. Pressman and Aaron B. Wildavsky, *Implementation (Berkeley:
University of California Press, 1973), p. xiv.*

a few mishandled firings precipitate the teachers' strike of 1968 could say much about the importance of undisrupted service.

The politics of jobs also influences the quality of government outputs. The precise relationship between employee competence and the excellence of an agency's service is hard to specify. Nonetheless, if administrators hire the adroit and weed out the inept, prospects improve that ghetto youth will experience rewarding recreation programs, that dangerous intersections will be appropriately marked, that criminals will face more obstacles, and that city services will generally improve.

Personnel decisions also dispense basic economic resources. As a result of such decisions, some get jobs and others do not; some earn more money to pay their bills than others. Moreover, with 70 percent of a city's budget often tied up in personnel, salary and manpower choices have implications for revenue policy. Many personnel choices siphon funds from the pocketbooks of city residents.

The politics of jobs also helps distribute self-esteem and status. Whether people are rich or poor, black or white they generally aspire to jobs which pay them enough to live comfortably. In our society, failure to find desirable employment tends to undermine self-esteem.[4] Daily hiring and firing judgments by city hall therefore make it easier for some to acquire and maintain self-respect than others. Other personnel decisions affect the status of individuals once they are hired. Salary decisions, for instance, not only permit bureaucrats to buy more amenities but often symbolize the employee's general prestige within the organization. Then too, the politics of jobs bestows special recognition or status on groups outside city hall. The percentage of city employees who are minority often indicates to members of the minority community just how much government cares about their problems.

The distribution of political power also stems in part from personnel decision making. Salaried employment in government is a kind of political participation which at times permits the job holder to exert substantial influence over policy out-

---

[4] See for example Leonard Goodwin, *Do The Poor Want To Work?* (Washington, D.C.: Brookings Institution, 1972) and Elliot Liebow, *Tally's Corner* (Boston: Little, Brown, 1967).

comes.[5] The job holder's capacity to shape the creation and implementation of policy increases with the number of personnel decisions he or she can control. The introduction of merit systems, for example, often boosts the power of city bureaucracies at the expense of political parties and elected officials. Where an agency employs large numbers of professionals and there is little interagency mobility among high department officials, the strength of city employees tends to increase further.[6] Professionals often use their expertise or reputations for it to escape control. Officials with long tenure frequently become committed to the agency's way of doing things; they also develop alliances which help them resist the wishes of elected officials. In some instances city bureaucracies gain so much autonomy within their areas of specialization that they resemble the political machines of old.[7]

Personnel choices are politically important. Administrators live with the politics of jobs day in and day out, aware that their success in other policy arenas often depends on their ability to cope with personnel issues. Frequently, such issues prove too tough to handle. A traffic engineer believes that traffic safety suffers because he cannot win new positions. A police chief wins new slots, but during economically prosperous times he cannot find recruits to fill them. A streets and engineering director believes that his department's performance is hurt because he cannot rid himself of inept employees. When city representatives sit at the bargaining table with employee leaders, they find themselves forced to pay more for the same old services. Such issues irritate local officials continually.

PERSONNEL POLICY AS A POLITICAL PROBLEM

Much current writing does not acknowledge the political nature of personnel processes. Writing in 1887, Woodrow Wilson helped establish the precedent for this view when he wrote:

[5] Bennett Harrison, "Ghetto Employment and the Model Cities Program." (Paper delivered at the American Political Science Association Convention, Washington, D.C., 1972.)

[6] See Fredrick Mosher, *Democracy and the Public Service*, (New York: Oxford University Press, 1968); Theodore Lowi, *At The Pleasure of the Mayor* (Glencoe, Ill.: Free Press, 1964); and Eugene B. McGregor, Jr., "Politics and the Career Mobility of Bureaucrats," *American Political Science Review* 68 (March 1974): 18-26.

[7] See Judith May, "Progressives and the Poor: An Analytic History of Oakland"

"Most important to be observed is the truth already so much insisted upon by our civil service reformers: namely, that administration lies outside the proper sphere of politics. Administrative questions are not political questions."[8] Wilson's view flavors much of the contemporary personnel literature. One student of personnel administration notes, for example, that the "working instruments of democratic politics as practiced today in the West are political parties." In his view administration becomes political primarily when party activists or elected officials influence decision making.[9] Another author discusses how "politics" presently poses less threat to merit practices than it did in the past. Throughout he assumes a dichotomy between political behavior and that found within true merit systems. That there is a politics of merit systems, apart from whether elected officials intervene, escapes notice.[10] Then too, a book aimed at helping officials manage the urban crisis features an article which suggests various techniques for selecting applicants and evaluating recruitment procedures.[11] The political aspect of the problem receives virtually no attention, however. Are any of the suggested options politically feasible? What are their implications for broader political values? Answers do not emerge.

Personnel decision making is too important to leave to those who view it as a technical problem.[12] The fact that personnel directors rather than ward bosses are often the pivotal players in the personnel game should not distract us from its political character.[13] Those who recruit, fire, allocate positions, and so

---

(unpublished paper, University of California, Berkeley, 1970), p. 61; and Theodore Lowi, "Forward," in Harold F. Gosnell, *Machine Politics: Chicago Model* (Chicago: University of Chicago Press, 1968), p. x.

[8] Woodrow Wilson, "The Study of Administration," *Political Science Quarterly* 56 (December 1941): 494.

[9] O. Glenn Stahl, *Public Personnel Administration* (New York: Harper and Row, 1962), pp. 362, 420. He notes that pressure plays by elected politicians have made it difficult for the bipartisan civil service commission to rid personnel administration of politics.

[10] Roger W. Jones, "The Merit System, Politics, and Political Maturity," *Public Personnel Review* 25 (January 1964): 28-34.

[11] Alan R. Bass, "Personnel Selection and Evaluation," *Management of the Urban Crisis: Government and the Behavioral Sciences*, ed., Stanley E. Seashore and Robert J. McNeill (New York: Free Press, 1971), pp. 299-341.

[12] A technical problem is one involving minute detail of little significance for broader values.

[13] See, for example, Dwight Waldo, *The Administrative State* (New York: Ronald

on may be bureaucrats but they are not simple cogs in the machine. Often they have significant leeway to choose among various courses of action. Officials sense that they must plot and mobilize power resources if they are to advance their ends. Among the resources that players may use to get their way are: *economic goods and services* (including money);[14] *legal authority*[15] which is the formal right to exercise an option (for example, as defined by an administrative code or the laws of society); *status*, which is having prestige as a result of some attribute; *the means of violence,* which is the capacity to damage human life and property in a direct, physical sense; *time,* which is the number of hours or days that an actor can spend on an issue without paying what he believes are prohibitive opportunity costs (the foregone benefits which result from engaging in one activity rather than another); *information,* which in more synthesized form becomes knowledge and expertise.

Information is particularly important to a decision maker. Without quality information about available alternatives and the consequences of using them, an actor has difficulty promot-

---

Press, 1948), pp. 120-129; and Michael M. Harmon, "Normative Theory and Public Administration: Some Suggestions for A Redefinition of Administrative Responsibility," *Toward A New Public Administration,* ed. Frank Marini (Scranton, Pa.: Chandler, 1971), p. 174. In the area of personnel administration, Robert D. Miewald, "Political Science and Public Personnel Administration," *Public Personnel Review* 30 (July 1969): 179, has made the same point. See also Robert D. Miewald, "On Teaching Public Personnel Administration: A Weberian Perspective," *Western Political Quarterly* 36 (March 1973): 97-108.

[14] I draw heavily on the typology presented by Warren F. Ilchman and Norman Thomas Uphoff, *The Political Economy of Change* (Berkeley: University of California Press, 1969), pp. 58-86.

[15] This definition of authority departs from that of other organization theorists. For example, Herbert Simon, *Administrative Behavior* (New York: Free Press, 1957), p. 125, affirms that authority "is a relationship between two individuals, one superior, the other subordinate. The superior frames and transmits decisions with the expectation that they will be accepted by the subordinate. The subordinate expects such decisions, and his conduct is determined by them. The relationship of authority can be defined, therefore, in purely objective and behavioristic terms. It involves behavior on the part of both superior and subordinate. When, and only when, these behaviors occur does a relation of authority exist between the two persons involved."

For my purposes formal authority exists whether subordinates obey orders or not. It is not causation, but a resource which may or may not be effective in molding behavior. The counter resource of a subordinate when confronted with an authoritative order is the ability to withhold legitimacy. Knowing who possesses what formal rights is not, of course, a description of an organizational power structure, but may explain part of the actual power configuration.

ing his ends. Problems increase further if the decision maker has few scorecards to orient him. A scorecard is a device which expresses in abbreviated and generally quantitative form how well an individual or group is performing;[16] in essence scorecards tell actors whether they are winning or losing in a given issue arena. In the private sector, for instance, documents containing profit margin information serve as scorecards. Without such indicators players cannot readily assess the precise payoffs of their tactics; adjusting behavior to foster greater attainment of objectives becomes more complex.

The information and other resources which actors possess, along with the objectives they hold, shape tactical behavior.[17] Since where one stands depends on where one sits, individuals who toil in different parts of the organization tend to develop different values and priorities. They want different things in different orders. Conflicts often erupt; bargaining ensues. Some exert more leverage over personnel outcomes than others.[18] Personnel processes do, then, feature many of the usual ingredients of politics.

A systematic study of the politics of jobs is overdue. A few studies have launched explorations in this direction. Raymond Horton's analysis of labor relations in New York during the Wagner and Lindsay years gives us a feel for the tactical maneuvering that occurs, as does Jay Shafritz's treatment of employee efforts to be upgraded in Philadelphia.[19] Case analyses

[16] For discussions of keeping score, see Herbert Simon, George Kozmetsky, Harold Guetzkow, and Gordon Tyndall, "Management Uses of Figures," *Public Budgeting and Finance,* ed. Robert T. Golembiewski (Itasca, Ill.: F. E. Peacock, 1968), pp. 15-23; and James D. Thompson, *Organizations in Action* (New York: McGraw Hill, 1967), pp. 83-98.

[17] Richard Cyert and James G. March, *A Behavioral Theory of the Firm* (Englewood Cliffs, N.J.: Prentice Hall, 1963); Aaron Wildavsky, *The Politics of the Budgetary Process* (Boston: Little, Brown, 1964); David Braybrooke and Charles Lindblom, *A Strategy of Decision* (New York: Free Press, 1970); Simon, *Administrative Behavior.* All these works discuss the ways in which decision makers cope with uncertainty.

[18] I define leverage as existing when one actor causes another to behave as the latter would not otherwise do. See also Kenneth J. Gergen, "Assessing the Leverage Points in the Process of Policy Formation," *The Study of Policy Formation,* ed. Raymond A. Bauer and Kenneth J. Gergen (New York: Free Press, 1968), p. 181.

[19] Raymond D. Horton, *Municipal Labor Relations in New York City: Lessons of the Lindsay-Wagner Years* (New York: Praeger Publishers, 1973); Jay M. Shafritz, *Position Classification: A Behavioral Analysis for the Public Service* (New York: Praeger Publishers, 1973); see also portions of Wallace S. Sayre and Herbert Kaufman, *Governing New York City* (New York: W. W. Norton, 1965).

of unusual series of events in various organizations also provide insight.[20] Yet on the whole the politics of jobs in urban bureaucracies remains a lost world to urban scholars. Existing studies do not describe and compare how city officials grapple with different kinds of personnel issues.

Greater insight into the politics of jobs will not only enhance our understanding of why local governments behave as they do, it should also sharpen our capacity to analyze policy proposals. In its rush to offer advice or make moral pronouncements, much of the personnel literature does little to describe and explain behavior; moreover it shies away from acknowledging that bureaucratic politics is an integral part of the personnel process.[21] Consequently, those who prescribe change frequently misjudge the impact of their proposals on the administrative systems they seek to improve and offer suggestions which officials find unattractive. Often they ignore the implications of their proposals for broader political values. In chapter 8, I will analyze these difficulties in greater depth.

OAKLAND AS A LABORATORY

City Hall in Oakland, California, provides a useful vehicle for analyzing personnel processes. During 1969 and 1970, I did

[20] Certain case studies do capture some of the flavor of personnel politics in the cities. Such studies, however, seldom use social science concepts to interpret data and are reluctant to suggest more general conclusions. Moreover, such studies generally deal with one unusual series of events in one organization rather than policy formation as it regularly emerges. See, for example, Frank Sherwood, *A City Manager Tries to Fire his Police Chief* (Indianapolis: Bobbs-Merrill, 1963); Frank C. Abbot, "The Cambridge City Manager," *Public Administration and Policy Development: A Case Book*, ed. Harold Stein (New York: Harcourt, Brace, 1952), pp. 580-617; Frank B. Sherwood and Beatrice Markey, *The Mayor and the Fire Chief: The Fight Over Integrating the Los Angeles Fire Department* (Birmingham: University of Alabama Press, 1959).

[21] Consider, for instance, how Stahl, *Public Personnel Administration*, pp. 146-167, treats the subject of position classification. The chapter begins with a discussion of duties and rank classification systems which different governments presumably use and presents what is "ideally" done in putting positions in a class. Finally, it briefly assesses proposals for adopting a rank system in the United States. There are, however, no answers to the following questions: Who cares about classification and why? How do they calculate and plot tactics? Who ends up controlling classification decisions? Nor is there much effort to assess precisely who benefits from "sound classification." For other examples, see almost any issue of the *Public Personnel Review* (more recently, *Public Personnel Management*).

part-time staff work for Oakland's personnel director and city manager. Simultaneously, I employed a standard array of participant observer methods to gather information for this book.[22] This research strategy gave me access to information which otherwise would have been difficult to obtain. From the start my purpose was exploratory. Knowledge about the politics of jobs was so minimal that hypothesis testing seemed premature. Instead, an effort to generate some concepts and propositions through an in-depth study of the personnel process seemed more appropriate.[23]

Given the research method employed and the focus on one city, this volume will not produce a proven theory of personnel politics. It will, however, contain some elements of a theory and serve as a step toward generalization. In this regard, it is important to emphasize that Oakland is not an unusual city. Its problems are the stuff of America's urban crisis—high unemployment, revenue shortages, poverty, racial tensions. Oakland's formal political arrangements moreover are common for a city its size. In many respects, then, the city is an all-American one.

Among Oakland's attributes, two are particularly important for understanding the politics of jobs: its substantial disadvantaged minority population and its reformed political institutions.

Race. Blacks, Chicanos, and Orientals comprise a substantial and rising percentage of Oakland's citizens. As Table 1 reveals, the city's population dropped by about 6 percent from 1960 to 1970 while its nonwhite component rose by well over 150

[22] I accumulated data through day-to-day observation, open-ended interviews, innumerable casual conversations with employees, perusal of documents, and careful scrutiny of the *Oakland Tribune* and the *Montclarion*.

[23] I am, of course, aware of the limits to the generalizations which case studies can produce. I would prefer to reside in the never-never land of social science where intimate knowledge of personnel politics in dozens of cities would be at my fingertips. But a researcher's resources have limits and acquiring information is costly. Furthermore, there is precedent for using one case to explore more general questions. Authors who have used this method to good advantage include: Jerome H. Skolnick, *Justice Without Trial* (New York: John Wiley, 1967); Alvin W. Gouldner, *Patterns of Industrial Bureaucracy* (New York: Free Press, 1954); and Alan Altshuler, *The City Planning Process: A Political Analysis* (Ithaca, N.Y.: Cornell University Press, 1970). Others have seen the utility of the case method. See, for instance, Arend Lijphart, "Comparative Politics and the Comparative Method," *American Political Science Review* 65 (September 1971): 691; Barney G. Glaser and Anselm Strauss, *The Discovery of Grounded Theory* (Chicago: Aldine, 1967).

percent. If the Census Bureau had classified Spanish surnames as nonwhite, the 1970 data would show that a majority of Oakland's residents are in minority groups.

TABLE 1: The Nonwhite Percentage of Oakland's Population Has Increased

Year	Total population	Percentage decline or increase	Nonwhite population	Percentage increase	Nonwhite as percentage of total population
1940	302,163	—	14,227	—	4.7
1950	384,575	+27.3	55,778	+292.1	14.5
1960	367,548	−4.4	97,025	+73.9	26.4
1970	361,561	−1.6	148,049	+52.6	41.0

Source: U.S. Census.

In terms of the proportion of its residents who are minority, Oakland ranks high among American cities. Of the roughly forty cities with over 250,000 population, only nine (Washington, Honolulu, Newark, Atlanta, Baltimore, New Orleans, Detroit, Birmingham, and St. Louis) had a higher percentage of nonwhite population than Oakland did in 1970. Limiting our attention (see Table 2) to places more nearly Oakland's size (those with a population of between 250,000 and 500,000), the city ranks fifth in percentage of nonwhite population.

TABLE 2: U.S. Cities of Between 250,000 and 500,000 with at least 20 Percent Nonwhite Population, 1970

City	Population	Percentage nonwhite
Honolulu, Hawaii	325,000	66.1
Newark, New Jersey	382,000	56.0
Atlanta, Georgia	497,000	51.6
Birmingham, Alabama	301,000	42.2
OAKLAND, CALIFORNIA	362,000	40.9
Norfolk, Virginia	308,000	30.2
Cincinnati, Ohio	452,000	28.1
Louisville, Kentucky	361,000	24.1
Miami, Florida	335,000	23.4
Jersey City, New Jersey	261,000	22.2
Buffalo, New York	463,000	21.3
Fort Worth, Texas	393,000	20.6
Tampa, Florida	278,000	20.0

Source: U.S. Department of Commerce, 1971.

Minorities not only comprise a key segment of Oakland's population; they also receive less of the good things in life.

The city's unemployment rate is generally twice that prevalent in the rest of the nation, with blacks and Chicanos being particularly hard hit.[24] Minorities have also had less formal schooling. While whites had a median education of 12.4 years, black and Spanish surnames had median marks of 11.0 and 9.9 respectively.[25] Though the number of minorities with a high-school diploma is rising, what they are learning is another matter. At three high schools with more than 70 percent minority student enrollment, for instance, roughly two-thirds of the students read at levels below the national norm.[26] Nor do minorities have housing comparable to that of whites. "A higher proportion of all black families, regardless of income, were inadequately housed when compared to white families in the same income and family-size categories."[27] Deprivations such as these have given impetus to complaints by various minority spokesmen. Convinced that city hall has done little to improve the plight of minorities, they have attacked recruitment and removal procedures.

Oakland features reformed government. In addition to racial unrest, Oakland features reformed political institutions. Urbanists generally define such institutions as including a city-manager form of government, nonpartisan elections where candidates run at-large, and broad civil service coverage of city employees.[28] Oakland has all these attributes. Reformed institutions are not unusual for cities Oakland's size. The council-manager form of government prevails in almost half the cities with populations of between 250,00 and 500,000.[29]

If Oakland's form of government is far from atypical, neither are the services it provides. (For an organization chart, see Appendix.) The bureaucracy devotes half its labor force to what we can loosely term public safety (such as police and fire protection, building and housing inspection), roughly one-fifth

[24] U.S. Department of Commerce, *Pocket Data Book, USA, 1971* (Washington, D.C.: U.S. Government Printing Office, 1971), pp. 48-49.
[25] Oakland, City Planning Department, *Options for Oakland*, 1969, p. 7.
[26] I am indebted to Jesse McCorry for these data.
[27] Oakland, City Planning Department, *Options*, p. 7.
[28] Bret W. Hawkins, *Politics and Urban Policies* (Indianapolis: Bobbs-Merrill, 1971) p. 19.
[29] Jeffrey L. Pressman "Preconditions of Mayoral Leadership," *American Political Science Review* 66 (June 1972): 515-516.

to culture and recreation, another sixth to various internal control and support functions (for example, budgetary review, building upkeep, purchasing, recruitment of personnel, and so on), and about one-eighth to street maintenance and repair (see Table 3). City hall does not run the educational or welfare systems. An independent district handles the former while Alameda county operates the latter.

TABLE 3: City Hall Devotes the Most Man-Years to Public Safety, Fiscal Year 1971/72

Department	Main functions	Number of man-years	Percentage of all man-years
Public Safety Units			
Police	Law enforcement, order maintenance	1014.3	28.1
Fire	Fire prevention and suppression	675.0	18.7
Building and Housing	Inspection of physical structures, and enforcement of codes	83.1	2.3
Culture and Recreation			
Parks and Recreation	Management of recreation programs and supervision of park areas	459.7	12.7
Library	Storage and lending of reading materials	189.0	5.2
Museum	Arrangement of historical, scientific, and artistic exhibits	88.6	2.5
Internal Control and Support			
General Services	Maintenance of electrical equipment, smaller purchases of supplies and equipment, care of city vehicles, provision of custodial services	375.3	10.4
Finance	Research and budget analysis, accounting, control of the electronic data processing facility	119.0	3.3

TABLE 3—*Continued*

Department	Main functions	Number of man-years	Percentage of all man-years
Civil Service	Search and selection; maintenance employee files; handling of employee complaints; classification studies	18.5	.5
City Attorney	Legal advice	18.0	.5
Other staff and clerical help	Auditing, record keeping	39.9	1.1
Street Maintenance and Repair			
Public Works	Sewer and street maintenance and construction, traffic engineering, appraisal and acquisition of needed property, architectural services	491.2	13.6
Other			
City Planning	Administration of zoning ordinance, short-term studies dealing with land use, development review, and updating of general plan	23.3	.6
Mayor-Council	Authorization of formal policies	14.0	.4
Associated Agencies	Stimulation and enhancement of interagency communication on problems of juvenile delinquency and antisocial behavior	2.0	.1

Source: Oakland Finance Office.

Formal institutional arrangements do, of course, allocate power resources and shape patterns of participation and leverage. In general, reformed institutions shift the center of personnel decision making to the bureaucracy. Reformed government strips power resources from elected officials and emphasizes that professionally trained experts should conduct much of government's business.

City employees are the main participants. Oakland's mayor and eight councilmen suffer from political poverty in the personnel arena. With the former receiving $7500 yearly and the latter about half of that each, all must rely on outside occupations for a basic livelihood. Naturally they devote little attention to city affairs, let alone to personnel questions. By and large, elected officials view personnel issues as insignificant relative to other matters.[30] As a result their knowledge of these activities is quite limited.

Even if they were keenly interested in the area, their lack of formal authority would inhibit initiative. To be sure, the council can legally set compensation rates, establish departments and positions, and layoff (not fire) employees. But in other personnel areas the charter draws a firm distinction between matters of administration and policy. It makes clear that the "Mayor shall have no administrative authority," and makes it a misdemeanor for him or the council to "take part in the appointment or removal of officers or employees in the administrative service of the city."[31]

The city manager and the department heads (whom he appoints) hold some rights at the expense of the council since they are the key proprietors of the so-called administrative sphere. The manager formally advises the council on how many men the city needs, how they should be allocated among departments, and what wage and fringe benefit settlements they should receive.

The manager, along with his leading agency officials, also has the authority to appoint and remove employees; but the large number of classified positions in the bureaucracy restricts these prerogatives. For classified slots, the Civil Service Commission holds formal authority over the initial screening of job applicants and can veto a decision to fire, demote, or transfer.

[30] Data from Heinz Eulau and Robert Eyestone, "Policy Maps of City Councils and Policy Outcomes: A Developmental Analysis," *American Political Science Review* 62 (March 1968): 137, point to the low salience of such issues for Bay Area councilmen generally.

[31] Oakland, *Oakland City Charter*, Article II, Sections 219 and 221.

Since nearly all Oakland's 3400 full-time positions are classified, the commission possesses a formidable power resource.[32]

The Civil Service Commission is not, however, as powerful as its supply of formal authority would indicate. This stems from the commission's limited expertise. Meeting four Tuesdays per month for two hours, Oakland's five commissioners do not know the intricacies of city hall administration.[33] Furthermore, they are unlikely to acquire adequate information through extended seniority. From 1961 to 1971 half of the members gave up commission posts before their terms expired, although they had each been appointed for six years. As of June 1971 the average tenure of each commissioner was roughly two and one-half years, with individual experience ranging from seven and one-third years to less than one month.

Nor are the private occupational backgrounds of board members especially likely to yield insights into city hall personnel processes. Of the fifteen commissioners who served during the period from 1960 to 1971, just under three-fourths were businessmen or lawyers. These vocations could potentially provide board members with information useful in making personnel decisions. On the whole, however, city hall procedures (such as the written testing program) are sufficiently unique to minimize a knowledge transfer from a private occupational role to that of commissioner.

The board's lack of expertise makes it dependent on the personnel director and employee leaders for information. The former, whom the commission appoints to head a staff of seventeen, serves as its chief adviser. He acts as master interpreter of the more than 40-page *Laws and Rules of The Civil Service Board* and is an expert on professional personnel trends. More than any other single actor, he is aware of what the board has done, what it legally can do, and what other jurisdictions are attempting. While the director's knowledge does not

---

[32] The picture changes only slightly if we consider part-time roles which, under civil service rules, are exempt. In fiscal 1970/71, the city used only 227 part-time man-years. Adding these to the number of full-time exempt slots, over 93 percent of all man-years are still classified.

[33] The mayor appoints commissioners.

invariably permit him to get his way, it gives him significant leverage over many commission choices.

The civil service office is not the only unit limiting the discretion of the council, manager, and agency heads. The rank-and-file employees (operationalized as those at least two steps down the chain of command from the department head) also possess resources. Of particular importance are the employee unions and associations which many bureaucrats have joined. Buttressed by a 1968 California state law which requires local officials to meet and confer in good faith, these groups are beginning to have considerable impact on personnel decisions. Well over three-fourths of all city employees belong to some union or association.

City employees within the bureaucracy are, then, the main personnel players in Oakland's reformed political setting. This is not to say that outside groups or events have no impact. For, as will become apparent, the national and state government, professional associations, job hunters, the electorate, educational institutions, the media, and local interest groups (particularly minority spokesmen) markedly affect the politics of jobs. Nonetheless, those who most consistently and consciously participate are within the bureaucracy's ranks.

How, then, do individuals and groups play the personnel game? What uncertainties do they face when they choose among options? What tactics emerge? Do dispersed or concentrated leverage patterns result? What impact do these patterns have on decision making? An examination and comparison of manpower, pay, recruitment, and removal arenas in Oakland will provide insights.[34]

These insights should in turn enlighten debate over how to improve civil service systems. Although long sheltered by merit symbols, personnel practices and the behavior of urban bureaucracies have come under increasing fire.[35] Two observers of New York's personnel system have charged for example, that it

[34] My research resources do not permit a more extensive probing of the incentives arena beyond the issue of pay and fringe benefits.

[35] See Alan Altshuler, *Community Control: The Black Demand for Participation in Large American Cities* (New York: Pegasus, 1970), pp. 151-173, 191; Susan S. Fainstein and Norman I. Fainstein, "Innovation in Urban Bureaucracies: Clients and Change," *American Behavioral Scientist* 15 (March/April, 1972): 511-532.

"prohibits good management, frustrates able employees, inhibits productivity, lacks the confidence of the city's taxpayers and fails to respond to the needs of citizens." They suggest that this situation is far from uncommon and that new personnel policies are essential.[36] Cures can be as bad as diseases, however. Misguided proposals for change are particularly likely if concern with what should be leads us to neglect what is.

[36] E. S. Savas and Sigmund S. Ginsburg, "The Civil Service—A Meritless System?" *The Public Interest* 32 (Summer 1973): 70-85.

2

The Politics of Manpower: The Manager Triumphant

> Organizational arrangements are not neutral. We do not organize in a vacuum. Organization is one way of expressing ... commitment, influencing program direction, and ordering priorities. Organizational arrangements tend to give some interests, some perspectives, more access to those with decision-making authority. ...
>
> Harold Seidman[1]

Officials in cities sporadically make choices that shape the formal role structures of local governments. They at least implicitly decide how to group certain sets of duties into positions (that is, promulgate a division of labor); they choose how many of the different kinds of positions the organization needs; and they determine where to situate work roles in the hierarchy of authority and among various departments. By so doing, officials influence the level of service the bureaucracy provides in different functional areas, the financial cost of local government, the level of work alienation among employees, the recruitment problems city officials confront, and so forth.

In appraising manpower decision making in Oakland, this chapter will focus first on the politics of numbers (for example,

[1] Harold Seidman, *Politics, Position and Power: The Dynamics of Federal Organization* (New York: Oxford University Press, 1970), p. 14.

choices concerning how many firefighter slots to fund). Budgetary and job classification processes will consequently receive considerable attention. Then I will analyze the factors that facilitate or impede position transfers among departments. As will become apparent, the manpower arena is the city manager's main personnel success story.

THE POLITICS OF MANPOWER NUMBERS

To an outsider, decisions on whether to add or delete certain types of jobs may seem complex. Who can be sure of the political, economic, and social costs and benefits of adding more patrolmen instead of recreation or museum personnel? Who can specify precisely the relationship between the number of people in different occupational roles and organizational effectiveness? While queries like these might trouble some, Oakland officials are generally little disturbed by them.

Consider the city manager, who, more than any other actor shapes personnel outlays. For Oakland's city manager, success in the manpower arena is comprehensible in terms of its implications for revenue policies. Reinforced by the attitudes of the mayor (a Republican in a formally nonpartisan role) and council, the manager considers the tax rate to be the crucial overall indicator of his performance. Since taking office in 1966, he has struggled to minimize the need for additional revenue, while whittling down the politically hot property tax. The manager has had some success in accomplishing the latter objective. During the period from 1966 to 1971, the property tax rate declined from $3.17 per $100 assessed valuation to $2.80, a 13 percent decline.[2] The search for money is, however, unending and the sense of fiscal crisis persists.

Given his revenue aspirations the manager naturally casts a jaundiced eye on any request which will further drain the city treasury. For him the basic concern is not whether a proposal will enhance organizational efficiency. Expanded out-

---

[2] During the same period, assessed valuation of property rose from $712,358,017 to $961,152,669, an increase of about 35 percent. Oakland, *City of Oakland Preliminary Budget*, 1971/72, p. A-10.

put at a lesser increment of increased cost is not the object. Rather, the point is to promote cost reduction efficiency, or on occasion simply to economize regardless of the impact on efficiency. The fact that fiscal inputs are relatively easy to measure compared to service outputs encourages this orientation. For as Anthony Downs has noted in another context, high certainty concerning costs and substantial ignorance concerning benefits often leads officials to undervalue the latter.[3] A city manager like Oakland's is all the more unlikely to seek efficiency through greater spending if there are no good productivity scorecards which tell him precisely what he is getting for spending more.

In his unrelenting war against greater costs, the manager believes that it is particularly important to resist work-force expansion. Personnel expenditures comprise more than 70 percent of Oakland's budget, in fiscal 1969/70, the city budgeted more than $45 million for employees. Furthermore, such expenses constantly threaten to mushroom. Once hired, a subordinate costs more each year. In part this is because the subordinate receives an annual step increase until he has been in the same position for five years. But it also stems from the pay and fringe benefit boosts employee leaders are constantly able to win.

Adding to the manager's problem is the "once hired, never fired" norm which pervades the organization. Civil service rules protect the tenure rights of employees after a probationary period; building the case necessary for firing consumes much time and energy. While the council and city manager have the authority to lay off employees (unlike firing, this means removing personnel for reasons other than poor performance) they are reluctant to use this resource. Concerned with showing fidelity to city bureaucrats and wishing to avoid conflict with employee organizations, council members and the manager prefer to eliminate slots only through attrition.

Even this kind of position surgery is difficult, as the experience of the Manpower Control Committee testifies. Created by the manager, this committee (consisting of the personnel director, finance director, and assistant to the city manager)

[3] Anthony Downs, "Why the Government Budget Is Too Small in a Democracy," *World Politics* 12 (June 1960): 541-563.

meets every Friday to decide whether to eliminate or refill vacant slots. While this body may raise questions and suggest careful review during the next budgetary cycle, it seldom weeds out a position. Committee members believe that they lack the data needed for sound judgment, and that they do not have the time or staff necessary to find out whether excessive manpower slack exists.[4] Another inhibiting factor is their awareness that constant challenges to department heads, particularly where the committee has flimsy evidence, might raise antagonisms. The city manager, then, faces difficulties in reducing the size of city hall's work force.

By contrast, the manager finds it much easier to prevent increases in man-years. In this regard the main threat to his cost-cutting goals arises during the budgetary process. By and large, Oakland's departments lend credence to the claims of Parkinson[5] and Downs that "all organizations have an inherent tendency to expand."[6] Attuned to professional norms and committed to better service, agency heads request more manpower year after year. In 1970, for example, 71 percent of Oakland's fourteen major departments sought additional personnel, 14 percent held the line asking for neither more nor less, and 14 percent requested fewer slots than the previous year. For most of these agency heads, the more slots attained out of those sought the greater the sense of having achieved success in this arena. (As will become clearer later, those who failed to ask for more men did so for broader strategic reasons, not because they had no aspirations to expand.)

Agency heads, then, periodically articulate manpower demands that threaten to push personnel costs upward. How does the manager respond to their challenge?

THE MANAGER'S BUDGET TACTICS[7]

In struggling to minimize position increases, the city manager relies on the finance office. Agency requests for support arrive

---

[4] The manager is not, of course, interested in perpetuating such slack as a hedge against uncertainty since it costs him money to do so.

[5] C. Northcoate Parkinson, *Parkinson's Law* (New York: Ballantine Books, 1964).

[6] Anthony Downs, *Inside Bureaucracy* (Boston: Little, Brown, 1967), p. 17.

[7] For an overview of Oakland's budgetary process, see Arnold J. Meltsner and Aaron Wildavsky, "Leave City Budgeting Alone! A Survey, Case History and Recommendation for Reform." (Unpublished draft, University of California, Berkeley, 1969).

in this office in January and February. Analysts then spend two to three months analyzing the department requests. To reduce decision uncertainty about manpower and other budgetary matters, the analysts will often visit the agencies and talk with officials there; but there are limits to the amount of information that can be accumulated in this and other ways. Time is short. Moreover all five analysts in 1970 had been with the office less than two years. Thus, they could not fall back on expertise born of seniority.

Standard decision rules help analysts cope with uncertainty. Although lacking knowledge concerning the precise consequences of their decisions, analysts make choices expeditiously through the use of orientation, trade-off, and slash rules. Orientation rules give initial cues as to how to approach the budget request; trade-off rules dictate that the analyst give up something in return for eliminating positions; slash rules lead the analyst to cut positions from requests without giving much in return. Chart 1 lists some manifestations of these types. The most basic of these rules is one which the manager repeatedly emphasizes: cut all requests for additional personnel. On occasion, analysts make exceptions to this norm, but overall it is the major factor molding their choices.

Once the analysts have made their recommendations, the finance director and the city manager may modify manpower outcomes slightly. By and large, however, the initial judgments of the analysts remain unchanged. This in large part reflects their adoption of some of the manager's values. The decision rules they use are those that the chief executive encourages.

Although the city council possesses ultimate authority over personnel expenditures, the body seldom challenges the city manager's recommendations.[8] The manager's expertise and prestige as a cost cutter give him considerable leverage over the budget's contents. The budget format (in use up to 1971) also helps him. Under this system, the council never learns what each department requests. Consequently, the city manager's recommendation comes across as representing a kind of unanimous bureaucratic decision, even though it is nothing of the sort.[9]

[8] Ibid., pp. 50-52.
[9] On the importance of unanimity, see Charles R. Adrian and Charles Press, "Decision

Orientation Rules—give initial cues as to how to approach the budget request.

1. Carefully scrutinize and cut low-status departments.
2. Disregard work-load data (analysts believe they are inflated and inaccurate and often have little significance because there are no good norms which establish proper workloads or manpower distributions).
3. Look for reference points and compare (e.g., the analyst reviewing the library knew that it had more book-binder positions than the Los Angeles library even though the latter was much larger).

Exchange or Trade-Off Rules—dictate that the analyst give up something in return for eliminating positions.

4. Trade position for position in a way that will cut costs.
5. Exchange positions for overtime allocations and vice versa.
6. Exchange positions for a promise that the slot will fund itself.
7. Cut positions and give machines in return.*
8. Get rid of positions for monetary contracts with private firms (e.g., hire a private firm to pick up garbage rather than having city employees do it).
9. Exchange a position at present for a departmental commitment to eliminate it later.

Slash Rules—lead the analyst to cut positions from requests without giving much in return.

10. Cut requests for new personnel.
11. Cut a little deeper than you actually feel is justified.
12. Eliminate vacant positions (the analyst reasons that if a department has been unable to fill a budgeted position throughout the previous fiscal year and has performed satisfactorily, this is an indicator that the department can get along without the slot).

Source: Oakland Finance Office

* See Judith May, "Budgeting in the Street and Engineering Department" (unpublished paper, University of California, Berkeley, 1968).

Of course, the council's basic commitment to holding the line on taxes does establish an expectation which the manager must meet. This, however, creates little tension for the city manager because he shares the council's value orientation. It is doubtful that the manager's choices would be much different if he suddenly had final authority over personnel allocations.

EXPANSIONARY BUDGET TACTICS

Year after year, then, the manager plays Scrooge with personnel. How do agency heads respond to an executive so stingy

Costs in Coalition Formation," *American Political Science Review* 62 (June 1968): 559; and Richard F. Fenno, *The Power of the Purse: Appropriations Politics in Congress* (Boston: Little Brown, 1966).

with man-years? The answer is mainly by asking for more personnel. In doing so, department heads tend to argue that work is increasing, that they have assumed new functions, or that manpower expansion will not cost more money.

We can't keep up with the load. The most typical department tactic is to contend that continued satisfactory performance of present duties necessitates adding personnel. One reason why agency heads keep work-load statistics is to make this expansionist argument more convincing. In their budget requests, agency officials will generally emphasize the statistics that most graphically illustrate a heavier work load. In 1967, for instance, the personnel director noted in his request that the number of positions in city hall had increased and that turnover would rise from 5 to 15 percent in the next two years. According to the director these increases meant that his staff would have to do more recruiting for line agencies; to keep up with the demand he would need three additional employees.

The finance office's response to the director's request suggests the common futility of claiming that work is increasing. In the year the director made this argument, the finance office not only rejected the plea for three new personnel staffers but cut one of the civil service office's regular employees as well. In general, budget analysts are suspicious of work-load data. They have little faith that agency statistics are accurate. Moreover, in the absence of clear norms concerning the amount of work an employee can do, analysts remain skeptical that such statistics demonstrate a need for more manpower.

We are doing something new. Another agency gambit is to claim that new responsibilities necessitate more manpower. Since Oakland City Hall seldom takes on new tasks, department heads rarely have the opportunity to use this tactic. If an agency does acquire a new function, however, officials will generally use the addition to justify a request for more slots. In making this kind of justification it helps the agency if the new function directly contributes to salient objectives of the manager and finance office. Thus, the head of the purchasing department, which contracts out for supplies and services, won a new position in order to "assist in a complete review of the entire purchasing system and to institute major changes which should be possible with new data processing capabilities."[10] The new data processing facility is a pet project of the manager and the finance director.

Let the manager have his cake and eat it too. At times the claim that work is increasing yields manpower payoffs for department heads. A surer means of getting more men is, however, the no-cost approach. This amounts to showing that positions will pay for themselves and, perhaps, raise revenue beyond cost. Use of the tactic, in a sense, represents a triumph for the city manager. Department heads keep an eye out for positions that will produce revenue. They become concerned with finding avenues toward fiscally costless personnel expansion.

Departments directly engaged in gathering fees for the city or ones dealing with functions which the federal government often subsidizes possess the greatest opportunity to use this approach. The traffic engineering and parking director, for instance, supervises the enforcement of parking laws, which is a money-making function for the city. In 1970, he justified a request for four new parking meter checkers on grounds that each would bring at least $35,000 to city coffers. He based his estimate on a study which showed that checkers wrote from nine to twenty-five tickets each hour. Assuming the tickets to be worth $2.00 each (the minimum fine), he estimated that each meter maid brought in $50,000 per year to the city. To be on the safe side, he reduced the figure to $35,000. The director and his assistant knew that beyond certain reasonable limits each checker could not produce this much revenue; but they believed the point of diminishing returns to be distant. They found support for this conviction in San Francisco which had twice as many meters as Oakland and almost four times as many checkers. Eventually the finance office gave them two new meter maids.

A request such as the traffic director's has appeal to budget analysts because they experience little uncertainty that the position will yield revenue. People parking in Oakland are unlikely to become more law abiding: the opportunity to write parking tickets will not dry up suddenly.

[10] Oakland, *City of Oakland Preliminary Budget, Fiscal 1970/71*, p. B-131.

Work-load and no-cost approaches are among the most common tactics for personnel expansion. There are, however, other ploys which agency heads can use. Such tactics are most likely to emerge in a bureaucracy, like Oakland's, which has a strong anti-expansionist leadership.

SELF-INFLICTED REDUCTIONS

However strategically sophisticated the department head, he is unlikely to win more positions. Not surprisingly, this has caused agency officials to lower their expectations, but has not resulted in a parallel reduction of aspirations. It is important in this context not to equate expectations with aspirations. Expectations are beliefs about what will happen. Aspirations are goals or future levels of performance which the individual wants to attain. Despite the fact that Oakland agency heads do not expect to procure many more slots, they still aspire to enlarge their work force. By and large this aspiration finds expression in their budget manpower requests.

This is not always true, however. At times reduced expectations have prompted agencies to ask for smaller personnel increases, to hold the line entirely, or actually to seek fewer men. When they practice such self-denial, it is usually out of a desire to secure some compensating benefit.

Belt tighten to invest in future status. When defeat seems inevitable, some administrators will ask for smaller personnel increases in an effort to build reputations for being "no fat" agency heads. By showing a willingness to restrain himself, the official hopes to build his status for economizing with the city manager and, perhaps, cash in on this enhanced prestige at some future point. In extreme form this type of belt tightening leads the department head to seek no new slots. The personnel director, for example, employed a "shame them and wait 'til next year" theme in his request for fiscal 1968/69. After noting that over the years the responsibilities of his staff had increased, he wrote: "Because of these various factors we asked in the 1967/68 budget for an increase in the staff of three positions. They were turned down without comment. Although the same situation exists this year as it has in the past, we are not asking for additional personnel since indications are for various reasons that they would not be granted." The personnel director hoped that this approach would enhance his status and would permit him to win personnel concessions in the future. The next year, however, he asked for new slots but did not receive any. This points to one reason why agency heads seldom use this tactic. Even if the city manager acknowledges their efforts to economize, he still may not grant them concessions in future years.

Trade personnel cuts for other budgetary concessions. Another self-denial tactic that is endemic to bureaucracies with an economizing leadership is to trade slots for nonpersonnel concessions. The fire chief used this approach in 1970, exchanging personnel cuts for capital outlay. The veteran chief, who heads a force of 684 persons, had for several years sought a $110,000 utility building. He wanted the structure in order to provide suitable space for fire-department training and the storage of apparatus. Year after year the city manager and finance office denied the request. Finally in his submission for 1970/71 the chief argued that the excellence of his fire prevention unit permitted him to cut two hosemen slots from his base of positions. In return the chief wanted the utility house. Convinced that the chief had shown a willingness to compromise and had displayed respect for economizing goals, the finance office and manager agreed. That they were impressed with the approach is evident from a later council session in mid-June 1970. One of the councilmen, chagrined at the lack of council control over the budget, suggested that he and his colleagues vote to eliminate the expenditure for the utility building. But the city manager defended the structure as a high-priority item stating that the chief was the only department head to request a cut instead of an increase in personnel.[11]

Exchange expensive slots for cheaper ones. Another variant of self-denial occurs when department heads try to trade expensive positions for cheaper ones. An agency head is more likely to attempt this infrequently used tactic if he has had difficulties in recruiting qualified personnel for a high-level

[11] A check of the budget requests indicates that the museum department also asked for fewer positions in 1970 than it had in 1969.

position. During fiscal 1969/70, for instance, the traffic engineering and parking director was unable to fill a budgeted
engineering position which had become vacant. He prodded
the civil service office, scanned the market himself, and placed
ads in professional journals but could find no satisfactory
applicant. The director valued the engineering position since
it was essential for planning and gave the department a skills
slack useful in meeting contingencies and boosting its professional status. At the same time, the director foresaw the
problems of continuing with the unfilled position. Obviously
the vacancy reduced the service his department provided; and
even if he suddenly succeeded in filling the slot, the director
believed that there would be persistent turnover in the future.
More fundamentally he knew that the budget analysts tended
to cut vacant positions. To avoid this eventuality and to ease
future recruitment problems, the director reluctantly asked
that finance eliminate the engineering position and substitute
a subprofessional senior engineering aide for it. The aide position was less expensive and called only for a high-school degree
with advanced mathematics and two years of experience. Subsequently, the budget analyst agreed to the exchange.

There are, of course, risks to the self-denial approach which
make its use infrequent. Many smaller departments believe that
they do not have men to give away. Furthermore an agency
head has to present a plausible excuse for being able to concede
a slot and then make a good case for receiving something in
return. Otherwise, he may find himself in a quandary comparable to that which the museum director faced in 1970. He
requested fewer man-years than he had had the previous year
in exchange for certain benefits; instead the budget analyst
cut even more slots and refused to grant him any concessions.
In short, pursuing self-denial tactics is an uncertain business.
The department gives up something at the outset and risks
getting little in return. Once a man is lost, it is difficult to
get him back.

Low expectations can at times, then, lead departments to
make more conservative requests—seeking smaller manpower
gains, holding the line, or even giving up slots. From the
manager's perspective this amounts to success. Responding to

his pressure, departments cut themselves and do not force the finance office either to spend time evaluating their requests or to wield its authority. This triumph does, however, bear the potential cost of information blockage for the manager. A budget request is one way those at the top of a hierarchy learn about manpower needs at the bottom levels. If agency heads believe that it is futile to seek more men, the manager risks losing touch with their problems. Given the general propensity of Oakland's agencies to continue to make requests, however, this is not a major managerial difficulty.

These, then, are the values and behavioral patterns which shape manpower determination decisions made through the budgetary process. Department heads play the game primarily to win more slots; the manager primarily to hold down fiscal costs. As will become even more apparent when we assess outcomes, the city manager generally prevails.

THE MANAGER'S CONCERN WITH CLASSIFICATION

The city manager's interest in the number of different kinds of positions city hall will contain does not end with the budgetary process. He has also considered the bureaucracy's position classification process. City hall has more than 300 classes of positions (for example, semi-skilled laborer, intermediate typist clerk, zoo keeper). The Civil Service Commission is formally in charge of keeping this structure accurate. Whenever someone consistently works outside his assigned classification, this body is supposed to reclassify him. For example the commission might conclude that an engineer had been doing the work of a subprofessional engineering aide and therefore downgrade him. In so doing, commissioners would eliminate a professional position and substitute another for it.

The city manager has a twofold interest in accurate classification. First, if the labels describe behavior he has a shorthand way of knowing what personnel in the organization actually do; it reduces some internal uncertainty. Second, accurate classification means that no one receives more pay than he should. Since class label determines salary, a failure to keep classification up-to-date can result in an employee being overpaid or underpaid. The manager suspects that the former is the more frequent occurrence.

Although the city manager values accurate classification, the existing array of forces makes such precision unlikely. The Civil Service Commission holds the authority to reclassify individuals but depends on the personnel director to bring the need for such decisions to its attention; the personnel director and his staff, however, seldom have much knowledge concerning which positions are misclassified. Moreover, they have little incentive to increase their information. The director senses that his status among department heads will decline if he constantly acts as a spokesmen for accurate classification. Since more honor flows to him if he focuses on recruitment the personnel director naturally sees little sense in spending time doing unwelcome exploratory studies. Furthermore, the director knows that even if he finds a position that needs reclassification, the Civil Service Commission may not approve the action. The commission dislikes moving employees downward in the hierarchy because it means that their salaries will be cut. The director can count on commission support only if he recommends an upward classification which would increase wage costs.

City departments also have few incentives for reporting inaccuracies. The incumbent in a position sees little reason to notify civil service that he is improperly labeled particularly if it would lead to downgrading and a resulting pay cut. Similarly, the supervisor or department head sees no advantage in consuming time and suffering a loss of prestige among subordinates by zealously searching for misclassification. To the extent that department heads become involved at all, it is mainly to get an employee upgraded; such reclassification gives them a position that has more skills associated with it. In sum, the actors in the civil service office's environment communicate about classification infrequently and then primarily when it costs the city more money.[12]

Aware of the tendency toward inaccuracy and the overgrading of employees, the city manager in 1969 successfully advo-

---

[12] For discussions of classification behavior, see Bernard H. Baum, *Decentralization of Authority in a Bureaucracy* (Englewood Cliffs, N.J.: Prentice Hall, 1961), pp. 89-129; and Jay M. Shafritz, *Position Classification: A Behavioral Analysis for the Public Service* (New York: Praeger Publishers, 1973).

cated hiring the classification consultant, Griffenhagen-Kroeger, for $40,000. Examining all agencies except police and fire, this firm suggested that city hall reclassify from 10 to 20 percent of all civilian employees, the majority of them downward.

The incentives pattern which fosters misclassification remains untouched. But the hiring of the consultant serves to illustrate further the city manager's interest in and leverage over manpower decisions. His commitment to shaping such choices goes beyond the budgetary arena.

THE POLITICS OF REORGANIZING POSITIONS

City officials at times change the location of positions in the formal authority structure; often the reorganization shifts positions from one department to another. Such activities are an integral part of manpower politics. The problems endemic to relocating slots are complex. Is it wise to decentralize? Should officials allocate positions in a way that promotes conflict and redundancy among agencies?[13] What is the relationship between grouping certain positions together and productivity? Convincing answers to these questions are in short supply. Many can only conclude that there is no one best way.[14]

Yet Oakland's city manager experiences relatively little uncertainty about the best way to structure positions within the bureaucracy. To be sure it is easier for him to compute the fiscal impact of adding or subtracting manpower than of reshuffling positions. This does not, however, drive him toward an administrative agnosticism with respect to relocating slots. The city manager feels that over the long run, adherence to certain principles will foster economy and efficiency in city hall. At the core of his credo is the belief that centralizing authority and reducing overlap will have desirable consequences. In his view, gaining authority more commensurate with his responsi-

[13] For an excellent analysis of redundancy see Martin Landau, "Redundancy, Rationality and the Problem of Duplication and Overlap," *Public Administration Review* 29 (July/August 1969): 346-358.

[14] See, for example, C. West Churchman, *The Systems Approach* (New York: Dell, 1968), p. 229.

bility, and making procedures and jurisdictions "neat and clean" are the essentials of sound management.

This attitude finds expression in his activities. On taking office in 1966, he was upset by the fragmented city bureaucracy which awaited him. At the time, there were over twenty departments, including five major ones run by semi-autonomous commissions (parks, recreation, museum, library, and civil service). Though his predecessor had warned him that efforts to place positions in these agencies directly under his authority would fail, the city manager soon set out to strip the commissions of their prerogatives. Emphasizing that reorganization would save the city $900,000, the city manager convinced the mayor, business leaders, the *Oakland Tribune*, and others to support a ballot proposition which would shift authority to him. In 1968, a narrow majority of the voters approved the proposition.

Position relocations involving charter revision are, of course, the exception rather than the rule. On other occasions the city manager has had an easier time fostering reorganizations. Using his authority, status, and expertise to good advantage, he has reduced the number of agencies by about one-third since 1968. Under his auspices, for example, parks and recreation departments merged and two superdepartments, the Office of Public Works and the Office of General Services, were created from smaller units. Through these mergers, the city manager hoped to reduce the overlap in functions among different agencies and improve coordination.

In arranging position shifts, the city manager has met no serious opposition. Unlike the president of the United States, the city manager has few worries about bureaucrats mobilizing outside constituencies or legislative committees to resist a reallocation of slots. Unless reorganizing positions involves charter change, the scope of conflict is usually limited to the manager and the agency heads. The city council seldom intervenes since it respects the manager as an administrative expert. Employee organizations abstain unless a move threatens the civil service office or increases the likelihood of layoffs. Citizen groups generally do not recognize the significance of transfers for broader policy questions.

It is, then, high-level department officials who believe that they have a direct stake in transfers. But how do they perceive these stakes? Taking a hint from Downs's contention that bureaucracies seek to expand, we might conclude that agency heads feel victorious whenever they gain positions. After all, securing more slots contributes to their prestige within the organization and increases their ability to provide services. In fact, however, department heads do not invariably view the acquisition of positions as a victory; an episode involving the Department of Traffic Engineering and Parking helps to illustrate this.

Agency heads may be reluctant manpower imperialists.[15] Prior to 1969 the traffic engineering department handled such routine functions as traffic surveys, curb and street lane painting, and the installation and maintenance of name signs, traffic signals, and parking meters. Then in 1968, the police chief gave the head of traffic engineering an opportunity to expand when he told the city manager that Oakland should employ meter maids rather than uniformed policemen to enforce parking regulations, and that the manager should remove this enforcement function from the police department. From the chief's perspective parking enforcement was a low-priority area that brought him hostile protests from ticketed drivers and businessmen who feared overzealous enforcement near their stores. By dropping this function, his department would suffer no actual loss in personnel and would rid itself of an activity that hurt police status.

The city manager, after discussion with the chief, tentatively decided to support the proposal. Shortly thereafter he suggested to the traffic director that his agency might supervise the activity. The city manager soon learned, however, that the traffic director had reservations about assuming the new duties even if it meant personnel expansion. While the director believed that planning and maintenance of meters belonged in his department's jurisdiction, he was uncertain about meter enforcement. He and his professional staff might pay opportu-

---

[15] For a general discussion of bureaucratic imperialism see Matthew Holden, Jr., "Imperialism in Bureaucracy," *American Political Science Review* 55 (December 1966): 943-951.

nity costs in supervising the meter checkers; time for planning
and professional duties was already scarce without taking on
lower priority tasks. Moreover the traffic director was aware
that absorbing the function would bring him the potentially
hostile constituencies of parking violators and local businessmen. While the director believed that meter enforcement did
relate to his agency's aspiration to promote traffic safety, he
was chary of taking over the function.

Faced with a reluctant, uncertain traffic director, the city
manager called for more study. He asked the agency head to
survey other cities to determine the practices they used. This
kind of study (which is standard procedure whenever Oakland
officials contemplate nonroutine change) would not only increase city hall's information but provide the traffic director
with time to reflect. The results of the research were far from
conclusive. Analyzing the practices of cities Oakland's size on
the West Coast, the director found that one-half of the sampled
governments placed parking enforcement in the police department and that about one-fourth put it under traffic engineering.

In the end the study was only one factor that shaped the
choice of the director. By the time of its completion the manager
had offered the director the accident analysis function if he
accepted parking enforcement. The director had long wanted
to assume the former activity. Faced with this enticement,
aware that a precedent existed for such a step in Seattle and
Portland, and not wanting to damage his reputation with the
manager by being troublesome, the director agreed to become
responsible for the meter maids.

The behavior of Oakland's traffic director suggests that an
agency head will view a transfer favorably if it provides him
with personnel: (a) who perform functions closely tied to major
agency goals; (b) who will not require substantial supervision
by his present staff; and (c) who will not involve him with
hostile external constituencies. Hence Oakland's traffic director
felt reluctant to add meter enforcement because he did not
believe it was as important as more basic traffic engineering,
because the new employees would require considerable surveil-

lance, and because outside groups were bound to complain about enforcement decisions.[16]

Taking factors like these into account, then, agency heads usually develop firm opinions about the desirability of a transfer. Whether these attitudes lead to action is another matter. As the case of the meter maids illustrates, resistance is difficult. Documenting a case against a proposed position shuffle is often impossible. If an agency head resists too emphatically, he risks developing a reputation for being uncooperative and uninterested in new responsibility.

Department imperialism succeeds if the manager approves. If transfers are often hard to resist, they are also perplexing to arrange. Many of Oakland's top bureaucrats are at least latent manpower imperialists. But acting on this disposition is difficult. For instance the traffic engineer would like to absorb street lighting and signal maintenance personnel from the Office of General Services. Despite this aspiration he has not attempted to obtain them. The traffic director feels that he lacks a good justification for imperialism since General Services has given his agency adequate support. A further barrier to action is his realization that the director of General Services enjoys considerable prestige with the city manager. (The chief executive at one point showed his faith in the director of General Services by making him his acting assistant.)

If, therefore, another agency head has preserved his status with the city manager, the imperialistic aspirations of an expansionist bureaucrat are likely to go unfulfilled. On the other hand, when the leadership of another agency has limited prestige with the city manager and the expansionist department head can appeal to the manager's basic organizing values (for example, centralization, reduction or overlap), the likelihood of a transfer increases. Thus the traffic director did persuade the city manager to shift five slots from the Off-Street Parking Commission to his agency.[17] The fact that commissioners re-

[16] Morton H. Halperin, "Why Bureaucrats Play Games," *Foreign Policy* 2 (Spring 1971): 80, discusses a similar phenomenon.

[17] Examples from the traffic engineering department in part come from interviews which Eric Sears conducted there in 1966 and 1967.

ceived their appointments from the mayor undermined their status with the city manager. By shifting personnel away from the commission's control, the city manager reaffirmed his faith in centralized administrative authority.

Agency heads can, then, occasionally encourage a desirable transfer but only if they can convince the manager that such a move is sound. As in decision concerning how many of what type of manpower to employ, the manager is the dominant figure. His veto power is secure. Unless a move requires charter change, what he initiates or approves will prevail most of the time.

OUTCOMES

What have been the results of this control pattern for outcomes? By looking at shifts in position allocations to departments since the city manager took office, we can begin to grapple with the issue. In terms of the overall work force, Table 4 shows that over a five-year period the manager has kept the bureaucracy from expanding rapidly. During this time the number of man-years rose by about 195, or 39 annually. This is an increase of only 5.7 percent, or slightly more than 1.1 percent per year. This rate is less than the national average for municipal governments, 2.9 percent.[18]

TABLE 4: MAN-YEARS INCREASE SLIGHTLY EACH YEAR, 1965–1970

Fiscal year	Full-time man-years	Part-time man-years	Total man-years	Increase over previous year	Percentage of increase over previous year
1965–66	3194.0	235.0	3429.0	—	—
1966–67	3228.0	237.8	3465.8	+36.8	1.1
1967–68	3250.2	235.8	3486.0	+20.2	.6
1968–69	3253.7	232.9	3486.6	+.6	.0
1969–70	3353.6	216.1	3569.7	+83.1	2.4
1970–71	3396.7	226.9	3623.6	+53.9	1.5

Source: Oakland Preliminary Budgets.

[18] International City Managers Association, *Municipal Year Book, 1967*, p. 228. Since it does not give data for the same period I examined, a comparison must be treated cautiously. It notes that from 1958 to 1968, the number of full-time positions rose from 1,372,000 to 1,813,000.

TABLE 5: Personnel Expanding, Maintaining, and Shrinking
in Oakland City Departments, 1966/71

Type of department	Formal function	1966/67 Man-years	1970/71 Man-years	Differ-ence	Percentage of increase over 1966/67
Expanding					
Finance	Accounting and bud-get preparation	8.0	104.5	96.5	1206.2
Traffic Engineering and Parking	Traffic planning, traf-fic marking upkeep, meter repair and en-forcement	34.1	63.0	28.9	84.8
Museum	Art, history, and science exhibits	61.0	87.6	26.6	43.6
Purchasing	Contracting for serv-ices and supplies	21.3	27.8	6.5	30.5
Municipal Buildings	City building main-tenance and security	107.9	135.0	27.1	25.1
Police	Crime prevention and law enforcement	909.9	1033.3	123.4	13.6
Maintaining					
City Attorney	Counsel and legal ad-vice to the city	17.0	18.0	1.0	5.9
Equipment	Maintenance of city mobile equipment	49.0	51.0	2.0	4.1
Civil Service	Recruitment and se-lection, employee records	18.2	18.5	0.3	1.6
Parks	Operation of city parks	198.1	199.2	1.1	0.6
Recreation	Recreational pro-grams and operation of recreational facili-ties	323.6	325.4	1.8	0.6
Fire	Fire prevention and firefighting	684.0	685.0	1.0	0.1
Electrical	Maintenance of city electrical facilities	72.0	70.0	–2.0	–2.8
Streets and Engineering	Construction and maintenance of streets, sewers and storm drains	450.6	428.4	–22.2	–4.9

TABLE 5—*Continued*

Type of department	Formal function	1966/67 Man-years	1970/71 Man-years	Difference	Percentage of increase over 1966/67
Building and Housing	Housing, building, plumbing, mechanical and electrical inspections	89.3	84.0	–5.3	–5.9
Shrinking					
City Planning	Zoning, planning for future in city	26.2	23.3	–2.9	–11.1
Library	Collection and lending of books and other media	250.5	205.0	–45.5	–18.2
City Auditor	Auditing of books, accounts, money, and securities of city	51.0	6.0	–45.0	–88.2

Source: Oakland Preliminary Budgets.

A focus on the particular agencies that have won or lost slots also provides insight into the manager's values. We can divide Oakland's departments according to whether they are expanding, maintaining, or contracting their work force. In Table 5 expanding departments are those that have increased their man-years by more than 10 percent over five years; maintaining departments have had man-year changes of from minus 10 percent to plus 10 percent; shrinking departments have lost more than 10 percent of their man-years. While the manager has initiated reorganizations during the period considered, most units have remained constant in identity. Consequently, while eight departments now fall into the larger Offices of Public Works and General Services, we can still identify the number of man-years allocated to the original department.

The changes indicated in Table 5 have occurred in part as a result of budgetary decisions and in part because of transfers. Of the six expanding departments, traffic engineering and parking, purchasing, and municipal buildings grew substantially through position shifts. The other agencies expanded by having portions of their budget requests granted. Another pattern is that, with the possible exception of the museum, changes are not a consequence of the city adding new functions or giving up old ones. Rather, they primarily reflect managerial reassessment of the number of men needed to perform long-standing activities.

In terms of more fundamental values, the patterns of growth and shrinkage reflect a desire to economize, to reduce internal organizational uncertainty for top management, and to minimize risk for Oakland citizens. The patterns also reveal a willingness to honor commitments that the manager's predecessor had made.

Reduce internal organization uncertainty and economize. The city manager's concern with reducing internal organizational uncertainty and with economizing accounts for the growth of at least three departments (finance, purchasing, and municipal buildings) and the contraction of two (library and city auditor). The finance office expanded because it is the manager's main weapon in his fight to control the rest of the organization. Among other things it is the arm that he uses to gather and synthesize information. In this capacity, its staff scrutinizes budget requests, carries out various studies aimed at saving the city money, and operates the new electronic data processing system. Some of finance's expansion came at the expense of the city auditor. Shortly after assuming office, the manager became convinced that the auditor's office had failed to supply him with necessary data. Moreover, since the auditor was an elected official, the manager exerted less power over the office than he wanted to wield. Consequently he persuaded the council to shift a net total of 45 positions from the auditor to the finance director. Finance has also gained 57.5 man-years in its own right, particularly for its electronic data processing unit, and for its other divisions as well.

His aspirations to economize caused the manager to enlarge the purchasing and municipal buildings divisions. Convinced that fragmentation had previously caused the hiring of more personnel than were necessary, he directed that the municipal buildings division take over janitorial services for the library branches and the new museum, and that purchasing absorb all duplicating functions in city hall. The purchasing unit also received new staff to analyze ways of enhancing efficiency in procurement and contract procedures.

The decline in library personnel resulted from the manager's belief that the department was inefficient. When outside and inside analysts confirmed the manager's suspicion, he and the finance department arranged to cut costs through reorganization and the elimination of professional positions through attrition.

The slight contraction of the city planning department also stemmed from a desire to economize, though in a different way. In 1964 the Area Redevelopment Administration of the U.S. Department of Commerce awarded city hall a grant for the preparation of a comprehensive development plan. With federal largesse coming in, the manager increased the staff of the city planning department. As the study neared completion and federal support began dwindling, the manager gradually eliminated slots from the agency.

Reduce risk for citizens. When a problem involves a serious risk to life and property, even fiscal conservatives become spenders. Thus, Oakland's police department, in an absolute sense, has increased its numbers more than any other agency. The reason for this expansion has been the manager's distaste for rising crime rates. The rate of serious crimes increased each year during the last half of the sixties, attaining a record 52 percent increase in 1968. Although uncertain about the precise causal relationship between more police manpower and safer streets, the manager believed that giving the police chief more positions was the most direct way to tackle the problem. Faced with a high-risk problem and the absence of persuasive, less expensive alternatives, the manager will add personnel. To modify Downs's theory,[19] then, remoteness and uncertainty of benefits need not necessarily produce an unwillingness to invest in a program. When dealing with high-risk areas such as defense or police work, the fear of doing too little may actually lead to an exaggeration of the return on an investment.

Commitment to an attack on major crime indirectly led the traffic engineering and parking department to expand. As indi-

[19] Downs, *Inside Bureaucracy*, 1960.

cated earlier, the city manager became convinced that police officers should concentrate on more serious criminal investigation and consequently shifted responsibility for enforcing parking regulations to the traffic engineering director.

Past commitments shape expansion. The traffic engineering department also has expanded because of commitments made before the present city manager took office. Dissatisfied with deteriorating traffic control, faced with new federal requirements for traffic planning, and concerned about the impact of the new Bay Area Rapid Transit system, the council in 1964 agreed to support traffic engineering expansion. Respecting this pledge, the city manager allowed the department six full-time positions his first year in office. The growth of the museum also stemmed from decisions made before the present manager took office. Voters approved a bond issue for a new museum in the early sixties and the manager felt obliged to expand services and maintain a high-status operation.

CONCLUSION

The city manager has shaped manpower trends in Oakland more than any other single actor. Wielding his authority and status, he regularly beats back department efforts to expand through the budgetary process. He is also the pivotal figure in most reorganizations. The city manager's considerable leverage, his widely understood commitments, and the presence of scorecards help reduce decision uncertainty. With leverage centralized, others have less to consider when anticipating the consequences of their tactics; agency heads, for example, need not ponder how elected officials will respond to their gambits. The city manager's persistent commitment to economizing also reduces uncertainty. Department heads need not wonder whether this year the manager will be pro- or anti-expansion; the manager consistently opposes increases in personnel. Scorecards also help players get their bearings. Changes in personnel expenditures and changes in the number of different kinds of manpower within city hall help players gauge the payoffs of their tactics.

Given the objectives of Oakland officials, manpower decision making poses few uncertainties for officials. The city manager believes that he knows how to resist bureaucratic expansion; department heads sense that they will win few positions regardless of what they do. By comparison, officials face more information deficits when they grapple with the politics of pay.

3

The Politics of Pay:
Policemen as Pace Setters

There are some employees who want everything yesterday.
> Past President,
> Oakland Firefighters' Local #55

Vowing not to strike is like sending a policeman into the streets without his gun.
> Past President
> Oakland Police Officers Association

Climate, supportive work groups, an interesting job, prestige, money, and countless other factors can entice people to work for local government.[1] Conceivably top city officials might worry about all these incentives and their relationship to productivity. In fact, however, only material ones usually receive much consideration from leading policy makers. One reason for this is that the law generally requires officials to set salaries and fringe benefits each year. Another reason for the disproportionate attention material benefits garner is that they are easily tallied. By comparison, for instance, high-level officials know much less about the level of supportive work-

[1] For a typology of incentives, see Peter B. Clark and James Q. Wilson, "Incentive Systems: A Theory of Organizations," in *The National Administrative System,* ed. Dean L. Yarwood (New York: John Wiley, 1971), pp. 277-278. See also, Chester Barnard, *The Functions of the Executive* (Cambridge: Harvard University Press, 1966), pp. 139-160.

group incentives present in the organization. A readily quantified incentive, particularly if the numbers are dollars, will tend
to capture more attention, even though other "softer" incentives may be equally significant for effective performance.

This chapter focuses on how Oakland City Hall deals with
salary and fringe benefit issues. Pay matters involve a broad
range of questions: Who should get how much more money?
What kind of insurance should the city provide? How many
hours should firemen work? Mundane as these queries may
appear, they all have political ramifications. For instance, the
higher the pay and fringe benefits, the more likely is city
government to attract competent people. On the other hand,
the more money paid for salaries the greater will be the tax
burden on Oakland citizens and the less likely is city hall to
expand services by hiring more people. The strategies various
actors employ in settling such issues also have political implications. The age-old issue of whether public employee strikes are
compatible with the functioning of democracy is illustrative.[2]

Three basic sets of actors participate in pay politics in
Oakland—the manager and his staff, the mayor and council,
and major employee organizations.[3] Table 6 lists three major
employee organizations along with some of their basic attributes, such as monthly dues levied, total membership, and the
percentage of eligible employees who belong.

Oakland's city manager and elected politicians do not play
the politics of pay purely to economize. While they wish to
hold concessions in check, they believe that pay rates should
be competitive. Most employee leaders, on the other hand,
prefer to be pace setters. For these leaders Oakland should
not stay with the pack in terms of material benefits: it should
lead.

These basic values shape the behavior of actors as they deal
with both procedural and substantive pay politics. The former
refers to interaction over the nature of the decision-making

---

[2] For discussions of the impact of employee organizations on democracy, see Frederick
C. Mosher, *Democracy and the Public Service* (New York: Oxford University Press,
1968) and Raymond D. Horton. *Municipal Labor Relations in New York City: Lessons
of the Lindsay-Wagner Years* (New York: Praeger Publishers, 1973).

[3] Conspicuous by their absence are material incentives actors who are quite active
in other cities—namely, people who bribe officials for favors (consider the case of the
New York City Police Department, for example).

TABLE 6: MAJOR EMPLOYEE ORGANIZATIONS IN OAKLAND, JUNE 1971*

Organization	Approximate membership in city hall	Types of employees who are eligible	Approximate percentage of eligible who are members	Approximate dues per month per member (excluding insurance) (dollars)
Oakland Police Officers Association	710	Uniformed policemen, captain or below	99	7.00
Oakland Firefighters Association	640	Uniformed fire employees	99	7.20
Oakland Municipal Civil Service Employees Association	850	All city employees except uniformed police and fire	41	4.50
United Public Employees Union No. 1 (AFL-CIO Affiliate)	475	All city employees except uniformed police and fire	23	6.00

* By major employee organization, I mean one with over 100 Oakland city employees as members.

structure; the latter refers to the maneuvers of actors as they attempt to influence directly annual pay and fringe benefit choices.

THE POLITICS OF PROCEDURE: THE MANAGER ATTEMPTS A HOLDING ACTION

Oakland's manager has not only faced the yearly problem of what pay boosts and merit raises to give, but has also felt compelled to confront basic questions concerning the appropriate decision process. Employee leaders have been responsible for this. Like groups elsewhere, they believe that a new collective bargaining period has dawned. Past ways of doing things must be abandoned. A procedural problem exists which cries out for solution.

When confronted with militant employees demanding "improved" procedures, a few chief executives might take the lead in sponsoring change. A devotee of participative management might do so, as would an executive who thought that concessions would earn him valuable cooperation from employee leaders at a later point. Many city officials do not favor participative decision structures, however; so too, many do not believe that employee leaders return favors. Such officials often see value in a holding action. Adopting this strategy a city manager or mayor denies that there is a problem and does nothing to change procedures until specifically challenged by an employee group or some other adversary. Then officials fight to preserve the status quo or make small concessions.[4]

Oakland's city manager opted for a holding action. The strategy has, however, brought him only partial success. In fact, he lost the first major structural battle he fought. Understanding the sense in which this is so requires a brief historical review.

Oakland has a system of pay setting by formula. When the present city manager took office in 1966, Oakland used formulae to set salaries. This approach to salary determination had come about as a result of action by the public safety organizations in 1958. In that year police and fire groups succeeded in their efforts to gain voter approval for Proposition C. This proposition was an amendment to the charter which linked police and fire department salaries to those of industrial workers in the Bay Area and, thereby, relieved the council of its authority to set wages (though not fringe benefits). Each year the California Division of Labor Statistics published data showing the percentage by which industrial wages had increased. Proposition C guaranteed public safety workers that their pay would rise at the same rate. The employees knew that the formula would not assure precise increases, but that it would probably enable them to keep up with the rising cost of living. In a sense the amendment enabled employee leaders to have their cake and eat it too. Workers in the industrial sector, represented by their unions, would win substantial pay raises. Police and firemen would not have to engage in militant bargaining, which was widely seen as illegitimate for them, but would benefit from negotiations in the private sector.

[4] A third basic strategy is to depart from the status quo by attempting to destroy or drastically undermine the union movement.

The Proposition C formula applied only to uniformed police and fire employees and not to the majority of city bureaucrats. The latter continued under the old decision framework whereby employee groups would lobby with councilmen for concessions. From 1959 on, however, city officials increasingly saw advantages in the formula method. By February 1962 the council had passed an ordinance (not a charter amendment) establishing the Reading Formula. This formula was applicable to all personnel other than uniformed police and firemen. It linked the salaries of these employees to the average paid for comparable work in thirteen other public jurisdictions.[5] Adopting this decision rule, the council believed that Oakland's salaries would be competitive but not excessive; pay rates would allow the city to compete for competent personnel but would not lead the field. Moreover, calculating yearly increases would become easier. For employees the formula meant that annual increases, while far from pace setting, would probably be forthcoming.

The introduction of "C" and the Reading Formula illustrate an important feature of pay politics in Oakland. Action by police and fire leaders is usually instrumental in producing a new salary setting phase. These two organizations (especially the police) press for innovation in the decision structure and the changes produced come to apply not only to public safety organizations but to other employee groups as well.

Support cumbersome change procedures. When Oakland's city manager assumed office in the mid-sixties, then, a system of salary setting by formula existed. As for fringe benefits (for example, overtime, vacations, retirement, equipment subsidies) council authority remained legitimate. Employee leaders would seek more perquisites but do little other than grumble if officials made no concessions.

Times were changing, however. Shortly after the city manager arrived on the scene, employee leaders became more assertive and vociferous. Some complaints came from union leaders who

[5] The Reading Formula drew data from thirteen jurisdictions: seven cities (San Francisco, Berkeley, Richmond, Alameda, San Leandro, San Jose, Hayward), three counties Contra Costa, San Mateo, Alameda) and three other jurisdictions (Oakland Schools, State of California, University of California). For "trade and crafts" workers, the city adds a fourteenth sample—union scale less any difference in the cost of city and private industry fringe benefits.

were trying to organize the less skilled workers in the bureaucracy. But as usual the more important catalyst for change
was the police association. Leaders of the association believed
that the prestige of police work had risen during the late sixties
as "respectable" citizens began to view officers as a bulwark
against crime and disorder. At the same time they felt that
their work had become more dangerous, unpleasant, and controversial. An excerpt from a letter which police association
spokesmen sent to the manager in part conveys their mood.

> The rigorous pressures and arduous demands faced by police officers
> during the working year should be countered with a vacation free from
> worry. Officers should be encouraged to travel with their wives and
> children to places of peace and serenity, and thoroughly enjoy their
> lives as they are unable to do during the rest of the year. The social
> deprivation and degradation that become daily experiences for officers
> present taxing emotional stresses to greater degrees than any other
> occupation, except perhaps the combat conditions of war.

Convinced that their lot was difficult and that respectable
people were according them more prestige as the "thin blue
line," policemen aggressively sought pay boosts. In 1968, they
asked the council to grant them salary concessions beyond
those authorized by "C." Police leaders argued that the formula
prescribed a minimum salary increase rather than the precise
amount.

The manager, mayor, and certain council members did not
want to modify "C," since it could only cost them more money
and cause them to spend more time setting salaries. They
contended that "C" specified the precise increase and not the
minimum. If police officers wanted to alter the rule, these
officials argued that they should take it to the voters. The
manager and his coalition believed that the police association
did not want to spend resources on an election campaign.
Holding out the ballot box as the only avenue of change might
well discourage public safety workers from trying at all. Thus
actors opposed to change will tend to support cumbersome
procedures which make change more costly to obtain.

While in 1958 the police association leadership saw advantages in having the formula written into the charter, its location

there now threatened to thwart them. Ultimately police spokesmen prevailed, however. Five councilmen decided to show
good faith and double the amount Proposition C decreed. Later
the courts upheld the action, thereby rejecting the manager's
procedural argument. Police success in reinterpreting "C"
meant the abolition of a previously firm decision rule and
thereby drove the manager toward more complex calculations.

As if his defeat by the police association had not been
sufficient, action by the state legislature weakened the manager's position further. In 1968 the California legislature passed
the Meyers-Milias-Brown Act which provided that the public
employer had to "meet and confer in good faith with representatives of recognized employee organizations." The act was
vague. Compared with other states which had dealt with labor
problems, the California statute gave considerable leeway to
local governments.[6] Uncertain as its impact was, however, local
actors viewed its passage as a victory for public employee
organizations.

As 1969 began, then, the manager and the council faced a
number of questions. Should they set up a new bargaining
representative? Should they allocate more time to discussions?
With which employee leaders should they bargain? What
should be the scope of negotiable issues? The new state law
suggested that local officials arrive at answers to all these
questions and more, but laid down few guidelines. Officials also
found it difficult to follow the leader by looking to other
jurisdictions.[7] Since employee relations throughout the country
were in flux, it was hard to locate a success story elsewhere
and apply the methods used there to Oakland.

Confronted with this situation, the city manager continued
to pursue his holding strategy and he chose to make no changes.

[6] David Bowen, Peter Feuille, and George Strauss, "The California Experience," in
Unionization of Municipal Employees, ed Robert H. Connery and William O. Farr
(New York: Columbia University Press, 1970), p. 123. They note "The evolving California system is clearly less legalistic than some others. There is no state-wide Public
Employment Relations Board to develop a body of law on its own, and indeed legislation
has created few rights which are litigable. Third party intervention . . . is relatively
rare. The parties have had to solve their problems themselves."
[7] In the face of uncertainty, organizations often look to others for cues as to proper
behavior. See Richard M. Cyert and James G. March, *A Behavioral Theory of the
Firm* Englewood Cliffs, N.J.: Prentice Hall, 1963), p. 102.

The fact that the new state law was ambiguous and state officials had allocated few resources to enforcing its spirit permitted use of this strategy, which from the manager's perspective had two main advantages: first, it promised to give him more time to assess precisely what his interests were; second, it forced employee leaders to spend resources to bring about change. They would get very little for free.

Ultimately employee spokesmen paid the costs necessary to produce procedural modifications. Once again, the police association played the major role in precipitating structural change. By June 1969 the manager, using old procedures, had settled with all employee organizations concerning salaries and had made a recommendation to the council concerning police benefits. But the police association refused to accept the decision. Matters dragged on through July and into early August when last-minute concessions by the manager and council prevented a strike.

The manager interpreted the near-strike to mean that resources were shifting in value and usage. He believed that the worth of council authority was declining as policemen displayed a greater willingness to deny legitimacy and withhold services. Consequently he decided to create a bargaining agent and commit more time to negotiations.

The manager creates an advocate he can control. A city manager who values internal control and economy will attempt to appoint his own collective bargaining representative and have that agent report directly to him. Thus Oakland's city manager moved quickly when the mayor and council took steps to establish an agent responsible to them. Disturbed by the conflict with the police, the mayor had appointed three councilmen to a special Employee Relations Committee in July 1969. At the time, one councilman thought that the committee might become a major forum for discussions between employees and top policy makers. The manager, however, did not want such a situation to develop. He doubted that the committee had the time and expertise needed to handle bargaining. Moreover the committee would prove to be a bothersome contingency for him. Council concessions to the police in 1968 had shown him how unreliable the body could be. As a result he appointed the finance director, the assistant to the city manager and the personnel director to a special Meet and Confer Committee which was to be in charge of negotiations. Except for the personnel director, who was under the authority of the Civil Service Commission, the committee consisted of close associates. As much as any group, it would serve as a conduit for his will.

The city manager's concern with establishing a compliant bargaining agent did not end with the appointment of the Meet and Confer Committee. It also led him to resist employee requests for compulsory arbitration, a procedure which would have given employees the opportunity to circumvent the city manager in the bargaining process. Compulsory arbitration, as proposed in Oakland, would have given arbiters the right to impose a settlement if city officials reached an impasse with employees. Union and association leaders had no illusions that compulsory arbitration would invariably lead to generous settlements. Nonetheless they believed that outsiders would be more liberal with concessions than the tight-fisted city manager. Above all, arbitration would have removed the need to rely on strikes. Even militant groups do not relish the costs and uncertainty of withdrawing services. The leadership faces difficulties rallying the rank-and-file behind such action; members may lose their salaries for the duration of the strike; the legality of such action is obscure; leaders risk their status when one occurs (in effect, they gamble that the extra concessions a strike wins will convince the union membership that the tactic was worthwhile). So great was employee leader distaste for the strike, that many promised to pledge never to take such action if the manager would grant them compulsory arbitration.

For the manager, however, prospects of soaring fiscal costs seemed greater if the council relinquished its authority. An arbiter would not have the same incentives to hold down concessions as the manager would. Moreover, an exchange of authority for guaranteed services hardly seemed worth it. It was too early to tell whether employee leaders were serious about striking. Employee spokesmen had made similar threats previously and nothing had happened. Thus, when elected politicians showed some signs of not knowing how to respond to a police request for arbitration in 1969, the manager's staff counseled against it. At an open session, the assistant to the city manager argued before the council that the public (specifically the taxpayers) would not receive adequate consideration under the plan. He warned council members that arbiters would be too far remove from Oakland to understand its problem. A majority of the council eventually backed the manager and has consistently denied the employee request.

Concede time reluctantly. One component of an employee relations holding strategy is to reduce negotiating time. Acutely aware that time is a scarce resource, Oakland's city manager felt reluctant to spend many hours with employee leaders after the passage of the state law.[8] Instead he followed the old practice of calling few meetings. For instance, the head of the firefighters noted that the manager had given his group only one-and-a-half hours of negotiating time the first year after the new state law went into effect. Another employee leader complained that his allotment was approximately one hour. Moreover, the chief executive tended to call meetings abruptly. The firefighters' president relates how the manager's office would call in the morning to set up meetings for the afternoon. The near-strike by the police association convinced the manager that more negotiations with all groups were inevitable.

In sum, a powerful employee group tends to force a city's chief executive to accept the principle of negotiation. The principle then begins to govern the executive's relations with less potent groups. Thus, the Oakland police association won procedural concessions and made city officials take notice. Weaker and less militant organizations then claimed equal rights.

Divide and rule. As part of his holding action, Oakland's city manager has practiced a strategy of divide and rule in response to the problem of union recognition. The Meyers-Milias-Brown Act required the manager to recognize certain

---

[8] California had had a labor law since 1961, when the legislature passed the George Brown Act. "This act merely established the right of all public employees to join organizations and required the governing body of the public agency to 'meet and confer' with representatives of employee organizations upon request, 'and to consider as fully as it seems reasonable such presentation' made by the organization." Under this law, the manager could avoid serious negotiation. Bowen, et al., "The California Experience," p. 110.

employee representatives as official bargaining agents. In response to the law, the manager did not immediately hold employee elections to determine once and for all which union and association leaders would have exclusive rights to represent certain classes of bureaucrats. Instead he recognized all employee groups presently operating in city hall. By so doing, the city manager encouraged unions and associations to compete for members in the same class of employees (for example, among janitors). In fact competition for new recruits was persistent and intense between the Oakland Municipal Civil Service Employees Association and the United Public Employees Union Local #1. From the manager's perspective this competition was useful. Bickering among these two major employee groups meant that they were unlikely to cooperate in a strike action. It meant that neither group could claim to speak exclusively for certain classes of bureaucrats. The city manager believed that this weakened both the union and association at the bargaining table and that, consequently, there would be less risk in denying their wage demands. Only in 1971, after local #1 made employee elections a central bargaining issue, did the city manager agree to poll employees and establish clear union jurisdictions.

Keep issue scope narrow. In addition to seeking leverage through a recognition policy based on divide and rule, the city manager has attempted to keep the scope of negotiable issues narrow. From the city manager's perspective, the fewer items he discusses with employee leaders the better. Of course the city manager knows that unions and associations have state guaranteed rights to negotiate some issues with him (for example, pay raises). There are, however, other matters, primarily dealing with the administration of fringe benefits, where the formal prerogatives of the rank and file are more ambiguous. Although employee spokesmen want to be consulted, the manager believes he can implement changes unilaterally.

Following this practice, the manager avoids overestimating the resources of his opponents and their will to resist. Employee spokesmen must earn every concession by spending time (and perhaps money,) contesting issues. They are constantly in the position of trying to overturn a choice which the manager has already made. To be sure, this tactic also has potential costs for the chief executive. If employee leaders do succeed in reversing a decision, it often means the disruption of a newly instituted practice. The opportunity costs that city officials paid to implement the change may be for naught. So too can unilateral action undermine the status of the manager with rank-and-file employees. Complaints of gross indifference to the welfare of the lower echelons at times result. On balance, however, the city manager thinks that the benefits of making the choice himself outweigh the costs.

Often the modifications he introduces go unchallenged. On occasion, however, employee groups have resisted. The issue need not be a major one to trigger conflict. For instance in 1970 the city manager ordered police captains living outside Oakland to stop driving city cars home at night. The manager had received a number of complaints from citizens concerning the practice. Moreover, regularly subsidizing transportation to surrounding communities seemed economically wasteful. But the captains perceived that the manager had no right to deprive them of their cars and soon appealed to the Oakland Police Officers Association for support. The association responded favorably, hiring the law firm of Davis, Cowell, and Bowe to handle the case. In court the police attorney argued that the city had "flagrantly violated its obligations under the Meyers-Milias-Brown Act by the unilateral action which changed an existing long established practice." In November 1970 a superior court judge sided with the captains and ordered city officials to meet and confer with them about the issue.

On occasion, then, employee leaders have picked up the gauntlet and have challenged managerial choices by enlarging the scope of conflict to include the courts. Often the judiciary has used its authority to force the manager to discuss matters fully when he has not wanted to do so. Such court decisions have not, however, defined once and for all which issues are negotiable. This ambiguity encourages the manager to continue with his unilateral decision making.

In sum, Oakland's manager has faced a constant struggle over the nature of the decision-making structure since taking office. By and large he has engaged in a holding action which at times helped him contain employee thrusts. But often employee groups, led by the Oakland Police Officers Association and abetted by the state legislature, have won.

BARGAINING OVER PAY

The manager and council only sporadically confront basic structural issues. Specific requests for salary and fringe benefit adjustments, by contrast, constitute a far more frequently recurring problem. The tactics which various actors use in confronting this problem are in flux; nonetheless, there are certain regular features. Each year in late February or early March, employee leaders send a letter asking for more perquisites. Discussions then ensue between each association or union representative and the manager's Meet and Confer Committee. If the various parties agree, they draw up a memorandum of understanding which the manager transmits to the council for passage prior to the advent of the fiscal year. Failure to concur causes the scope of conflict to expand as the council more actively intervenes. When this happens, resolution may not come until August or later. We will consider some of the tactics actors employ as they participate in this decision process.

EMPLOYEE TACTICS

Varied as employee groups are, the formulation of a request is a tactical exercise which they all take seriously. The request is important because it demarcates the boundaries of discussion and affects what employee groups will have to trade once bargaining begins. Furthermore an astutely written petition can build the reputations of employee advocates not only with members of their own group but with unaffiliated bureaucrats and those persons who belong to competing unions or associations. Prestige with nonmembers is particularly important to leaders of the civil service employees association and the public employees union #1 who seek to enlarge their following.

Aware of the request's significance, employee representatives assign the chore to special task teams, whose members generally have considerable expertise vis-à-vis pay issues. Many task team

participants have past experience writing such petitions; a few
have taken special collective bargaining courses.

Find supportive reference groups. Working over roughly a two-
month period, team members hammer out the official group position. In doing so, they could make judgments without extensive research. Team members might, for instance, arbitrarily
decide in fifteen minutes that a 20 percent salary increase would
be appropriate. In Oakland, however, they do not operate in
this way, but rather spend time searching for information about
the views and practices of others. As the writings of social
psychology predict, they look for and are most receptive to
data which support their general beliefs and values.[9] But they
do not search simply to reinforce what they know is the
appropriate pay aspiration. The data that they accumulate also
removes uncertainty concerning how large an increment they
should seek; the data function as a guidepost for them. Furthermore, team members believe that the information accrued will
lend credence to their arguments when they deal with the city
manager's Meet and Confer Committee.

For team members, then, the object of the material incentives
game at this early point is to find a friendly reference group.
In procuring data they tend to rely on the decision rules
suggested in Chart 2.

Once committee members have sifted through various information sources, they generally adopt a shotgun approach to
the final formulation of the request. Their practice is to ask
for many different concessions. In 1970, for instance, the Oakland Municipal Civil Service Employees Association sought
twenty-one separate concessions including more pay, better
retirement benefits, expanded sick leave privileges, more holi-
days, an ampler educational incentives allowance, more generous uniform subsidies, and more extensive insurance coverage.[10]

[9] See, for example, Jerome M. Levine and Gardner Murphy, "The Learning and
Forgetting of Controversial Material," *Readings in Social Psychology,* ed. Eleanor
E. Maccoby, Theodore M. Newcomb, and Eugene L. Hartley (New York: Rinehart
and Winston, 1958), p. 100. They reiterate the widely supported finding that "an
individual notes and remembers material which supports his social attitudes better
than material which conflicts with those attitudes."

[10] Not all fringe benefit issues are subject to simple negotiation. Many retirement
system rules are in the city charter so that a decision to modify them requires voter
approval. Charter provisions are quite detailed. For instance, one section deals with
the impact of "hernia, heart trouble and pneumonia" on disability pay.

CHART 2: EMPLOYEE LEADERS LOOK FOR SUPPORTIVE DATA

Decision rule	Example
1. Scan publications put out by state and national employee groups.	The fringe benefits committee in the police association surveys documents released by the Police Officers Research Association of California (the Oakland chapter is an affiliate) and the Fraternal Order of the Police. A comparable committee, comprised of firemen, relies on materials sent to them by the International Association of Fire Fighters such as *Economic Needs of the Fire Fighters.*
2. Scrutinize some Department of Labor data.	The firemen's committee often pegs their salary request to the highest standard of living mentioned in the Bureau of Labor Statistics publication, *Three Standards of a Living Budget.* The police association takes into account cost-of-living increases.
3. Reject data put out by "pro-management" groups.	The police association leaders will not use information supplied by the League of California Cities because they believe its sympathies are with councils and managers.
4. Get data on cities which have a reputation for paying well.	Fire fighters pay particular attention to what their counterparts receive in San Francisco and Los Angeles.
5. Search through past demands and reiterate them.	Employees leaders in general feel that persistence pays off and resubmit unsatisfied requests.
6. Secure data on material incentives allocated to comparable classes in Oakland; strive for parity.	Though they ask for a specific pay boost (e.g., 12.7 percent in 1970) fire leaders also emphasize maintaining parity with the salary police officers receive. The leadership of union local #1 draws on salary data from the Port Commission when it bargains with city officials. The Port Commission has independent salary setting authority and sometimes pays more than city hall for comparable work.
7. Be sensitive to what the membership wants.	Committee members usually claim that they pay attention to the wishes of the elected executive body as well as to the rank and file. One police official boasted that most association requests originate in the locker room. A past president of the fire fighters' association claimed that he

CHART 2—*Continued*

Decision rule	Example
	did as much as he could to placate more militant members "who want everything yesterday." Precise evidence on the linkage between the membership and special committees is missing but it is apparent that committees try to reflect the aspirations of the rank and file.

Employee spokesmen see the shotgun request as the logical bargaining gambit. They have no reputation for economizing to protect with the manager, and they need to present something that they can give up in the move toward a compromise settlement. Furthermore, employee leaders do not believe that asking for a lot and getting a little undermines their status with the membership. Most of the time they can attribute failure to the insensitivity of the city manager. By asking for much, employee representatives hope to raise their prestige as vigorous advocates for the rank and file.

When basic objectives are crystallized, employee group leaders usually set some priorities among them. Aware that this knowledge might give city officials an advantage, they keep the information to themselves. Shortly thereafter, executive secretaries (in civilian groups) or lawyers (in public safety organizations) help draft the official request to city policy makers. At a minimum, members of the Meet and Confer Committee, the city manager, and mayor receive copies.

Publicize demands in the face of resistance. Employee leaders may attempt to publicize their demands in the press. For instance, in 1970, police leaders sent their request to the publishers of the *Oakland Tribune* and weekly *Montclarion*. Both newspapers gave the document coverage, quoting verbatim its opening paragraph:

Let us take a close look at an Oakland police officer and attempt to define him—lest we forget. An Oakland Police officer is a bullet ridden body staring blankly to the night sky because he substituted his conscience for the apathy of others. An Oakland police officer is a lonely man searching a darkened warehouse for a hidden burglar so the owner can get a full night's sleep. An Oakland police officer is the man who returned your son's bicycle.

An Oakland police officer is the man who studied two years for a promotional examination—and lost because another officer studied harder. An Oakland police officer is the man who underwent oral surgery because he turned the other cheek. An Oakland police officer is the nice looking young man that addressed your women's club last week. An Oakland police officer is a pig that the college professor describes to his students. An Oakland police officer is the man who arrested John Doe for petty theft ... and burglary, and robbery, and rape and murder. An Oakland police officer is your servant.

The article then went on to mention the pay increase that the police sought.

Behavior such as that of the police association is more likely if employee spokesmen anticipate a protracted, bitter struggle with city officials and believe that a strike may result. This is in line with a more general proposition which Wilensky has suggested. To paraphrase him, the more an organization is in conflict with its own immediate environment, the more resources it will allocate to making contacts with important segments of the public either to transmit or gather information.[11] Hence, the police leadership sent out its message the year after the association almost went on strike. Anticipating trouble again, police representatives sought to boost their status with the public at an early point.

Similar considerations shape employee behavior if no settlement has emerged as the new fiscal year approaches. When this occurs, group leaders appear before council meetings and seek press coverage. They strive to justify their claims on the city's purse and they utter vague warnings. At such times militant employee groups also tend to use informational picket lines. In May 1970, for example, from 50 to 100 members of union local #1 picketed outside City Hall during the Tuesday evening council session, carrying such signs as "Slaves went out with Lincoln," "Don't make us strike," and "Can't buy bread with promises."

Through such pickets, employee leaders hope to: (a) induce public sympathy and make councilmen aware that their reputations as responsive officials are on the line; (b) persuade elected politician that employee spokesmen feel strongly about

[11] Harold L. Wilensky, *Organizational Intelligence* (New York: Basic Books, 1967), pp. 10-11.

the issue and that, in the case of pickets, the rank and file support the leadership; (c) rally member support by intensifying feelings of polarization; and (d) generally build their reputations as employee advocates.

Some use the strategic threat. Open displays of disaffection are fairly common among Oakland's employee leaders. Strategic threats are not.[12] Strategic threats involve more than vague utterances about withdrawal of services. Instead, such threats specifically note a time when action will be taken unless further concessions are forthcoming. Employee leaders are more likely to use a strategic threat if they believe: that the threat, per se, will produce satisfying concessions; that the union membership will deliver on the threat if city officials prove recalcitrant; and that carrying out the threat (for example, striking) will produce satisfactory benefits. If these condition do not hold, employee representatives fear that the strategy could backfire and produce a decline in their prestige.

Among Oakland's employee representatives those in the police association are the most confident about their capacity to use the strategic threat effectively. In 1969, for instance, the police leadership asked the Alameda County Central Labor Council for strike sanction in early August. Simultaneously, the leadership called a general membership meeting for the following Tuesday in order to hold a strike vote. By so doing, police spokesmen "bound themselves" to a time and place for a tactical decision and, thereby, laid their status as leaders on the line.[13] If the council granted no more concessions and the rank and file voted down such action, the prestige of police leaders as representatives of a constituency would sag. The very fact that police spokesmen were willing to "burn their bridges" in such a visible way made council members more open to compromise.[14] Eventually, the police won additional overtime concessions and a special pay boost for lieutenants.

[12] There are various kinds of strategic threats. A group can make a minor threat, warning of a slight modification of services if city officials are obstinate. A threat geared to increments is also a pledge to take a small step but it links the move to more basic action. An all-out threat is one where employees show a willingness to use their basic resource, the strike, or possibly violence. See Thomas C. Schelling, *The Strategy of Conflict* (New York: Oxford University Press, 1963), p. 42.

[13] See Schelling, *Ibid.*, p. 22.

[14] A recent strike in nearby Vallejo, California, also lent credibility to the threat. The disruption went on for a week and despite court injunctions, police and firemen won much of what they wanted and were not punished for their actions.

MANAGER AND COUNCIL TACTICS

Facing various employee gambits, the manager and, at times, the council counter with a set of their own. During the early phases of the game, the manager is particularly active.

Reduce uncertainty. When confronted with a salary request, city officials initially attempt to reduce uncertainty about it. In Oakland the city manager and his staff gather data concerning the cost of the proposal, practices of other jurisdictions, and employee priorities.

Oakland's assistant to the city manager works closely with a finance office staff member to determine how the requests will affect the city's budget. The assistant and the staff specialist make no effort to do an analysis of every request, but instead focus on those items that they believe will be central during bargaining sessions. (Once negotiations begin, the manager's assistant will seek additional information as the need arises.) In general, determining how much a specific proposal will drain city coffers is easy, but this is not always so. Some requests are perplexing to estimate even over the short run. For instance, in 1969, the police association sought time-and-a-half pay for overtime worked. (Previously policemen had received one hour off for each extra hour put in.) The manager's assistant found it difficult to attach a price tag to this proposal because data were not readily available on how many extra hours police officers had worked in the past. The eventual pact officials negotiated reflected this uncertainty. The city council agreed to pay officers at this rate up to the amount of $50,000. After this sum had run out, policemen would get an hour-and-a-half off for each extra hour worked.

The city manager searches for cost data because he wants to know how much his efforts to economize will be hurt. By contrast he orders his staff to collect information from other jurisdictions primarily because he wants to stay in the salary race with other governments. The amount that enables city hall to compete becomes the maximum desirable concession. In order to obtain information concerning pay rates elsewhere, the manager continues to have the civil service office gather statistics from Reading Formula jurisdictions. This provides him with salary data. Good fringe benefit information takes more time to accumulate and synthesize since many different

programs exist and since there is seldom an accurate expression
of their overall dollar value available. Consequently the manager's staff usually check into prevailing fringe benefit practices
elsewhere when it learns which issues will be salient during
bargaining sessions.

In addition to tapping other jurisdictions and the finance
office, the manager's staff gets a small amount of information
from the police and fire chiefs. These department heads receive
particular attention because, as we have seen, employee groups
in their agencies are the strongest in the city. In discussions
with them a staff member usually asks: Which employee demands are justified? Which ones are employees serious about?
For the two public safety officials, such questions produce some
ambivalence. They do, after all, want their subordinates to
receive ample pay since they believe that it helps their agencies
attract and keep first-rate personnel. Despite these sentiments,
however, they do not become major proponents of employee
values. Sensitive to the chief executive's cost-cutting aspirations, the two officials point to a few requests which seem
particularly justified and express some hunches as to association priorities.

With this information, as well as that from other sources,
the Meet and Confer Committee (in consultation with the
manager) develops a first-round counteroffer. As is commonly
the case, the committee offers employee leaders less at the
outset than it ultimately expects to give.

Keep information from employees. A more direct adversary
relationship between employees and city officials causes the
latter to place greater emphasis on secrecy. In the course of
compiling data and making calculations, Oakland's city manager is increasingly aware of the value of information as a power
resource. He is sensitive to what others have observed: that
"information violates the law of conservation, since sharing
it does not diminish its quantity, though its value may decline
as more people possess it."[15] With the dawn of the bargaining
phase, the manager prizes secrecy more than ever. Thus in
1970 he ended the practice of sharing the results of the Reading

[15] Warren F. Ilchman and Norman Thomas Uphoff, *The Political Economy of Change*
(Berkeley: University of California Press, 1969), p. 67.

Formula salary survey with employees. Since losing this aid
to calculation, the rank and file no longer know what they
have coming to them under a previous decision rule. Changes
in the budgetary form also reflect the manager's concern with
creating uncertainty for opponents. Until 1970 the preliminary
budget which the finance office made available in June contained a salary increase reserve category. This specified the
amount top officials had set aside for a possible employee pay
boost; but after 1969 this figure no longer appeared. The
manager wanted to keep employees guessing about how much
he could afford to give them. From his point of view the more
ignorant they were of contingency funds the better. The experience of Oakland's manager suggests, then, that when one
resource declines in value as a means of attaining ends (for
example, authority), actors tend to become more skillful in
manipulating others (for example, information).

Concede the merit pay raise. In considering the counteroffer
which the manager formulates, it is important to realize that
it is above and beyond a raise he has already agreed to grant
to a substantial number of bureaucrats. This ensues as a result
of city hall's merit pay system. Each year most of Oakland's
classified employees receive a seniority or step increase which a-
mounts to about a 2 1/2 percent hike over their previous year's
salary.[16] While some persons in city hall call the increase a
"merit" raise, it is so automatic that the term is inaccurate;
officials rarely deny employees the boost. In preparing the
budget, the analyst assumes that all eligible employees will
receive the increases and adjusts personnel expenditure figures
accordingly.

The manager and some finance staff members are unenthusiastic about the automatic quality of the pay boost. While
they would like to see step increases which are based more
on merit, and which are far less automatic, they have not
seriously pushed for this "reform." Instead Oakland officials
have adopted what Wildavsky and Singer (in their discussion
of foreign policy) have called an averaging strategy. This
strategy "rejects creating special policies for each" case and

[16] Once an individual reaches the top step in a salary ladder he does not receive
an increase.

"maintains the same policy for an entire class" of instances. "The rationale for adopting the same policy for an entire class ... is that the results would, on the average, be better than trying to work out specific policies for all or a few of them. ... Averaging strategies originate as a response to conditions that make it prohibitively expensive to calculate new policies for each situation."[17]

From the manager's vantage, a serious effort to administer a merit pay plan would have substantial costs. Since there are norms against doing it capriciously, it would require more systematic employee evaluation than bureaucrats presently carry out. In addition, administrators would have to spend considerable time making calculations about whether to grant each employee a raise. Still another cost would be increased discontent and conflict within the organization. Employee leaders would protest. There would be unpleasantness. A special appeal mechanism to handle complaints about the rating might be necessary. Given disadvantages of this nature, awarding an average increase to everyone has a compelling logic even if it leads to overpayment and a failure to reward quality performance.

In general, then, where employee groups are strong and good performance information is scarce, officials will try to reduce conflict by adopting an averaging strategy.

Elected officials dispense justifications. In attempting to resolve differences concerning other pay issues, the city manager works through his Meet and Confer Committee. During this bargaining phase politicians are minimally involved and will remain so if employee leaders accept an offer which comes close to what the manager originally expected to give. If consensus occurs, the city council generally rubber-stamps the agreement. To ignore the recommendation of the Meet and Confer Committee would lower the status of the committee in negotiations; elected officials would have to spend more time bargaining; moreover, prospects are minimal that councilmen could convince employee groups to settle for a smaller pay package.

It is when the manager cannot forge a settlement that elected

---

[17] Aaron Wildavsky with Max Singer, "A Third World Averaging Strategy," in *The Revolt Against the Masses and Other Essays on Politics and Public Policy*, ed. Aaron Wildavsky (New York: Basic Books, 1971), p. 474.

politicians tend to intervene more actively. Relying on the manager for data and advice, they seek to justify publicly city hall's position while at the same time they search for a new problem solution.

Initially, the mayor and councilmen respond to employee discontent by trying to enhance or preserve their status as competent government officials. To this end, they defend the offer that city hall has extended and question the propriety and accuracy of employee statements. The 1969 remarks of the mayor to the police association indicate themes which city officials repeatedly use. First, the mayor claimed that disruptive tactics would be a "grave disservice" to the citizens; this was the public interest theme. The mayor aimed a second contention at a particular group—the taxpayers. He claimed that these people, particularly the old living on fixed income, would foot the bill if the city granted police demands. Third, the mayor emphasized a reference group argument that the "grass was not greener" elsewhere. He noted that fringe benefits in Oakland were higher than in any city across the nation and he cited four California cities in support of this contention. Finally, the mayor sought to reduce the status of police leaders in the eyes of the public, arguing that they were not "truly representative" of the rank-and-file policemen.

While justifying themselves publicly, top policy makers also assess the need to search further for a problem solution. In general, the resources they are willing to commit to a renewed hunt for a solution increase with their perception of employee organization strength. The greater cost and uncertainty they believe an employee group can create, the more loquacious and the more interested in new data they become. For this reason, they pay more attention when the police association is unhappy than when local #1 is complaining.

Search for new information. When confronted with a strong group and a stalemate, the manager and council at times promote a fact-finding mission. This tactic meshes nicely with the faith Oakland council members have in "the big round table" method of conflict resolution.[18] It assumes that if men

[18] Jeffrey Pressman, "Preconditions of Mayoral Leadership," *American Political Science Review* 66 (June 1972): 519.

of good will have the facts and sit down to discuss matters, they can agree. The possibility that good communication and excellent information may exacerbate differences is not widely understood. The manager and council also appreciate this tactic because it buys additional time. They can avoid an immediate ultimatum to come to a decision and accordingly can assess their stake in the issue more thoroughly.

The quest for new data need not have all the payoffs that the council would like, however. In July 1969, for instance, city officials and the police leadership agreed to visit seventeen jurisdictions in hopes of coming up with data to justify one claim or the other. Fact-finding did not produce agreement, however, because negotiators saw the new information through different lenses. The material incentives goal of the council has long been to follow the leader, that is, to stay competitive but not to pay more than "necessary."

The police felt that their professional excellence and the hazards they faced entitled them to top pay. Consequently, when the council and city manager noted that the Oakland police received more fringe benefits than most of the seventeen sampled cities, they thought that this fact supported their idea that the police association request lacked justification. Police leaders took a different view. They fought to the end for a 5 percent night differential pay even though none of the seventeen sampled cities had such a policy. Where basic values differ, new information often means little.

Information gathering is, then, unlikely to produce a solution particularly when the council confronts a high-resource employee organization committed, if necessary, to the strategic threat. At such times, only concessions to employee leaders in areas which they deem important are likely to bring peace. This brings us to a basic question: How have the Oakland manager and council fared in their efforts to keep down pay increases? During the manager's term of office the city has moved from a formulae phase into a bargaining period. Have employee groups extracted larger pay boosts as a result? Data limitations prevent definitive answers to these queries, but some tentative conclusions are possible.

OUTCOMES

Financial costs per man-year provide one clue. Such data not only incorporate salary increases but certain kinds of fringe benefit concessions as well. Table 7 shows that cost per man-year had risen by $3347 over a four-year period, an increase of 31.5 percent. Table 7 also indicates that increases were more substantial after the bargaining phase began. In the formulae period, costs per man-year rose by .3 and 8.9 percent respectively; with the advent of 1969, increase amounted to 9.7 and 9.8 percent. Limited as the data are, they do suggest that in the transition to the new phase, the manager has had to pay more for services. In passing, one can note that these increases do not simply reflect cost-of-living boosts. During this time, the consumer price index indicates that the value of the dollar went from $1.029 in 1966 to $.86 in 1970 (1967 = $1.00), a decline of 16.4 per cent.[19] Costs per man-year rose by just under twice that rate.

TABLE 7: Fiscal Cost per Man-Year Has Increased, 1966–1971

Fiscal year	Man-years	Personnel expenditures	Cost per* man-year	Percentage of increase in man-year cost over previous year
1966/67	3465.8	$36,858,264	$10,634.85	—
1967/68	3486.0	37,171,541	10,663.09	.3
1968/69	3486.6	40,493,519	11,614.04	8.9
1969/70	3569.7	45,463,769	12,736.02	9.7
1970/71	3616.2	50,562,095	13,982.11	9.8

Source: Oakland Preliminary Budgets.
* This is far from a perfect indicator for some purposes since it incorporates certain retirement costs. As the number of retired employees rises, this figure tends to go up as well.

Not surprisingly, certain types of employees have profited more than others. Table 8 presents salary levels for a cross-section of positions, including public safety, clerical, professional, skilled and unskilled categories, and reveals that police and firemen have recorded the most substantial gains. Patrolmen

[19] *Statistical Abstract of the United States, 1971* (Washington, D.C.: U.S. Government Printing Office, 1971), p. 332.

and hosemen won pay hikes of 35 percent; increases for the other groups ranged from 22 to 25 percent. This finding lends support to the claim that the police association exerts pace-setting leverage. While hosemen in the fire department have received comparable gains, their success has rested on an ability to maintain pay parity with the police. (Note that this parity does not extend to fringe benefits.) Data on man-year costs all show police increases to be above the mean. While the increase for all bureaucrats was 31.5 percent from 1967 to 1971, police costs per man-year went up by 49 percent. (In absolute terms, the dollar outlay per man-year of police work rose from $10,927 to $16,269, a boost of $5,342.)

TABLE 8: SELECTED SALARIES HAVE RISEN

	Salaries at Lowest Step per Month				
Class	1966/67	1968/69	1970/71 (Dollars)	Amount increase	Percentage hike
Patrolman	711	823	960	249	35
Hoseman	711	797	960	249	35
Electrician	824	910	1,029	205	25
Semi-skilled Laborer	541	598	669	128	24
Intermediate Typist Clerk	433	478	535	102	24
Assistant Engineer	845	910	1,043	198	24
Assistant Planner	784	845	956	172	22

Source: Oakland City Hall Salary Ordinances.

Since taking office, then, Oakland's manager has granted substantial pay concessions, particularly to public safety workers. Employee leverage in the material incentives game has been much in evidence.

CONCLUSION

The pay arena's less centralized (and recently, more fluid) leverage pattern creates more decision uncertainties for high officials than they face in the manpower sphere. The city manager cannot as readily anticipate employee reactions to his pay maneuvers as he can department head responses to his manpower gambits. He therefore has less confidence in his capacity to pick the most satisfactory alternative available.

As in the manpower arena, however, the city manager and others have access to scorecards which help them assess how well they are doing. Dollars and the number of workdays lost are the major tallies for keeping track of victory or defeat. While this numerical feedback may not help officials assess the value of a specific tactic it helps them determine the overall results of their strategies.

In the personnel arenas examined so far, Oakland's city manager has been a key participant. In turning to recruitment, we will find that the city manager is a much less pivotal force and that leverage is more decentralized.

4

The Politics of Recruitment: Publicity Tactics

> It is the policy of the City . . . to attract to municipal
> service the best and most competent person avail-
> able; to assure that appointments will be based on
> merit and fitness as ascertained by practical compet-
> itive examination and by records of achievement; and
> to provide the employees security of tenure, with
> advancement or promotion within the service where
> practicable from among employees having appropri-
> ate qualifications. . . .
>
> Oakland City Charter[1]

Oakland bureaucrats are sensitive to the importance of recruitment. As one might expect of reformed governments, attracting
skilled employees is a highly salient objective. To be sure, racial
and other ascriptive considerations affect recruitment decision
making (as I will show in chapter 6); yet much hiring behavior
in city hall can still be understood in terms of the value officials
place on attracting the competent while simultaneously conserving scarce resources.

Skill is facility at performing some task. Given this definition,
we can conceive of employees as displaying skills congruence,
mismatch, deficit, or slack. Chart 3 captures the meaning of
each of these concepts. The circle with the solid line reflects
the minimum work-related skills the occupational role demands. The dash line shows the skills an incumbent possesses

[1] Oakland, *The Charter of the City of Oakland,* Article VIII, Section 800.

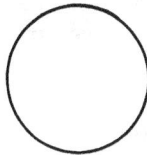

Skills Congruence

Skills congruence is present when the abilities employees have equal those that their organizational roles demand (e.g., a worker knows only how to fix cars and that is what his agency expects of him).

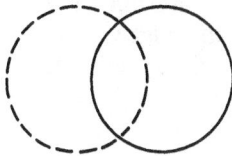

Skills Mismatch

Skills mismatch exists when there is some overlap between the skills ordinarily demanded and those employees possess, but where employees have slack abilities in some areas and deficits in others (e.g., a personnel analyst has more knowledge than is necessary in advertising vacancies, but does not know how to construct examinations, for which he is also responsible).

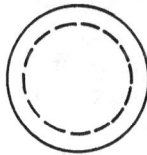

Skills Deficit

Skills deficit occurs when employees lack the abilities which organizational roles normally require (e.g., the city hires employees to program a computer, but they do not know how).

Skills Slack

Skills slack exists when the work related abilities of employees exceed those which organizational roles demand (e.g., a man hired to take care of the park lawns not only does so with ease, but also understands mechanics and carpentry).

with respect to the particular role he occupies and with regard to other jobs in the organization as well.

Generally, officials believe that slack is the most desirable state, followed by congruence, mismatch, and deficit. The reasons for this are clear. When an employee displays skills deficit, top bureaucrats have only costly options available. They can: (a) spend time trying to remove the employee and find a replacement; (b) stick with him and put up with poor performance, which could undermine departmental service and prestige (tolerance of incompetence in public safety units is particularly risky); or (c) commit resources toward bringing the individual into a condition of skills congruence or slack (for instance, city hall might spend resources training an employee hired to fix traffic signals who had proved to be inept).[2] Officials find skill mismatch slightly more attractive than deficit because it opens up another alternative. If the employee fails at one job, they may be able to transfer or demote him to one where he will perform adequately.

Not surprisingly, Oakland bureaucrats find skills congruence and slack most appealing. Presence of the former means that the job will get done. The existence of the latter means not only that the job will get done but also that the organization has a hedge against uncertainty. An employee with skills slack can often utilize his talents when he runs into unusual problems. One particularly important contingency is the vacancy at the higher level.

When promotion from within is the prevailing norm, leaders hope that employees at one hierarchical level will develop sufficient slack to display skills congruence in the position above them. In short, they want bureaucrats to be promotable. For these, and other reasons, Oakland officials generally strive to foster skills slack. To be sure the quest for such slack often has limits. Bureaucrats in the public works office would look askance on a Ph.D. who wanted to work as a semi-skilled laborer if for no other reason than that the Ph.D. would be likely to quit soon after taking the position. Nonetheless, agency officials do strive for some slack.[3]

[2] Amitai Etzioni, *Modern Organizations* (Englewood Cliffs, N.J.: Prentice Hall, 1964), pp. 68-70, has noted the relationship between control, selection, and socialization.

[3] In discussing skills level, it is useful to remember that the concept applies to individuals in roles and not to organizations.

In their efforts to attract skilled manpower Oakland officials employ publicity and selection strategies. The former refers to the transmission of information to the environment and internal organization in an effort to attract applicants. The latter deals with the processes involved in accumulating data on job hunters and choosing the ones most likely to foster skills slack. Of course, the distinction between publicity and selection is in at least one respect misleading. Publicity tactics, after all, lead to de facto selection, since someone who never hears of an opening will fail to get the job no matter how well qualified. Yet I believe the distinction is useful in pointing to the main phases of city hall's search for skilled personnel.

This chapter will deal with the publicity facet of search; the next will assess selection; and the following one will analyze the minority challenge to recruitment procedures. Throughout, the spotlight will be on hiring to the classified civil service rather than the tiny number of exempt slots at the top of the pyramid. While employment practices at the higher levels affect organizational performance, so do those processes which bring in the vast majority of city employees. Moreover, social science literature generally tells us less about rank-and-file hiring than recruitment to elite slots.[4]

THE CLASSIFIED CIVIL SERVICE

In fiscal 1970/71, more than 98 percent of city hall's full-time positions were classified.[5] Even if we add part-time positions (which are exempt) to the rest, over 93 percent of all man-years are still classified. This high percentage affects the recruitment leverage pattern by giving the civil service office substantial clout. As usual, then, rules strengthen some actors at the expense of others. Often in political life those whose freedom the rules restrict try to alter them. In Oakland, however, only a few minor skirmishes have emerged over issues related to

[4] For data on elite recruitment, see Richard Fenno, *The President's Cabinet* (New York: Random House, 1959); Theodore Lowi, *At the Pleasure of the Mayor: Patronage and Power in New York City, 1898-1958* (Glencoe, Ill.: Free Press, 1964); Dean E. Mann, "The Selection of Federal Political Executives," *American Political Science Review* 58 (March 1964): 81-99.

[5] Data are from Oakland Finance Office documents.

the classified civil service. Elected politicians, often presumed to be the natural enemy of such a system, have shown no interest in expanding the number of exempt slots.

Elected politicians adopt a hands-off policy. Oakland's mayor and council have paid little attention to rank-and-file hiring. They are content with the authority to appoint the city manager and members of various commissions and have not tried to increase the number of exempt slots or circumvent the rules to award jobs to their followers. Patronage appointments to temporary or part-time positions in evidence elsewhere, are nowhere to be found in Oakland.

The fact that the mayor and council are low resource recruitment actors in part accounts for their hiring inactivity. However, their basic value orientations afford a more powerful explanation. Having imbibed the "good government," antiparty culture so much a part of Oakland's local government tradition, they have little desire to influence bureaucratic appointments and removals. The city has been formally nonpartisan and had a civil service office since 1911. It has never had a vigorous machine that sustained itself by giving jobs to party regulars.[6] Patronage played a minor role in the success of Oakland's only version of a conventional political boss, Mike Kelly. From 1915 to 1930, he used his influence with Mayor Davie to get public works contracts awarded to certain firms. In exchange, the contractor would, among other things, agree to employ some of Kelly's supporters. But even this limited form of patronage went out with the adoption of the council-manager form of government in 1931. At present, a nonpartisan ethos pervades. The mayor and councilmen are content to leave most recruitment in the hands of bureaucrats.[7]

Few support exemptions. The city manager on the other hand does favor more exempt positions because such slots enhance his control over hiring and removal. Few, however, share the manager's view. Employee leaders oppose exemptions because

---

[6] For perspective, see Martin and Susan Tolchin, *To the Victor: Political Patronage from the Clubhouse to the White House,* (New York: Random House, 1971); Harold F. Gosnell, *Machine Politics: Chicago Model,* (Chicago: University of Chicago Press, 1968); Raymond Wolfinger, "Why Political Machines Have Not Withered Away and Other Revisionist Thoughts," *Journal of Politics* 34 (May 1972), pp. 365-398.

[7] One cannot gainsay the importance of a nonpartisan culture. See Edward C. Banfield and James Q. Wilson, *City Politics* (New York: Vintage Press, 1963), pp. 207-208.

such a designation increases uncertainty over job tenure and promotions for their followers. If a position is exempt, its incumbent cannot appeal a dismissal to the Civil Service Commission; nor does the rank-and-file bureaucrat receive priority over outside applicants when applying for a high-level exempt post. Civil service commissioners also oppose more exemptions because such labeling diminishes their authority and because they sympathize with rank-and-file concerns. Even high officials who occupy exempt slots are usually not interested in seeing more of them created. The great majority of these bureaucrats gradually worked themselves up through the hierarchy and sympathize with the value subordinates place on security and promotional opportunities. Furthermore, agency heads think that the classified civil service helps protect professional values. The head of the housing division believes, for instance, that "the influential" would benefit if more positions were exempt. On matters of code enforcement, friends of the councilmen might ask for special favors. Employees, insecure about tenure, would bend the rules to accommodate them. Faced with few constituencies which back increased exemptions, the city manager seldom fights for more unilateral hiring authority.

Recruitment to Oakland City Hall does not, then, feature elected politicians and the manager as primary players. Rather the main protagonist is the civil service office. In essence, its staff practices a mediating technology which links "clients or customers who are or wish to be interdependent."[8] Its main customers are an amorphous constituency of job seekers in city hall's environment, municipal employees eager for promotion, and top department personnel who want to fill vacancies quickly with competent people. How, then, do these and other players respond tactically to the recruitment game?

CIVIL SERVICE PUBLICITY TACTICS

Publicizing a vacancy consists of transmitting information concerning government manpower needs to people. Of all the

[8] J. D. Thompson, *Organizations in Action* (New York: McGraw Hill, 1967), p. 16.

actors in the bureaucracy, the civil service office is the most consistently involved in the publicity process. The formal organization chart holds the office responsible for assuring that city hall attracts skilled applicants, and personnel analysts devote considerable time to it.

Department heads are the main clients making recruitment demands on the personnel director. They are well aware that shrewd publicity campaigns can make the differences between getting a run-of-the-mill (albeit acceptable) candidate and one with skills slack. Agencies vary in the amount of service they seek from the civil service office. One element of their demand is the total number of employees they need, which stems from turnover and manpower allocation decisions made during the budgetary process. Table 9 provides a limited overview of hiring demands in Oakland. High-demand departments are those that wanted 75 or more positions filled during the year; moderate-demand agencies called for from 25 to 74 recruits; and low-demand, 24 or less.

While the data are from only one fiscal year, they do show the variation among agencies. The police department accounted for more than one-quarter of the city's needs and the three high-demand departments for more than one-half. The overall need pattern only partly reflects the size of the agency. Police, public works, and parks and recreation rank first, third, and fourth, respectively, in the number of man-years they incorporate. The fire department, which is the second largest unit in the city, is a moderate-demand agency.

Vacancy totals are, of course, only one index of the work load which departments create for the civil service office, since some slots are far more difficult for a personnel analyst to fill than others. Generally, professional positions and certain hazardous ones like patrolman pose the most vexing problems, particularly in times of economic prosperity. Considering this factor, the problems posed by the police department increase in magnitude.

Table 10 shows that almost half the police slots (47 percent patrolmen) typically pose search problems, whereas in the case of public works and parks and recreation, less than one-fifth of the vacancies (that is, the professional-managerial) create

TABLE 9: DEPARTMENTS VARY IN PERSONNEL NEEDS, FISCAL YEAR 1969/70

Department	Size of department in full-time man-years 1969/70	Number of full-time employees leaving positions refilled in 1969/70	Departmental position gains in 1969/70 budget	Total number of full-time positions needing filling	Percentage of government recruiting needs
High-demand departments					
Police	988	105	88	193	27.5
Public Works	456	91	12	103	14.7
Parks and Recreation	403	82	8	90	12.8
Moderate-demand departments					
Fire	687	62	3	65	9.3
General Services	274	53	5	58	8.3
Museum	83	42	16	58	8.3
Library	186	44	0	44	6.3
Finance	94	34	6	40	5.7
Limited-demand departments					
City Auditor	6	12	1	13	1.9
Building and Housing	83	12	0	12	1.7
Civil Service	17	8	0	8	1.1
City Planning	21	7	1	8	1.1
Retirement Administration	5	5	0	5	.7
City Manager	7	2	0	2	.3
City Attorney	17	1	0	1	.1
City Physician	2	1	0	1	.1
TOTAL				701	99.9

Source: Civil Service Office and Oakland Preliminary Budget, 1969/70.

difficulties. The police department, then, places the greatest demand on the civil service office in more ways than one.[9]

Rely on standard operating procedure. In focusing on publicity, the personnel director mainly seeks to manipulate his resources to satisfy department heads. His activities also reflect a sense of obligation to job hunters, however. Merit principles dictate that qualified individuals be given a chance to compete for government positions. Job hunters must therefore have a means of learning about vacancies and must have a reasonable time to apply. To these ends, civil service rules require personnel

[9] The police department fills almost all managerial and professional slots through promotion. Consequently, the civil service office experiences few search problems with respect to them. Public works and parks and recreation contain far more entry level managerial and professional slots, which create more search burdens.

TABLE 10: HIGH-DEMAND DEPARTMENTS NEED DIFFERENT TYPES OF PERSONNEL, FISCAL YEAR 1969/70

Job type	Percentage of total vacancies in the Police Department	Percentage of total vacancies in Public Works	Percentage of total vacancies in Parks and Recreation
Professional and Managerial (above Patrolman Level in the Police Dept.)	11	16	18
Secretarial-Clerical	17	14	5
Paraprofessional and Skilled Workers	19	29	43
Patrolmen	47	–	–
Semi-Skilled	7	41	35
TOTAL	101 (n=193)	100 (n=90)	101 (n=102)

Source: Civil Service Office.

analysts to publicize vacancies in an official newspaper (the *Oakland Tribune*) for three days and to accept applications for at least ten days. Rules like these at times cause city hall to spend more effort publicizing vacancies than is necessary to attract the human resources it needs.

Whether fulfilling obligations to job seekers or department heads, the formal goal of the civil service office is to attract the most competent applicants available. How close the agency comes to attaining this goal is a mystery. How can the staff be sure that communications flow to the right spots in the environment with the right message and the right medium at the right time? The number of applicants who show up and pass the tests provides one clue. But who knows which tactics produce these outcomes or whether another strategy would lure more talented applicants?

Ordinarily, the personnel director does not worry much about these uncertainties. Rather he responds to this situation of intrinsically complex choices by adhering to certain decision rules which have fostered satisfactory performance in the past and have not damaged his status. Chart 4 captures the nature of these rules. It indicates that analysts first attempt to avoid publicizing the vacancy at all by picking someone from the eligible list. If the staff member cannot fill the slot this way,

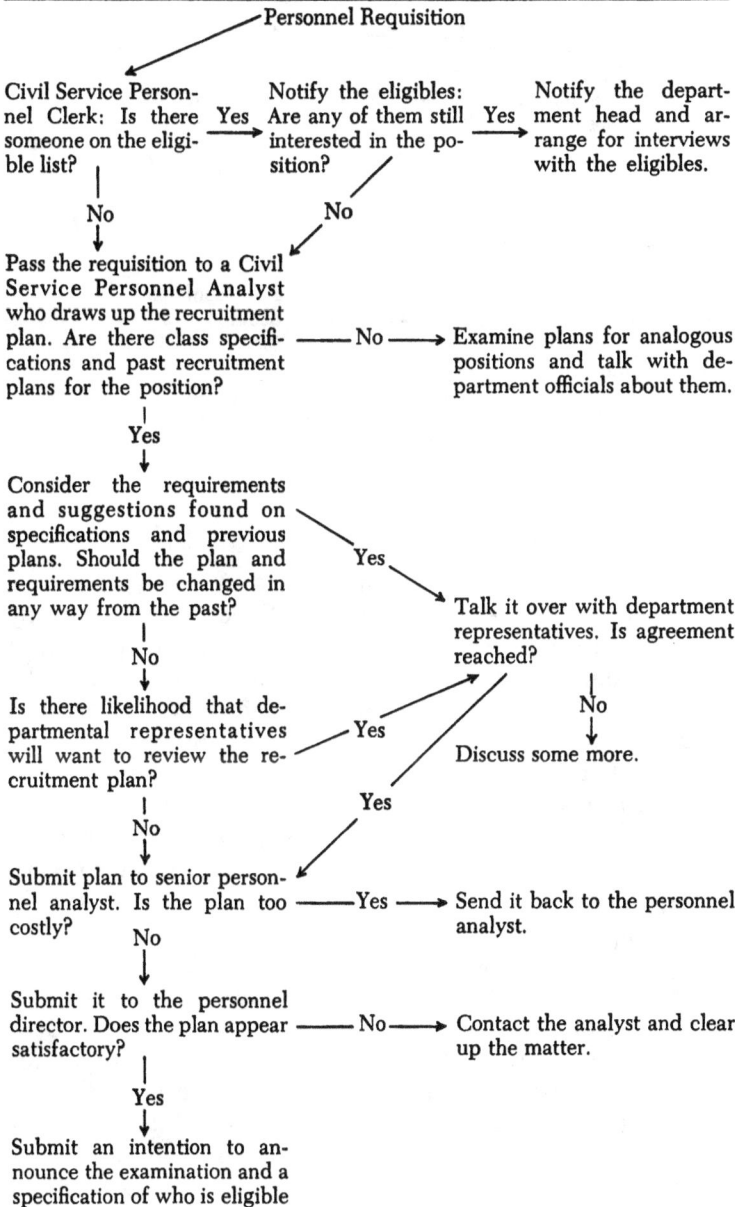

Personnel Requisition

Civil Service Personnel Clerk: Is there someone on the eligible list? — **Yes** → Notify the eligibles: Are any of them still interested in the position? — **Yes** → Notify the department head and arrange for interviews with the eligibles.

No ↓

No (from "Notify the eligibles")

Pass the requisition to a Civil Service Personnel Analyst who draws up the recruitment plan. Are there class specifications and past recruitment plans for the position? —— **No** —→ Examine plans for analogous positions and talk with department officials about them.

Yes ↓

Consider the requirements and suggestions found on specifications and previous plans. Should the plan and requirements be changed in any way from the past? —— **Yes** → Talk it over with department representatives. Is agreement reached?

No ↓

No ↓

Discuss some more.

Is there likelihood that departmental representatives will want to review the recruitment plan? — **Yes** →

No ↓

Yes

Submit plan to senior personnel analyst. Is the plan too costly? —— **Yes** —→ Send it back to the personnel analyst.

No ↓

Submit it to the personnel director. Does the plan appear satisfactory? —— **No** —→ Contact the analyst and clear up the matter.

Yes ↓

Submit an intention to announce the examination and a specification of who is eligible

CHART 4—*Continued*

to take the examination to the
Civil Service Commission. Do ——— No ——→ Discuss it with commission.
the commissioners approve?

   |
   Yes
   ↓

Have clerk send announce-
ments to standard contacts
and whoever is on the recruit-
ment plan. Does the recruit-   Feel confident that present
ment plan lead to attraction ——— Yes ——→ decision rules are satisfac-
of an adequate supply of   tory.
eligible candidates?

   |
   No
   ↓

Begin thinking about the ways
in which more complex and
distant search can be conducted.

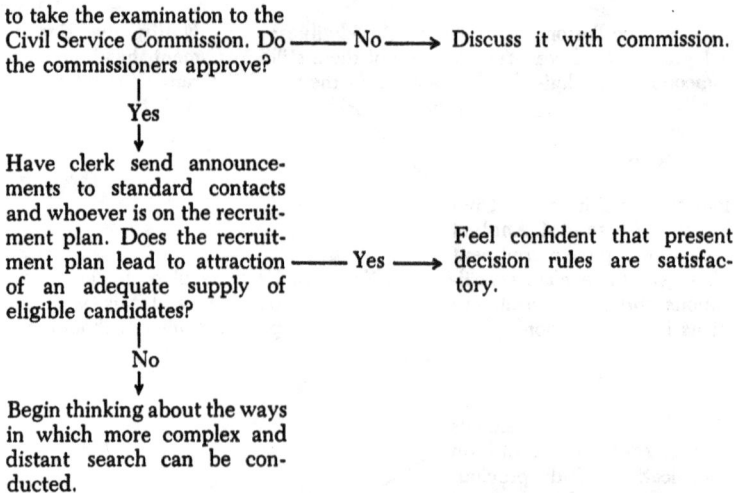

he looks to past practices, perfunctorily contacts departments,
and then draws up a publicity plan. Following a review by
his immediate superiors, his proposal receives the approval of
the Civil Service Commission. Personnel clerks then put the
plan into effect. Only if the publicity effort fails to produce
enough acceptable applicants do calculations become more
complex and time consuming. At such moments, the civil
service office often uses a wider range of media and transmits
more messages greater distances. Having provided this overview, we will now appraise publicity tactics in greater detail.

Keep search cheap. One of the personnel director's main
aspirations is to keep a search from consuming his staff's time
and resources. Extended, complex publicity campaigns take
effort away from test construction, classification studies, performance evaluations, and search for other replacements. Consequently, the cheaper the publicity, the better. One way his
staff reduces costs and simplifies its task is through the use
of an eligible list which specifies those individuals who previously have passed a civil service examination. Whenever
personnel analysts give a test they anticipate future needs by
passing more applicants than there are vacancies. The surplus
candidates go on the list which becomes an informational

resource for the office. The next time a vacancy occurs, the civil service staff checks the eligible list to learn precisely where to look for a replacement. Civil service secretaries then write and phone eligibles until they find three who still want the job. A department official subsequently chooses one of the three.

Use precedent and information from clients. Whenever the list is empty, very near depletion, or two years old, personnel analysts conduct more elaborate publicity campaigns. At such times, they first draw up a recruitment plan which specifies whom they will contact, by what means, and with what message. In performing this task analysts do not rigorously assess costs and benefits of alternative tactics. Rather, they rely on standard operating procedure and in particular on one main formal decision rule—adopt the recruitment plan used in the past. The civil service office has a rudimentary memory system, one component of which contains files of previous publicity blueprints. These documents contain routing rules which specify "who will communicate to whom about what."[10] Unless another good recruiting source immediately comes to mind, the analyst basically adopts the previous plan.

In addition to doing this, he also orders a secretary to send an announcement to locations which automatically receive notification of almost all civil service openings. These contacts number about 75 and include Bay Area employment offices, educational institutions (for example, University of California, Berkeley, Laney College in Oakland), social service agencies (for example, rehabilitation offices, the YMCA), and some minority organizations (for example, Mexican-American Political Association).

The civil service staff does not strictly rely on information in its files to guide its behavior; it also draws on some which its clients furnish. Before completing the blueprint, the analyst contacts a department official for publicity suggestions. The official will often recommend placing advertisements in certain journals or getting in touch with certain institutions. The building division executive will, for instance, tell him to adver-

[10] Richard Cyert and James G. March, *A Behavioral Theory of the Firm* (Englewood Cliffs, N.J.: Prentice Hall, 1964), p. 109.

tise in the *Daily Pacific Builder*. The city attorney will on occasion advise him to contact certain law firms. The analyst discusses matters with departments not only to enhance his expertise; he also wants to coopt the agency into the publicity process. In case applicants prove difficult to find, he reduces the tendency of the department to blame him for the failure. Under such circumstances who has the "buck" is more difficult to determine.

The civil service staff also builds information by recording inquiries from job hunters. At times someone will come to the office to determine whether a position is available. If one is not, the clerk at the reception desk asks the job seeker to fill out a small green card which specifies the type of position he wants and where he can be reached. When a slot of this type opens, the analyst glances at the card and contacts those who indicated interest. This card file simplifies search problems by pinpointing where likely applicants are in city hall's environment.

Maintain the rules. Whether engaged in hiring or other activities, bureaucrats generally attempt to reduce the burdens of calculation by maintaining their decision rules. Hence, in the recruitment arena, Oakland's personnel director is reluctant to authorize special publicity campaigns unless programmed procedures fail to turn up enough applicants to fill vacancies. He is wary of department claims that their needs are unique and require special attention by his office.

Department officials will, for example, occasionally ask the personnel director to conduct an extensive search before the eligible list is empty. By getting him to do this they hope to improve the quality of candidates available for appointment. If an eligible list is old the remaining successful applicants on it are often those "dregs" at the bottom, who just managed to pass the examinations. If the personnel director opens a new recruitment drive a department head may avoid having to hire a "barely satisfactory" applicant and can instead pick from three highly competent candidates. Then too, when a department head believes that turnover in his agency will rapidly deplete the existing eligible list, he often asks the personnel director to publicize vacancies before the rules require it. By persuading the personnel director to get a jump on a publicity campaign, the agency head can avoid delays in filling vacancies.

The personnel director, relying on his status as an expert, could persuade the Civil Service Commission to authorize such "premature" publicity efforts. Moreover, he has some incentive to do so since the action would build his prestige with favored departments. But he also pays costs for making such concessions. The time it takes to conduct such campaigns might be devoted to more immediate problems. Furthermore, if he gives in to one agency, others might bury him under requests. Consequently, the director generally sticks to his office decision rule: do not reopen the search unless the eligible list is empty; in short, maintain the rules unless they produce bad results.[11]

Prerequisites for rule breaking. This is not to say that the personnel director inevitably turns down special requests for nonprogrammed publicity efforts. For rare, "once only" cases where costs are not excessive and where the prospects of enhancing his prestige with powerful constituents are good, he will deviate from standard decision rules. For instance, the finance director, who has considerable say over the civil service office's budgetary allocation, asked the personnel chief to help him find an accounting officer. Since the position was exempt, the personnel director was under no formal obligation to contact anyone. But in order to boost his status, he agreed and eventually secured applications from several individuals. But at the last minute the finance director got a call from a friend in Houston, Texas and hired him. As a result, the personnel director felt that his office had received little credit for its efforts. Even so, he believes that such favors often promote good will.

The civil service office also departs from its routine when applicants are hard to find. At such time, the staff deliberates more and will often use such tactics as campus visits, more elaborate media advertising, and personal contacts aimed at community groups. For example, during the mid-sixties when unemployment was low and the aerospace companies booming, computer programmers and engineers were often difficult to

[11] *Ibid.*, p. 121.

find. Officials consequently spent some days touring college campuses. But by October 1970, unemployment in California had hit 7.2 percent and the aerospace industry, in particular, suffered. As a result, the civil service office had plenty of applicants for those positions and more expanded, elaborate publicity efforts were unnecessary. In sum, personnel staffs tend to engage in more complex calculations and more elaborate publicity campaigns if there is labor market scarcity or a high-prestige constituent asks for a special favor which would involve spending a relatively small amount of resources.

DEPARTMENT PUBLICITY TACTICS

While the civil service office is the main actor involved in attracting a candidate, top department officials also participate. Their involvement is, however, a reluctant one. "Let someone else do it" characterizes their attitude. They prefer not to eat up time publicizing vacancies and on occasion refuse requests by the personnel director to participate. In this way, they try to keep the "buck" with him. For example, though the city attorney wants better recruits, he shuns suggestions by the personnel director that he visit law schools. He does not see himself as a "personnel man" and believes that he would be "in a hell of a spot" if he went to campuses because it would divert attention from other responsibilities.

Departments publicize openings as a last resort. Some department personnel do broadly publicize vacancies. Overall, department officials more readily publicize openings if they feel that the civil service office cannot assure them a supply of talented applicants quickly enough. Convinced that the personnel director "lacks the horses" to meet their needs, bureaucrats in the police and parks and recreation departments have, for instance, long been recruitment activists. So too the city planner found that the secretarial-clerical help which the civil service office provided him was unsatisfactory—generally older women who wanted to get on the city payroll so they could draw good retirement benefits. Rather than accept this, he has scanned the environment on his own for competent secretaries, and has earned a reputation in city hall for invariably having skilled and attractive ones.

At times a department head feels that a special effort to locate "quality" personnel is necessary to assure social integration in his agency. For example, the fire chief is well aware that his men spend considerable time together. They work, eat dinner, play ping-pong, watch television, and sleep in the same room. Because for brief periods firemen live in a virtually communal atmosphere, the chief feels that social compatibility is particularly important. Consequently, he encourages his staff to search for those who will fit in.

In scanning the environment the relatively few department heads who make contacts rely on a number of decision rules Chart 5 presents some of the rules they use, and examples of each. As the chart indicates, proximity to Oakland, professional reputations of schools, past hiring successes, college back-

CHART 5:

DECISION RULES OAKLAND DEPARTMENTS USE IN PUBLICIZING VACANCIES

Decision rule	Example
1. Contact those institutions with a reputation for being strong professionally.	The police chief focuses on the schools and universities with police science programs because he believes that people in such programs are more committed to police work and oriented toward desirable police behavior.
2. Search in close proximity to Oakland. (Communications are easier and cost less at close range. Local search may be good for the image of the department.)	Engineers from the Department of Public Works visit the University of California, Berkeley, rather than making more time-consuming trips to the California Institute of Technology in Pasadena.
3. Contact institutions with which you are personally familiar, especially alma maters.	Since they know professors there and probably nurture affection for the school, some search at their alma maters. A former budget and research officer had received his B.A. at San Jose State College and an M.A. from the University of Pittsburgh. He kept in close touch with these schools and recruited at least two analysts from Pittsburgh and one through an old professor at San Jose State.

CHART 5—*Continued*

Decision rule	Example
4. Contact places where you succeeded in the past. (Through learning, past experience becomes a guide to future action.)	The city planner, after recruiting excellent secretarial help at business schools plans to return there to search. Similarly, the police chief has been reinforced by the success of his visits to campuses with police science majors. In the words of one official, after this much success one would have to be a "nut" not to return.
5. Where social integration is a major concern and present interpersonal conflict in the department is low, have subordinates recruit their friends.	Each time the examination for entry level hosemen positions opens, the fire chief distributes a vast number of announcements to the more than 650 employees in his department. He urges his men to find him applicants who will bring "honor" to the department. In the fire department the "friends and relatives" approach has been elevated to the status of formal search policy.
6. Contact skilled individuals about to leave previous jobs.	The police department has focused some attention on the Oakland Army Terminal and Travis Air Force Base. Soldiers are used to the rank system, have had some relevant training, and often are looking for jobs when they leave the service. Furthermore, the Pentagon has offered military personnel "early out" from their military obligation (by three months) if they work for law enforcement agencies.
7. Rely on a business contact or professional associate to help you search. In this way you enlarge the scope of search at no financial cost to yourself.	When the finance director was looking for someone to head the electronic data processing unit, the IBM salesman with whom the city dealt made a considerable number of inquiries on the city's behalf. By being coopted into helping, the salesman hoped to build his status with those in city hall. It was from the IBM salesman that the present incumbent first received word of the opening.
8. Do not search where you will create trouble for other jurisdictions.	In conducting tours to college campuses, Oakland police representatives have been plagued by student disturbances. For instance, in April 1969, 100 students at Michigan State University staged a dem-

CHART 5—*Continued*

Decision rule	Example
	onstration against Oakland police recruiters. When Oakland officials were going to recruit at California State College in Fresno, the police there anticipated trouble. Rather than precipitate problems and overtime compensations for Fresno police officials, Oakland's chief cancelled the visit.

grounds, and knowledge of turnover in other organizations are among the factors shaping department publicity efforts.

Top officials are not, of course, the only agency personnel influencing city hall's publicity process. Sketchy data (for example, from the fire department) indicate that the rank and file play an important part in disseminating information.[12] The employee who is aware of a vacancy will often do his friends and relatives a favor by tipping them off about an opening. Consequently, those who know city bureaucrats have special access to information concerning employment opportunities.

A wide array of actors do, then, exert leverage over the publicity process. Having assessed the pervasiveness of the classified civil service and the tactics which the civil service office and others use to attract applicants, I will next focus on how city hall evaluates those who want jobs.

[12] See Richard Wilcock and Walter H. Franke, *Unwanted Workers* (New York: Free Press, 1963), p. 129; Harold L. Sheppard and A. Harvey Belitsky, *The Job Hunt* (Baltimore: John Hopkins Press, 1966), p. 187.

5

The Politics of Recruitment: Selection Tactics

Disabuse yourself of the fiction ... that employers
necessarily know what they are doing when they hire.

Richard Irish[1]

Selection is a guessing game. Obtaining and interpreting good
information about the ability of a job hunter is extremely
difficult. Problems begin with defining skill itself. Often the
criteria and standards of excellent performance are so vague
that no one is sure what to look for in an applicant. (Those
familiar with never-ending discussions concerning "what makes
a good teacher" will quickly understand the point.) Even if
decision makers firmly grasp what skilled performance is, they
may not be able to predict which applicant will display such
behavior. Who can be sure that Candidate X will be more competent than Candidate Y? Officials typically lack proof that
their selection practices give jobs to the most adroit.

Oakland's personnel analysts and certain department officials are sensitive to many of the uncertainties involved in
selection. Yet many of them feel that their hiring tactics
produce at least satisfactory results. Most Oakland officials
believe that they can distinguish the very bad and very good
applicants. Some have great faith in the predictive power of
certain hiring standards.

[1] Richard K. Irish, *Go Hire Yourself An Employer*, (Garden City, N.Y.: Anchor
Press, 1973) p. xxii.

Chart 6 presents an overview of the technology which Oakland officials use in trying to reduce uncertainty about appli-

CHART 6: OAKLAND'S ENTRY LEVEL SELECTION PROCESS

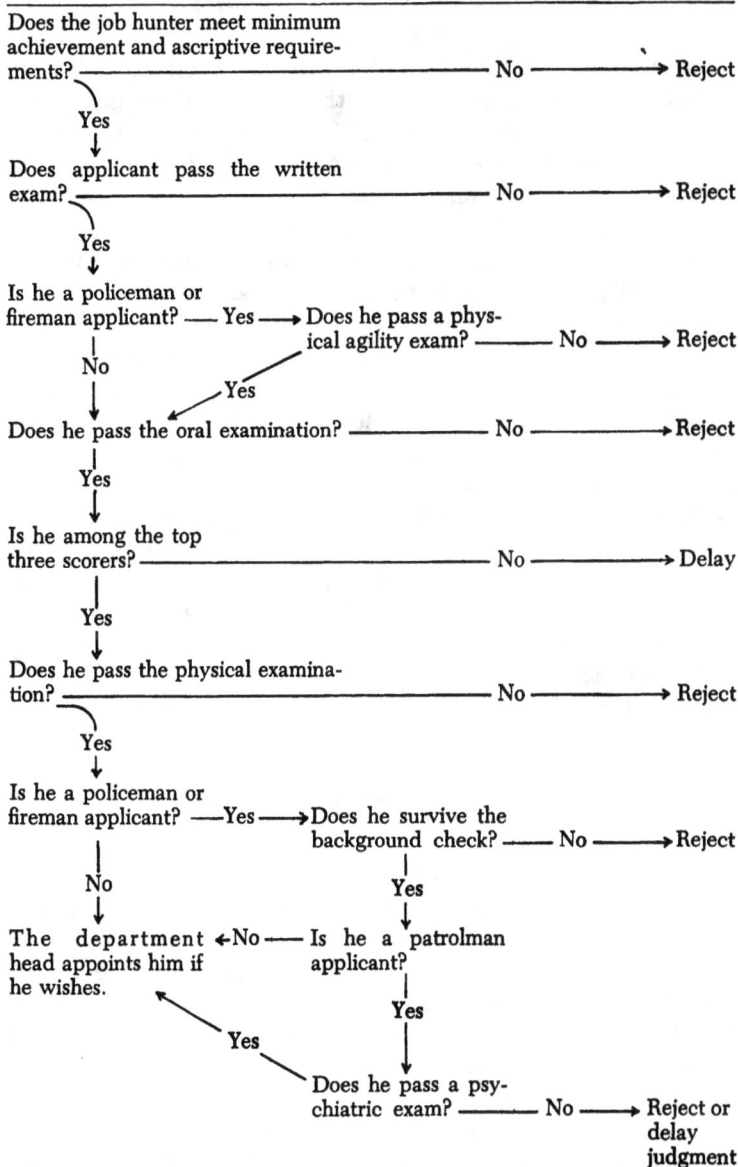

Does the job hunter meet minimum
achievement and ascriptive require-
ments? ─────────────────────────── No ───────→ Reject

   Yes
   ↓

Does applicant pass the written
exam? ─────────────────────────── No ───────→ Reject

   Yes
   ↓

Is he a policeman or
fireman applicant? ── Yes ──→ Does he pass a phys-
       | ical agility exam? ───── No ───→ Reject
   No
             Yes
   ↓
Does he pass the oral examination? ───── No ───────→ Reject

   Yes
   ↓

Is he among the top
three scorers? ─────────────────────── No ───────→ Delay

   Yes
   ↓

Does he pass the physical examina-
tion? ─────────────────────────── No ───────→ Reject

   Yes
   ↓

Is he a policeman or
fireman applicant? ──Yes──→ Does he survive the
       | background check? ──── No ──────→ Reject
   No   Yes
   ↓   ↓
The department ←No── Is he a patrolman
head appoints him if   applicant?
he wishes.
                  Yes
        Yes   ↓

               Does he pass a psy-
               chiatric exam? ───── No ───→ Reject or
                                   delay
                                   judgment

cant ability. It shows that the process is more elaborate for some positions than for others. Almost all job hunters must have certain background attributes and pass written, oral, and physical examinations, and a final interview. But only certain applicants are subject to a background check, a psychiatric examination, and a physical agility test. More complex selection structures correlate positively with the amount of money the city spends training the recruit and the possible impact of employee performance on life and property. For this reason, selection procedures for patrolmen are the most extensive. Abuse of police authority or simple incompetence often have grave implications for the administration of justice. Furthermore, the police department spends close to $4,000 training each patrolman.

Though formal organization charts confer recruitment responsibility on the civil service office, control over selection is fragmented. Civil service employees and department officials share clout over the establishment of minimum education and experience requirements; while personnel analysts exert more power over the written examination, the departments substantially control the oral test, the final interview of the three eligibles, and the background investigation. Professionals from other jurisdictions enter the decision process for promotionals, and medical doctors hold veto power over physical and psychiatric examinations. Below, I will explore in greater depth city hall's tactical response to selection and the resulting leverage pattern.

BACKGROUND REQUIREMENTS:
THE INITIAL GATE

One way administrators try to promote sage hiring decisions is through the use of background information (such as job experience, education, police record, and age). While they have no data to confirm their view, officials believe that many of these indicators are useful in predicting the future performance of applicants. Moreover, personnel analysts appreciate them because the criteria lighten their work load. The plethora of background standards eliminates about one-fifth of the job seekers prior to testing. This proportion, which is substantial in itself, becomes even more significant if we remember that it underrepresents the number of people screened out. Many do not even bother to apply since they perceive that they lack the necessary attributes.

Diplomas and experience: What is past is prologue. All requirements eliminate some job hunters, but in this section we will focus primarily on the minimum education and experience that city hall demands. Department heads and personnel analysts see these two attributes as of prime importance for screening purposes. Education and experience probably also have the greatest implication for lower and working-class job seekers who comprise a substantial segment of Oakland's work force. Table 11 shows the average minimum education and experience requirements for positions in various Oakland departments.[2]

Stringent departments each have a mean educational requirement exceeding 12.5 years. These units provide legal ser-

TABLE 11: EDUCATION AND EXPERIENCE REQUIREMENTS VARY BY DEPARTMENT IN OAKLAND, OCTOBER 1970

Department	Number of fulltime man-years fiscal 1970/71	Average education requirement (Years)	Average experience requirement (Years)
Stringent			
City Attorney	18.0	15.5	1.9
City Planning	21.0	14.7	2.1
City Auditor	6.0	14.7	.5
Civil Service	18.0	14.0	2.8
Museum	85.0	13.1	2.3
Finance	104.5	13.0	1.8
Library	176.0	12.9	1.1
Moderate			
Building and Housing	84.0	12.2	2.8
City Clerk	5.0	12.0	2.0
Retirement Systems	6.0	12.0	2.2
Police	1030.0	12.0	1.0
Fire	685.0	12.0	1.4
Parks and Recreation	379.0	11.7	1.5
Permissive			
Public Works	481.0	10.9	2.0
General Services	284.2	10.3	2.0

Source: Oakland Civil Service Office.

[2] The data are approximate since the Civil Service Commission asks for so much education and experience "or some equivalent combination." Also note that I have equated a requirement that the applicant be able to read and write with a sixth-grade education (to facilitate numerical averaging).

vices, recruit personnel, administer fiscal policy, and offer cultural services. Officials in these agencies believe that college degrees are essential for most of their slots. Only the presence of secretarial and clerical staff lowers their averages below sixteen years (a college diploma).

Moderate departments ask for at least 11.5 years of education on the average but do not demand more than 12.5. Three of the department in this group (building and housing, police, and fire) enforce laws on codes and generally provide for the public safety. These agencies insist that virtually all bureaucrats have a high-school diploma. Officials in the tiny city clerk (recording and storing information) and retirement (handling the investment and administration of retirement money) departments have similar educational aspirations. In the moderate category only parks and recreation has heterogeneous requirements. Many of its slots, such as recreation directors and supervisors, call for a college degree, but it also has a number of positions which demand only the ability to read and write for instance, high climber, tree trimmer, golf-course maintenance man, nursery man, truck driver, and utility stage hand.

Positions in permissive departments require no more than 11.5 years of schooling on the average. Public works and general service which fall into this category, are responsible for physical construction and maintenance. The former does this on Oakland's streets and terrain and the latter on the physical structure of city hall. Both have substantial numbers of positions which do not require a high-school diploma. For instance, semi-skilled workers, who comprise about a quarter of the public works staff, need only an eighth-grade education. Similarly, about 30 percent of the slots in general services are janitorial positions which do not demand a twelfth-grade diploma.

Putting the city government's educational requirements in broad perspective, 8.4 percent of all full-time positions do not require a high-school degree; 11.2 percent ask for at least a college degree; and about 80 percent demand a high-school education (and in some case special kinds of vocational training as well).

As for experience, all departments, except the city auditor's require on the average at least one year. City planning, the civil service, the museum, building and housing, and retirement systems prescribe a mean of more than two years. These figures reflect the fact that all higher level slots demand time on the job for an employee to be eligible for promotion. Many entry level jobs also require some experience. Yet, 40.7 percent of all full-time positions ask for no specific work experience. This high percentage stems from the presence of 559 patrolmen and 399 hosemen slots which require no particular job history.

In Oakland, then, the overall picture is one of a bureaucracy which requires a high-school degree of most applicants and some work experience. These educational and experience standards do not rest on an overwhelming consensus among bureaucrats that present practice is appropriate. Oakland officials view the utility of these criteria in different ways. Department heads aspire to make application demands more stringent while personnel analysts often value movement in the opposite direction.

Department heads want to boost requirements. Oakland's high department officials comprise the main group supporting stringent background requirements. Only one agency head, the city planner, defends lowering standards. (He feels that this will promote minority hiring.) But his department has the second highest educational requirement in the city at 14.7 years, and also one of the highest experience demands at about two years per position. Among other officials one cannot find even a latent disposition to reduce standards. This commitment to ample education and experience has roots in four basic assumptions.

One is that greater education and experience predicts technical competence (that is, abilities which do not involve mastery of human interaction). Diplomas and work history presumably show that the applicant has either already internalized important technical decision rules or has the ability to do so.[3] An applicant with a college diploma in accounting is likely to know how to audit books. A man with five years experience as an auto mechanic is likely to be a useful addition to the city's equipment division.

[3] See Richard M. Cyert and James G. March, *A Behavioral Theory of the Firm* (Englewood Cliffs, N.J.: Prentice Hall, 1964), p. 105.

Department heads also assume that job history and education predict interpersonal competence (for instance, the ability
to get along with others). This quality can be particularly
important to a department head in his relations with groups
outside the department. For instance, both division heads in
the building and housing department, which enforces city codes,
feel that the ability to deal smoothly with code violators is
essential. The housing division head wants an urban renewal
representative who can do a "sell job." He has to be able to
convince a property owner that even if a particular defect has
not caused a mishap in forty years, "it might cause one this
afternoon." Agency heads also realize that interpersonal competence helps promote the internal integration of their departments. Someone who rubs people the wrong way can heighten
conflict, decrease internal communications, reduce supportive
work group incentives, force the agency head to intervene in
petty squabbles, and generally undermine services. Better to
find someone who gets along with others than to put up with
this.

Top bureaucrats also assume that greater experience and
education reveal a willingness to conform to schedules and
organization rules. Agency heads wish to avoid hiring employees
who will do such things as drink on the job or fail to show
up for work on time. Disobedient behavior like this threatens
their capacity to provide services and their supply of power
resources.

The concern with amiability and self-discipline helps explain
why requirements for menial jobs are often high even though
the technical skills demanded by the role are low. Consider
the case of semi-skilled laborers who do basic road repair work.
An employee needs little education and experience to perform
such tasks. Despite this, requirements for the position are either (a) an eighth-grade education and five years of relevant
work experience, or (b) a high-school diploma and one year's
experience.

A fourth assumption of agency officials is that high background requirements boost their professional status. Most
department heads see themselves as professionals. They receive
journals which warn them of the complexity of their tasks and

the merits of hiring high ability people. Such literature extolls the efforts of other departments to get "top notch," well credentialed personnel and assumes that "professonalized" agencies are effective ones. By raising educational requirements, then, high officials boost their own self-image and raise the status of their department vis-à-vis those in other cities.

Overall, the quest for skills slack has caused almost all department heads to support high background requirements.⁴ Further encouraging agency heads is the fact the city hall does not pay a direct financial cost for hiring better certified employees. Some systems, such as schools, automatically pay a recruit with a B.A. less than someone with an M.A.; in Oakland, the salary ordinance does not require this.

Despite their commitment to high requirements, however, agency heads are generally content to "live with" the status quo. Many believe that requirements are "good enough"; most do not want to pay the opportunity costs necessary to get changes approved by the civil service commission. Yet, some do push for modifications.

High requirements and scarcity. Among Oakland department heads the police chief is one of the few who has actively espoused higher educational standards. This commitment largely arises from the internal control problems he faces. The chief well understands that lower echelon patrolmen wield considerable discretion and that supervising their behavior is difficult. James Q. Wilson captures the problem in a nutshell. Because the chief "cannot in advance predict what the circumstances are likely to be or what courses of action are most appropriate—because, in short, he cannot be there himself—he cannot in advance formulate a policy that will guide the patrolman's discretion by in effect eliminating it."⁵ Adding to

---

⁴ For an account of the increasing trend toward "professionalism" in government, see Frederick C. Mosher, *Democracy and the Public Service* New York: Oxford University Press, 1968), pp. 101-110. Randall Alfred Collins, "Education and Employment: A Study in the Dynamics of Stratification" (unpublished Ph.D. dissertation, Department of Sociology, University of California, Berkeley, 1969), found that Bay Area firms are concerned about the interindustry status implications of their job requirements. See also Ivar Berg, *Education and Jobs: The Great Training Robbery* (Boston: Beacon Press, 1971).

⁵ James Q. Wilson, *Varieties of Police Behavior* (Cambridge: Harvard University Press, 1968), p. 66.

the chief's problems is the fact that misbehavior by one or two officers can greatly undermine his prestige.

Since joining the Oakland Police Department as a patrolman in November 1947, the present chief has on numerous occasions observed the problems of inadequate high echelon control. During the 1950s, for instance, corruption plagued the department when a number of officers took kickbacks. He also recalls the bleak day in 1967 when two of his patrolmen illegally shot up the Black Panther headquarters. Confronted with abuses like these and worried about skills deficit, the chief has emphasized more extensive education as a means of promoting the proper exercise of discretion. By stressing professional police work and attracting better credentialed employees, the chief hopes to reduce uncertainty concerning lower echelon behavior.

Consequently, the head of the police department went before the Civil Service Commission (which has the authority to modify requirements) in December 1968, to suggest that it raise educational standards from a high-school diploma to two years of college. He told the commissioners that the complexities of modern law enforcement demanded high-quality policemen well versed in "sociology, political science, history and philosophy." The commission delayed a decision and as of early 1972 had taken no action.

In response to scarcity, publicize more; don't lower standards. It is important to realize that Oakland's chief has espoused this view despite difficulties in filling vacancies. Observing the chief's behavior, one finds little backing for the "supply and demand" proposition that employer standards will go down as applicants are difficult to find. Instead the chief's approach supports the finding that firms in the Bay Area do not lower formal requirements in response to a tight labor market.[6] At least over the short run, they and the chief respond to scarcity by intensifying publicity efforts.

Officials take this action to reduce the risk of skills decline. While personnel officials are uncertain about the consequences of adjusting both specific publicity and selection tactics, they are more willing to depart from current alternatives in the case of the former. To fail at publicity is to have vacant slots

---

[6] Collins, "Education and Employment," pp. 159-165.

standing open; to fail at adjusting selection standards downward is to create skills deficit in positions. (In this regard, the police chief is particularly aware of the damage that "one bad apple" can do.) At least in reformed, professionally oriented bureaucracies, like Oakland's, officials will view skills deficit among those employed as more costly than vacancies (up to a considerable vacancy level). Officials do not, then, lower standards in response to labor market scarcity but instead publicize more.

In speaking out for higher requirements, the police chief is the exception rather than the rule. One reason why most agency heads do not spend time doing so is their anticipation of civil service office opposition.

The civil service office: opponent of higher requirements. In reformed contexts, like Oakland, a civil service staff will generally oppose raising educational and experience requirements. While in unreformed settings, personnel analysts often devote their energy to professionalizing the bureaucracy and fighting patronage, in council-managed governments this is less likely to be true. Professional orientations will often be so widespread within reformed bureaucracies that personnel analysts will focus more on keeping job requirements from skyrocketing.

Oakland's civil service office provides insight into the origins of resistance to greater credential demands. The personnel director and his staff frown on departmental tendencies to "shoot for the moon" on requirements. While they are not crusaders on behalf of lowered standards, they feel that in many cases requirements could be reduced. Personnel analysts believe there are costs to pay for too much selectivity. For one thing high requirements can create search difficulties for them. If they have a hard time filling patrolmen slots when they demand only a high-school education or the equivalent, calling on applicants to have two years of college can only increase their burdens. The personnel director believes that excessive "professionalism" creates a "false labor market." He recalls his years with the civil service office in Nevada where top-flight highway engineers had reached that level by working themselves up through the hierarchy rather than by having status university degrees.

A sense of duty to employees also leads personnel analysts to oppose extravagant requirements. On the whole staff members come from an educational background and are absorbed into a work culture which emphasizes that employees should gain fulfillment and satisfaction from their jobs.[7] Staff members believe that if background requirements are excessive, overqualified people obtain jobs and subsequently become alienated from their work. In a related vein, analysts worry that high requirements increase discontent by cutting off promotional opportunities. Bureaucrats with a high-school diploma will feel thwarted if all the slots above them in the hierarchy demand a college education.

A final factor encouraging staff opposition to stringent requirements is the concern with hiring more minorities. I will explore this further in the next chapter.

Despite these sentiments, the civil service staff under ordinary circumstances does little to lower requirements. The personnel director does not want to appear as an obstructionist in the eyes of department officials. Persuading them to lower requirements consumes time which could be devoted to pressing, day-to-day matters. Furthermore, if he is too arbitrary with departments, conflict might result and his image as a competent administrator might decline. Lowering requirements might win the director the support of such constituencies as the personnel professionals and minority leaders. But generally, these groups do not do him much good if departments become hostile.

Ordinarily, then, there are few forces at work which would push the organization to change standards. Neither the personnel director nor department officials find the minimum requirements completely satisfactory. But they are unwilling to pay the costs necessary to bring about change.

Performance risk spurs the quest for information. In assessing the achievement attributes of job hunters, personnel analysts and other bureaucrats generally rely exclusively on data which appear on the application form. They note educational credentials and job history but to reduce expense they do not spend time interviewing previous employers and teachers to

[7] Of seven professionals in the office, three hold advanced degrees in industrial psychology.

learn more about the applicant. Only when the risks involved in making a selection mistake are substantial do officials go beyond this in building their expertise. Hence, the police and fire chiefs authorize more extensive background investigations, since both believe that hiring errors can be costly in terms of financial resources, departmental status, and human life.

The standards for evaluating the information turned up by the check are still far from crystallized. As of 1970, however, the presence of any of the following would incline the police to reject an applicant: (a) incorrect information on the application form when it appears to be the result of deliberate falsification; (b) the applicant has a bad reputation with his neighbors; (c) the job hunter has had a disciplinary problem in high school, in the army, or with a previous employer; (d) the applicant has gone through bankruptcy or been "irresponsible" in paying off his debts or alimony; (e) the job seeker has received a "large" number of traffic citations, failed to pay parking fines promptly, or generally shown disrespect for the law.

These rules aim at filtering out those who tend to lose their "cool" or refuse to respect authority. The latter factor is particularly important. Departments concerned with enforcing the law and which internally stress the significance of rank as embodied in the chain of command, will attempt to recruit those who have always bestowed legitimacy on authority structures. Those who have ignored the decrees of courts about alimony, the instructions of high-school teachers, or the commands of an army sergeant are suspect. Overall these background rules cause from 5 to 10 percent of the police applicants, who have passed written and oral examinations, to be eliminated.

Background data do, then, play an important role in the efforts of bureaucrats to filter out the inept. But these indicators are not the only ones used.

INFORMATION GATHERING THROUGH TESTING

In the federal government and elsewhere, personnel agencies have increasingly discarded written examinations as a criterion of selection and relied on background attributes and interviews

instead.[8] In this way civil service offices have yielded substantial
screening powers to schools and universities. In Oakland, however, there is little evidence of this trend. The city, as of 1971,
filled almost all classified jobs through the use of written tests.
Furthermore, it is unlikely that the Civil Service Commission
will soon modify this practice since supporters of the procedure
outnumber opponents. Employee leaders back written tests out
of a conviction that they reduce favoritism in appointments
to higher level slots. Agency heads generally believe that the
tests provide them with useful information for entry level
appointments.[9]

The personnel director and his staff also perceive that written
tests are useful. This is not because they have proof that the
instruments are perfectly valid, that is, predictive of future
performance. Procuring evidence with respect to this issue is
costly. To understand whether their tests are valid, they would
have to give examinations to a sample, and without telling
the subjects their scores (to avoid self-fulfilling prophecy),
permit those who passed as well as those who failed to work
under comparable conditions. Then, they would need a fairly
good measure of performance to determine the correlation
between skill and test scores. Since the civil service office gives
distinct examinations for many different slots, a large number
of validity analyses would be necessary to assess the technology.
Faced with many demands, the personnel director does not
want to spend the time and resources such research would
require.

Despite the paucity of precise evidence, the personnel director and his staff see some value in written tests. First, they
believe that the examinations do reduce uncertainty about the
ability of an applicant. Since most people city hall hires do
not get fired and seem to perform satisfactorily, he suspects
that the instruments are somewhat predictive. In contemplat-
ing the issue, the director gains some confidence from his
knowledge that Oakland uses roughly the same test construc-

___

[8] See Mosher, *Democracy and the Public Service.*
[9] Though the parks and recreation department is under no formal requirement to
give a written examination for part-time positions, it does. Officials believe tests to
be a useful basic screening device.

tion methods as other jurisdictions.[10] Apart from whether tests tap ability, analysts appreciate them as a means of reducing opportunity costs. The technology enables the staff to classify large numbers of job hunters in a short time. Oral tests, by contrast, consume many more hours. Then too, analysts believe that examinations boost the prestige of the civil service office. The device conveys to some segments of the public and certain internal bureaucratic constituencies that analysts use "objective, merit" standards in appraising applicants. In the words of one personnel staff member, tests are a "crutch" which make hiring look less arbitrary. Finally, tests reduce prospects that elected politicians will attempt to shape hiring decisions. Personnel analysts assume that intervention by elected officials will lead to the hiring of the inept; written tests provide a defense against this source of skills deficit.

Convinced of the benefits of written examinations, the civil service staff has continued to construct them. Chart 7 suggests some of the decision rules personnel analysts use and the rationale behind each. Like countless other political decisions, test writing rules have a firm foundation in power resource concerns. For instance, many of them explicitly aim at conserving agency time. Some reflect analyst awareness that they lack needed expertise. Still other decision rules have their roots in a desire to protect agency prestige and the legitimacy of its authority by appearing "objective."

The civil service office sets performance standards. Personnel analysts not only wield discretion in constructing examinations but also in applying standards of adequate performance. Civil service rules indicate that the applicant needs a score of 70 to pass. But this does not necessarily mean 70 percent correct. Through weighing parts of the examination differently, the analyst at times passes applicants who get only 60 percent correct. Though they have considerable discretion, analysts assume that an applicant must answer well over half the items correctly if he is ever to display skills congruence, let alone slack. Within this basic constraint, analysts vary standards

---

[10] Cyert and March, *A Behavioral Theory,* p. 102, note how concerned firms are with general industry practice.

Rule	Rationale
1. Purchase outside tests when measuring aptitude or particularly esoteric skills (e.g., personnel analysts administer standard intelligence exams, such as the Army General Classification Test to patrolmen, security guards, and a few others; they rely on tests used by the electronics industry to screen computer programmers.)	Analysts perceive that they do not have the expertise and time to construct these kinds of tests.
2. Primarily use multiple choice questions. (Only tests for certain professional positions such as assistant city planner call for essays.)	Grading this type of test requires little judgment and can be accomplished by a computer. This saves time for the civil service staff and reduces prospects that test takers will charge them with being "subjective"; in this respect, it helps preserve the legitimacy of civil service authority.
3. Extract some items from the national test exchange.	Analysts believe that an inflow of new data broadens their perspective and makes test writing easier.
4. Use questions from past tests.	This conserves time since personnel analysts do not have to think up a whole new batch of questions every time they give a test.
5. Consult with departments concerning the correct answers to the test questions and what information the test should probe.	Agency officials have more expertise than personnel analysts concerning technical aspects of the exam. By consulting with them the civil service office may gain some status as being responsive to department interests.
6. Particularly when writing promotionals, ask questions only directly related to the job (e.g., an Oakland plumber should not have to know about frozen pipes.)	By doing this, analysts avoid trouble with employee leaders and some department heads. Employee representatives have insisted that professional tests tap specific knowledge of city hall procedures since this gives their main constituency an advantage. Agency heads have shared this

CHART 7—*Continued*

Rule	Rationale
	view on grounds that it reduces the time they must spend socializing an employee. They assume that someone with specific knowledge of the role will adapt to it more effectively.

slightly. Staff members are less likely to be demanding if: (a) it is hard to fill vacacies; (b) all applicants had difficulties with the test (that is, even top scorers got many wrong); and (c) they can thereby avoid giving the test again in the near future. Pass-fail decisions, then, respond slightly to labor market conditions, the overall performance of the applicants, and the desire of the civil service office to build up a long eligible list which will postpone the need for renewed search.

Through the construction, administration, and grading of multiple choice tests (with an occasional essay), personnel analysts screen out more than half the job hunters taking the examination. Department officials move to center stage when less than 30 percent of the original job seekers remain.

Orals: find someone who can get along. The main way in which department personnel exert selection leverage is through the official oral examination. For entry level slots, the oral board consists of two or three officials from the department and one from the civil service office.[11] Oral examinations typically eliminate about one-fifth of the job hunters who make it to this selection gate.

The civil service office attempts to structure the thinking of department representatives in the oral. It gives them rating sheets which specify important factors and call for officials to give the applicant a score on each. The criteria vary according to the position but usually contain five or six categories somewhat like the following:

1. Appearance, manner, and self-expression.
2. Social adaptability ("Is he at ease, friendly, confident? Does he appear to have the tact and adaptability necessary to deal with citizens,

[11] The major exception to this occurs in the handling of secretarial and clerical applicants where personnel analysts control both the written and oral tests.

and co-workers under trying conditions? Or would he tend to be too submissive, abrupt, impatient, or overbearing?").

    3. Alertness and judgment.

    4. Suitability of experience.

    5. Interest and enthusiasm.

    6. Attitudes ("Is she businesslike? Do her manner and responses indicate that she wants to do a job, or does she appear to look upon this as just another job?").

Obviously, the above hardly comprise rigorously operationalized procedures for evaluating anyone. But the criteria do provide some general guidelines. In particular, department officials probe the ability suggested by item two. While bureaucrats pay some attention to technical knowledge, many assume that the written examination has measured this skill and, therefore, focus on interpersonal competence in the oral.[12] In sum, then, where local officials use written tests to screen applicants, they will primarily use the interview to determine whether an applicant has the ability to get along with others; to a lesser degree, they will probe the candidate's orientation toward work rules and a career.

The attitudes of the statistical service officer show how important amiability can be. He would rather hire a mediocre programmer who is easygoing and pleasant than a very able one who is abrasive—who "makes waves and stirs up trouble." On one occasion he served on an oral board which was interviewing a young lady. In terms of the applicant's computer knowledge, she was clearly superior to all the other applicants. But he and the other board members felt that she was too "aggressive and dynamic." There was too much "hostility" in her replies and, consequently, they flunked her.

Others use the oral in an effort to find out whether an applicant will conform to work rules. Concerned with this, fire officials, for example, often ask an applicant what he plans to do with his leisure time. Since a hoseman works one day and then has two off, officials worry that he may be tempted to "chase and carouse" during his free time. This may make

[12] Analysts who have seen the significance of social skills include: Charles H. Coates and Ronald J. Pellegrin, "Executives and Supervisors: Informal Factors in Differential Bureaucratic Promotion," *Administrative Science Quarterly* 2 (September 1957): 215, and Edward C. Banfield, *The Unheavenly City* (Boston: Little, Brown, 1970), p. 102.

the employee late for work or guilty of other rule infractions. Generally, officials believe that an applicant is less likely to misuse his time off if he expresses interest in attending junior college or has such hobbies as hunting and fishing.

Other questions probe the career aspirations of the applicant. Officials wish to avoid hiring those who will quit shortly thereafter or who will show little interest in winning promotion. Since department heads sink costs in training employees and it takes time to recruit new personnel, they dislike quitters. Thus, if an applicant cannot justify his constant shifting from one job to the next oral examiners will give him low ratings. Agency personnel are also suspicious of those few job hunters who are unenthusiastic about promotion. In their view such employees are unlikely to develop skills slack. In bureaucracies, like Oakland's, where promotion from within is the prevailing norm, officials will see a lack of career ambition as particularly threatening.

Whatever the orientation or skill they are trying to tap, various officials emphasized the importance of "being hard." The statistical services officer was particularly emphatic on this point. He is aware of the tendency to pass applicants with border line abilities simply to encourage them. But he also knows that such "just pass" applicants wind up at the bottom of the eligible list and may eventually come up for appointment. Consequently, he guards against being "humanistic" and fails those whom he does not want to hire.

Though most department officials have a theory of interviewing, they admit that their tactics are fraught with uncertainty. While they believe they can pick out the very bad, they generally lack confidence in their ability to discriminate beyond this. Most can recall some mistake. Thus, while officials wield considerable leverage over interviews, either to veto an applicant or place him high or low on the eligible list, they are not sure that their decisions maximize bureaucratic skills level.

Promotion orals: barrier for agency heads. Reformed political institutions, with their strong civil service offices and emphasis on written tests, stripped hiring leverage from elected politicians. By so doing, these institutions in certain respects undermined the power position of top department officials as well. In Oakland, agency head weakness is particularly evident in the promotional process. Not only does the use of written examinations for advancement curtail a top official's discretion; the civil service requirement that "experts" from outside the city administer the oral examination for promotion also reduces agency head leverage.[13]

Where formal rules restrict the ability of department heads to promote whom they please, these officials will attempt to manipulate the system through informal means. This is what occurs in Oakland. Agency heads are not completely powerless over promotion boards. One tactic they use to encourage better outcomes is to suggest proper interviewers to the personnel director. The assistant fire chief, for instance, asks the director to contact fire officials affiliated with what he believes are professional departments. These include San Jose, Sacramento, Berkeley, and Orinda. Oakland fire officials hold San Francisco in less repute. They can recall times when San Francisco officials gave high scores to low caliber applicants. The fire leaders attribute these poor choices to the tendency of San Francisco firemen to be "politically minded." Too much in San Francisco depends on "who you know" rather than on other more relevant criteria. Consequently, they have spoken out against having representatives from across the bay on the boards.

Another tactic departments use to get a "favorite son" promoted is the temporary appointment. When a position opens, civil service rules permit the agency head to appoint whomever he pleases for ninety days, during which time the personnel office will fill the position through usual procedures. By appointing someone temporarily, the department anoints the favored and gives him experience which might help him accumulate more information and earn a higher score on the promotional examination. While, most of the time the temporary appointee wins the slot, on occasion he does not. The city planner, for instance, made an interim appointment only to see the individual fail the examination.

Delay in filling a vacancy is another approach used to

[13] Experts include one individual from another personnel agency and two from the department's area of specialization.

manipulate the promotional system, as the behavior of the statistical services officer in 1969 illustrates. At that time, the civil service office gave a promotional test for a high level computer programmer position. On hearing the examination announced, the statistical services office immediately encouraged a favored employee to take it. Only one other subordinate in his division competed with her, a man who had less experience and in the mind of the statistical services officer was much less qualified. To the division chief's distress, his anointed employee failed the test and the unsuitable one passed.

Faced with someone he did not want to promote, the division head procrastinated. But the statistical service officer knew he could delay only for a limited period since it hurts morale to deny an employee a promotion after the latter has earned it by passing the test. Furthermore, the statistical services officer needed someone to fill the slot. Fortunately a vacancy for a systems analyst suddenly opened in his agency, and he convinced the subordinate who passed the earlier test for senior programmer to apply for it. Again the man passed the test and the statistical services officer promptly promoted him. This left the senior programmer position open again with the prospect that the favored applicant might retake the test for it.

The promotional system can, then, create difficulties for department heads. They may ultimately win but often they must pay substantial opportunity costs.

Background inspections, written examinations, and interviews are the main ways that bureaucrats acquire knowledge in an effort to promote skills slack. They also use such devices as psychiatric, medical, and physical agility tests. But these filtering devices play a minor role compared to the three already presented.

Less than 10 percent win jobs. As Table 12 indicates, city hall's multiple evaluation system eliminates most applicants. Less than one-fifth of those who apply pass and get on the eligible list. City officials reject more than 60 percent; another 20 percent lose by default since they fail to show up for examinations. While precise data are not available, officials estimate that during economically prosperous times, when

TABLE 12: CITY HALL FILTERS OUT MOST APPLICANTS

	1966		1967		1968		1969		Total	
	Number applicants	Percentage of original	Number applicants	Percentage of original	Number applicants	Percentage of original	Number applicants	Percentage of original	Number applicants	Percentage of original
Submitting applications	7,497	100.0	5,494	100.0	6,525	100.0	6,166	100.0	25,682	100.0
Applications accepted	6,200	82.7	4,192	76.3	5,357	82.1	5,315	86.2	21,064	82.0
Taking the examinations	4,638	61.9	3,247	59.1	4,012	61.5	3,741	60.7	15,638	60.9
Making the eligible list	1,308	17.4	841	15.3	1,099	16.9	1,205	19.5	4,453	17.3

Source: Oakland Civil Service Office.

turnover is higher, they will have enough openings to employ roughly half those who make the eligible list. This means that less than 10 percent of the original applicants eventually wind up on city payrolls. During recessions this proportion dwindles.

In broad perspective, then, Oakland's selection process represents the triumph of reformed government. The process involves many hurdles which, among other things, shift leverage away from elected politicians, and disperse power broadly. In assessing applicants, officials rely heavily on education and experience credentials, written examinations, interviews, and other devices. Even though uncertain about the precise payoffs of these techniques, Oakland's bureaucrats believe that they have recruited an adequate supply of manpower. In the late sixties, however, outsiders challenged this conviction. City hall's environment grew more turbulent as minority spokesmen asserted that race should be a selection criterion, that modes of evaluating candidate capability had been spurious, and that officials should conduct special search for blacks, Chicanos, and Orientals. In the next chapter, I will assess the impact of the Civil Service Commission's newly aroused client on recruitment behavior.

6

New Trends in Recruitment Politics: The Minority Challenge

> The civil service law is the biggest fraud of the age.
> It is the curse of the nation. There can't be no real
> patriotism while it lasts. How are you goin' to interest
> our young men in their country if you have no offices
> to give them. . . ?
>
> George Washington Plunkitt[1]

Recent court and legislative actions have made it almost impossible for city officials to seek out competence while ignoring the race and sex of applicants. In its Duke Power Company decision of 1971, the Supreme Court ruled that Title VII of the 1964 Civil Rights Act forbade an employer from using credentials or tests for screening purposes when: employers could not show that these selection criteria predicted job performance, the criteria disproportionately screened out minorities, and there was evidence of past discriminatory practices. With the Equal Employement Opportunity Act of 1972, Congress put state and local governments under provisions of the 1964 Civil Rights Act, thereby making the Duke decision binding for city officials.

Most of my observations in Oakland occurred prior to the Duke decision. Nonetheless, I had ample opportunity to watch officials incorporate new racial considerations into their calcu-

[1] William L. Riordon, *Plunkitt of Tammany Hall* (New York: E.P. Dutton, 1963), p. 14.

lations.[2] The increased racial concern within the bureaucracy
largely stemmed from community unrest over city employment
practices. The purpose of this chapter is, then, to analyze how
Oakland officials reacted to the minority challenge. Questions
of importance include: What changes did bureaucrats resist
and what changes did they promote? Why? What success did
officials have in fostering racial representation while attempting
to minimize the risk to skill? Before dealing with these questions
it is useful to describe briefly the sources and nature of the
minority attack.

MINORITY ADVOCATES COMPLAIN

Job hunters seldom exert direct pressure on a personnel
director to change procedures other than through the labor
market mechanism of supply and demand. Potential applicants
who do not hear about a vacant position in time to apply seldom
have the resources or inclination to attack the legitimacy of
city hall's publicity process. Then too an applicant rarely
understands whether the selection process has treated him
fairly. Since the job hunter knows so little about competing
applicants, how can he be sure that the personnel agency failed
to live up to merit standards when it did not hire him? Even
if an applicant believes that recruiters cheated him, economic
pressures to look for another job plus his limited supply of
power resources make him reluctant to fight city hall.

When spokesmen for minority job hunters challenged Oakland's personnel director it was not, then, business as usual.
The challenge received impetus from the federal government.
In August 1969, a well-publicized report by the United States
Commission on Civil Rights noted that Oakland was the only
major jurisdiction among seven metropolitan areas studied in
which the three main minority groups were greatly underrepre-
sented on city employment rosters. The report stressed that
while Oakland's population was almost 50 percent minority,
city hall's employees were only 15.3 percent Negro, 1.5 percent

[2] Groups seeking more employment for women were not active at the time of my
study.

Spanish-surname, and 1.6 percent Oriental. The federal report
was only the tip of the iceberg. Shortly thereafter, leaders from
the Oakland Black Caucus (a coalition of black organizations
including CORE, the NAACP, and the Urban League), the
East Oakland-Fruitvale Planning Council (a neighborhood
group concerned with representing the interests of the poor),
an other local organizations attacked recruitment policies in
the police department.

City hall jobs in particular were important. The reasons why
minority spokesmen were interested in city hiring policies are
not as obvious as they might seem at first glance. To be sure,
like federal officials, minority leaders wanted to mitigate Oakland's unemployment problem. Minority unemployment ex-
ceeded 10 percent and was generally twice the white rate.[3]
Minority advocates felt that city hall, as the eleventh largest
Alameda County employer, could help attack this problem by
providing jobs.[4] But their concern went beyond this. After all,
if it was just jobs that interested them, city hall had no
monopoly on the supply, with roughly 3500 full-time positions.
By comparison, Kaiser Industries employed 9000, Alameda
County, over 7000, and Pacific Telephone, 6000. Why not focus
on these organizations instead?

Minority leaders focused on city hall recruitment in large
part because they saw it as a means of securing control over
policies which city hall, alone, provided. They felt convinced
that various city agencies, particularly the police department,
had been insensitive to the needs of minorities. They assumed
that more black and brown faces in city hall would help make
local government more responsive to the city's ghetto dwellers.
Furthermore, minority advocates believed that by winning
something in the recruitment arena, they could set a precedent
for concessions in other issue areas. As one minority spokesman
put it, victory in the recruitment sphere would be a means
of getting "a toe in the door" more generally.

Assuming, then, that minority advocates feel politically effi-

---

[3] The national picture for minority unemployment is about as bleak as Oakland's.
See *The Report of the National Advisory Commission on Civil Disorders* (New York:
Bantam, 1968) p. 253. See also, Alan M. Ahart, "An Economic and Demographic Study
of Oakland, California, 1960-1966, With Comparisons to Other Cities." (Unpublished
paper, University of California, Berkeley, June, 1970), pp. 18-19.

[4] *Ibid.*, Index, P. 1.

cacious, their tendency to challenge civil service recruitment procedures will increase if they: (a) believe that certain departments have few minority bureaucrats; (b) perceive that minority employees will be more responsive to the needs of the minority community; and (c) believe that a victory in the recruitment arena will facilitate challenge in other policy spheres.

Minority tactics. In making their attacks on city hall, minority leaders faced many tactical quandaries. Those who wrote the tests that screened out most were not "street level" bureaucrats but were cloaked in anonymity.[5] Furthermore, the decision rules these officials used to shape publicity and selection processes were a mystery to minority advocates. In fact the very utility of some selection tools partly rested on secrecy—on job hunters and the public being unable to predict precisely what questions would turn up in a written test or an interview. Unlike many other policy spheres, then, minority leaders could not even claim that they had a legitimate right to know the specifics of the process.

Faced with a complex, secret technology, minority leaders refused to pay opportunity costs trying to understand it. Instead, they adopted two basic tactics. First they persistently focused on the racial scorecard, which the federal government had initially provided, and urged officials to do better. Second, they attempted to set up participatory recruitment structures which would either give them direct access to information or permit them to hire professionals who could gather data and make suggestions. These two basic strategies ran through the course of events which emerged from August 1969 into 1971.

The new museum received the initial attention of minority leaders. In mid-summer 1969, the museum commission fired the department's director whom minority advocates had viewed as an ally. Consequently from August well into early November 1969, members of the Oakland Black Caucus appeared at various museum commission and city council meetings to demand proportional representation of minorities on the museum staff particularly at the higher administrative levels. Failing to get this and other guarantees, they called for a boycott of

[5] Michael Lipsky, "Street-Level Bureaucracy and the Analysis of Urban Reform," *Blacks and Bureaucracy,* ed. Virginia B. Ermer and John H. Strange (New York: Thomas Y. Crowell, 1972), pp. 171-184.

the agency. Only after the new museum director appointed a black to a top position in mid-1970 did the caucus call off the boycott.

Long before this occurred, other minority spokesmen attacked police recruitment policies. On October 15, 1969, roughly two months after the first volleys at the museum, representatives of the Black Caucus and East Oakland-Fruitvale Planning Council argued before the Civil Service Commission that its written tests were racially biased. They asked the commission to establish a citizen's advisory committee to overview an inquiry into recruitment procedures. For the Civil Service Commission, this request was only the beginning. Two weeks later, the Alameda County Legal Aid Society filed a suit charging that present tests emphasized white middle-class values and, therefore, discriminated against minorities.[6]

In January 1970, minority advocates received encouragement. Despite extensive lobbying against an advisory committee by the police chief and personnel director (who saw the proposal as a front for "community control"), a majority of the civil service commissioners approved the "concept" of such a committee. Two black commission members, a lawyer and minister, were particularly sympathetic to the goal of hiring more minority policemen and did not view the proposal as a threat to merit. In part as a result of this commission decision, an umbrella organization called the Task Force on the Police emerged in early 1970. Spearheaded by the East Oakland-Fruitvale Planning Council, its nucleus also included representatives from churches, the Legal Aid Society, and the Urban League. Attendance at task force meetings usually ranged from 20 to 40 people.

While working on a proposal for an advisory committee structure the task force strove to get funding for it. In early February 1970, a legal assistant with the East Oakland-Fruitvale Planning Council wrote to the Association of Bay Area Governments announcing intent to submit an application for a grant of $150,000. Responding to this letter, Bay Area government officials urged the task force to submit a grant application

---

[6] Faced with other demands on its resources and believing that city hall had made some effort to be responsive, the legal aid society later abandoned the suit.

but noted that it required the endorsement of both the Oakland Civil Service Commission and the city council.

In June, the Civil Service Commission made its decision concerning the grant. Faced with opposition from the personnel director, police chief and mayor, the two black commissioners could not sustain their initial coalition. Consequently, the commission voted three to two against backing the grant application. Three months later, the commissioners ruled against having any kind of advisory committee whatsoever. The chairman of the commission captured the feelings of the dominant faction when he noted: "you don't step blindly into deep water where civil service rules and regulations are connected."

The failure of the task force to establish a citizen's advisory committee did not produce tranquility in city hall's environment. In April 1970, less than a year after the initial assault on the museum, about twenty organizations concerned with police problems created another umbrella organization called the Police-Community Clearing House.[7] Funded in part by the Methodist Church, the clearing house persistently claimed that the police force should racially reflect the 50 percent minority population in Oakland.

THE SEARCH FOR TACTICS TO RESIST

Oakland City Hall, as the preceding description indicates, responded to the minority challenge in large part by resisting Oakland's personnel director and others were reluctant to relinquish any control over hiring to an advisory committee comprised of critics. Such behavior is hardly surprising. Local officials generally resist when the demands of challengers pose

[7] The membership included nine religious groups (East Bay Lutheran Advisory Council, Bethlehem Lutheran Center, South-East Oakland Parish, American Jewish Congress, East Bay Ministerial Alliance, J.S.A.C. East Bay Committee, Shattuck Avenue Methodist Church, Downtown Oakland Christian Parish, and the Jewish Community Relations Council), three legal groups (the Oakland Lawyers Committee Project, the NAACP Legal Defense Fund, and the American Civil Liberties Union), and various other organizations (Oakland Social Service Bureau, East Oakland-Fruitvale Planning Council, the East Bay Urban League, the Oakland Citizens' Task Force, Community Organizations United for Progress, Oakland League of Women Voters, and the Model Cities Program).

a threat to bureaucratic autonomy in issue areas, like recruitment, which vitally affect the flow of power resources into city departments. Top policy makers also opposed the minority proposal for a special committee because they adhere to a localized version of the domino theory. Where officials believe that negotiations with challengers will be continuous over a wide range of issues (as in the case in Oakland) they will view a concession in one arena as weakening their position in another. Thus, key officials believed that setting up participatory structures in the recruitment arena would only whet the appetites of minority spokesmen for more.

In dealing with minority advocates, Oakland officials had ample authority to block the challenge. Civil Service Commission approval was essential for the creation of an advisory committee; funding would require not only commission sanction but city council support as well. Despite their capacity to deny flatly the minority quest for participation, officials did not wish to be so direct. Such behavior might promote an image of unresponsiveness within the minority community. Thus, officials searched for resistance tactics which stopped short of a formal ruling against challengers.

DELAY

Putting off a decision is almost always an attractive first tactic for officials; it gives them time to reduce uncertainty; it may permit them to defeat challengers without ever having to assume responsibility for saying "no." As Lipsky notes:[8]

> The effect of postponement, if accompanied by symbolic assurances, is to remove immediate pressure and delay specific commitments to a future date. This familiar tactic is particularly effective in dealing with protest groups because of their inherent instability. Protest groups are usually comprised of individuals whose intense political activity cannot be sustained except in rare circumstances.

Though the various groups clamoring for more minority employment were not protest groups in Lipsky's sense of the term, his comment is apropos. Many meetings with few results do

[8] Michael Lipsky, "Protest as a Political Resource," *American Political Science Review* 62 (December 1968): 1157.

little to encourage followers and serve as a barrier to expanded membership. Beyond this, even among those committed to the cause, delay can impose substantial opportunity costs. The leaders of the task force and police community clearing house did not have large chunks of free time. When city hall put them off, spokesmen felt they paid a price since the hours consumed here could not be used for other ends.

While elected politicians and bureaucrats in almost any context can exploit delay, in organizations such as Oakland City Hall it is easier than in others.[9] Generally, the more dispersed the distribution of authority and the more part-time high level positions, the more officials will delay.

Dispersal of authority facilitates buck-passing. As I have already mentioned, recruitment authority in Oakland City Hall is dispersed. This gave officials ample opportunity to delay action by passing the buck. For example, when Black Caucus members told the museum commission that there should be a training and career program for minorities and that the museum staff should be more racially representative, the commission flatly denied that it had any authority over recruitment.[10] Later in September 1969, minority spokesmen made a similar demand to the city council, only to have the mayor clarify that civil service rules prevented any council action.

This pattern was also apparent in minority dealings with the police department. Task force and clearing house members often could not understand whether the personnel director, Civil Service Commission, or police chief had the power to meet their requests. Each official minimized his ability to act. The chief claimed he had exclusive powers only over the background check. The commission had considerable authority yet depended heavily on the advice of the personnel director. The latter, however, could argue that he possessed no real authority and would not usurp commission prerogatives. Some minority spokesmen, such as a young lawyer for the Alameda County Legal Aid Society, sensed that the chief and personnel director

[9] See also Andrew McFarland, *Power and Leadership in Pluralist Systems* (Stanford: Stanford University Press, 1969), p. 327, and Thomas C. Schelling, *The Strategy of Conflict* New York: Oxford University Press, 1963), p. 33.

[10] Lipsky, "Protest as a Political Resource," 1968, p. 1156, notes how target groups may appear constrained.

could produce changes if they wished. But even he found that the system's complexity posed strategic difficulties.

It is little wonder that one frustrated minority spokesmen, after dealing with the museum commission, likened the bureaucracy to a "monolithic multi-headed hydra—when we approach one head, it always tell us that the other head is responsible." Or, as one participant in a meeting of the clearing house commented, "In Oakland the buck never stops."

The "vanishing authority" syndrome facilitates delay. Another city hall attribute which caused postponement was the part-time employment of elected politicians and commission members. This practice serves to divorce ultimate authority from expertise. It means that the initial response to any request that is slightly out of the ordinary is often a time-consuming study. For instance, busy with their day-to-day occupations, Civil Service Commission members do not devote much time to personnel matters beyond the regular Tuesday afternoon meetings. Typically lawyers, labor representatives, businessmen, or ministers are unfamiliar with most testing technologies. Consequently, when the task force challenged the fairness of the patrolman examination, it is understandable that the commission's reaction was to try to get more information. To this end, they underwent briefings by the civil service staff and took the patrolman test. After using this tactic, however, commission members were still baffled. The staff talked in the language of test technology which they found enigmatic. After seeing the exam, commissioners speculated that some of its questions were irrelevant, but felt that they could not make an overall assessment. Unable to fathom the technology, they concluded that an outside consultant was necessary. From the standpoint of commission members, the two months they took to boost their knowledge was simply an effort to promote rationality. But in the eyes of some minority leaders, it was another manifestation of the "study you to death" approach. Time is lost and no changes occur.

Part-time bodies make stalling for other reasons easier as well. The fewer the hours officials are formally expected to devote to city affairs, the easier it is for these officials to make themselves inaccessible. Late in June 1970, for instance, the task force leadership appeared at a commission meeting to discuss the possibilities of an advisory committee. While the commission had denied it funding, the committee still might function in some form. But explaining that many board members would be away on vacation during the summer months, the commission chairman postponed any further consideration of police hiring issues for sixty days. For change advocates, then, a part-time commission creates problems of access. If you strike out one week, you may have to wait awhile for another turn.

STATUS ENHANCEMENT TACTICS

In resisting challengers, bureaucrats will also tend to consider such status enhancement tactics as verbal justification of onself, denunciation of the opposition, cooptation, or a "safe" formal study. Such tactics help officials preserve or increase their prestige without involving any effort to solve the problem posed by adversaries. In dealing with minority advocates Oakland officials considered all of these options.

Verbal justification and denunciation. The propensity of officials to use verbal justifications and denunciations increases with the prospect that the media will focus on the dispute. With media coverage, the scope of conflict is more likely to expand and officials wish to control that expansion. While Oakland's television station and newspapers paid scant attention to the minority challenge, at those times when media coverage seemed likely, officials were quick to justify themselves and blame minority spokesmen. In doing so, bureaucrats and elected politicians repeatedly emphasized the importance of competence and professionalism. Responding to early complaints about inadequate minority representation, for instance, the personnel director warned that "a city is responsible to the taxpayer and it can't afford to hire people not capable of doing their jobs."

Similarly, the police chief and personnel director resisted suggestions that they "reduce" standards for patrolmen applicants. Convinced that such a step would create lower echelon control problems, the chief defended requirements. In this effort he has had the support of the city council. For instance, at a council meeting on May 11, 1971, the chief labeled the efforts of the Police-Community Clearing House "destructive." When a spokesman for the clearing house attempted to clarify what the chief meant, a councilman commented, "it would be disruptive if you had the chief hire unqualified personnel and that is exactly what he means."

Pass the buck to minorities. In addition to reaffirming "professional" values, bureaucrats have attempted to undermine the status of minority claims by insinuating that minority leaders themselves are to blame for inadequate racial representation in city hall.

This response was readily apparent as bureaucrats dealt with the Police-Community Clearing House. Both the police chief and personnel director blamed some of their recruitment difficulties on the failure of the clearing house to cooperate with them. For example, at a meeting of the council in May 1971, the police chief claimed that "the real problem we have in our recruiting efforts is the inability to get community people to do something to cooperate with the Police Department and the Civil Service Department in the recruiting effort." He advised the clearing house to "do less planning and suggesting of programs and more active encouragement of persons to apply for the exam." Rather than "tearing down" his efforts, they should "go out there and talk to people, black persons, and encourage them to become applicants." This would be the "proof of the pudding" concerning their sincerity.

From the standpoint of city officials, such pass-the-buck tactics could be beneficial in two ways. First, by making the charges highly visible to the press, they could undermine the status of minority advocates by putting the monkey on their backs. It was one way of saying that if there were not enough minority cops, the community was to blame. At the same time, if the task force or clearing house responded by searching for applicants, city hall would benefit. Officials would not give up any control over hiring decisions, but would have the assistance of an outside group in spreading word about vacancies to the minority community.

Sponsor a safe study. In addition to uttering verbal justifications and denunciations, officials at times sponsor a safe formal study. A safe study is one which does not provide adversaries with information they can use to bolster their attack on city hall. While such studies are unlikely to generate remedies to problems which concern challengers, officials hope that they will make bureaucrats look responsive. Oakland's personnel director was sensitive to the uses of such low-risk studies. Consequently, when presented with the opportunity to shape a research project, the director attempted to keep it safe, first, by controlling the appointment of consultants and, second, by shaping the focus of the research so that it only indirectly dealt with the problem minority advocates had raised.

The personnel director had a long-standing interest in police issues. Since 1963 his office had gathered data on intelligence test scores, civil service written examinations, psychiatric evaluations, and personality tests (the last is not part of the selection process). In his view, by relating these and other variables to the eventual performance of police recruits, useful information would accrue to him and the chief. Moreover, it would be a "feather in his cap" in professional circles. In June 1969 (before the planning council and others began their attack), the director gained managerial approval and applied for a study grant. Later, when the Legal Aid Society and planning council challenged the written examinations, he realized that winning the federal money might serve the additional function of improving his reputation with minority spokesmen. The director could claim that he had already taken steps to make sure that his selection methods were fair.

Eventually, federal coffers opened. In July 1970, the city council unanimously approved a $63,000 grant from the California Council on Criminal Justice and appropriated $47,000 of city money to support data gathering efforts. In making appointments to the research team, the personnel director used professional and racial standards. Of the ten consultants he named in mid-September 1970, seven had Ph.D.s and half were minority. In essence, then, minority activism gave the personnel director additional leverage in securing funds which he had long wanted.

But task-force leaders did not accord the study much respect. Excluded from any control over the hiring of consultants and the definition of problems to be studied, they repudiated the research at the outset. Before the city council, they charged that the grant would be "irrelevant" to the issue of inadequate minority representation on the police force.

Attempt cooptation. Concerned with this rejection, the personnel director tried to coopt them into meeting with the consultants. In the fall of 1970 he asked an Urban League representative active on the task force to submit a list of community people who would meet with the research team periodically to discuss developments. But when the league spokesmen sent a letter, it contained names which the personnel director did not want—for example, a Ph.D. social worker, and a criminology professor from Berkeley whom the director viewed as too "far out" on community control issues. Rather than risk dealing with those who might possess the expertise and inclination to make judgments far different from those of the other professionals, he decided to invite only the urban league official.

The difficulties the personnel director had in attempting cooptation help explain why the tactic received limited attention. Cooptation is "the process of absorbing new elements into the ... structure of an organization as a means of averting threats to its stability or existence."[11] But where, as in Oakland, officials perceive minority advocates as skilled and as having values markedly at odds with their own, they are likely to reject cooptation as an alternative. Under such circumstances, incorporating new groups into the organization poses more of a threat to its stability than leaving them outside.

THE SEARCH FOR RESPONSIVENESS

The search for alternatives to mitigate the problem posed by minority advocates would in many instances end with the selection of resistance tactics. In Oakland, however, search extended beyond this point as certain city officials attempted to modify the recruitment structure in order to hire more

[11] J. D. Thompson, *Organizations in Action* (New York: McGraw Hill, 1967), p. 35.

minorities. Why, then, did Oakland officials attempt to be responsive? What tactics did they employ and with what results?

The propensity of urban bureaucrats to strive for responsiveness when dealing with challengers generally increases if: (a) officials believe that challengers hold important hostages; (b) officials sympathize with the challengers' cause; and (c) responsiveness scorecards are present.

Hostage scarcity. Hostages, as William Muir notes, are an actor's valued possessions, of which some other individual or group can deprive him.[12] Among the possessions which bureaucrats value are their jobs, authority, time, and prestige with citizens. What characterizes spokesmen for disadvantaged groups is, of course, their difficulty in convincing bureaucrats that they hold hostages. This problem tends to be particularly acute for challengers where attracting sympathetic media coverage is difficult, where intervention by outside authorities seems unlikely, and where reformed political institutions prevail. All three of these conditions existed in Oakland.

Extensive sympathetic media coverage of a challenge generally nurtures an impression among bureaucrats that a broad public is observing their behavior and that their professional reputations are on the line.[13] Such coverage also heightens their fear that the scope of conflict will expand in a way detrimental to bureaucratic interests. In Oakland's case, however, media coverage of the minority challenge was minimal. Television and radio stations devoted almost no time to the issue. To the extent that the conservative *Oakland Tribune* and the more liberal weekly *Montclarion* covered the challenge at all they buried it on the back pages. Since there was limited media coverage and minority advocates did not seem to have a broad community following, officials suspected that the challengers did not hold significant hostages.

Nor did Oakland bureaucrats worry much that minority leaders could undermine their status or the legitimacy of their authority by calling on other government units to overrule city

---

[12] William Key Muir, Jr., "The Development of Policemen." (Paper delivered at the American Political Science Association Convention, 1970).

[13] Lipsky, "Protest as a Political Resource," 1968.

hall. Keep in mind that the events in this case took place before the Supreme Court made its Griggs v. Duke Power Company decision.

Finally, Oakland's reformed political institutions raised doubts that minority advocates held hostages. For one thing reformed structures generally insulate bureaucrats from those who have the greatest cause to fear for their job security: elected politicians. Oakland's mayor and councilmen have few power resources with which to control hiring processes even if they want to do so. Reformed governments also weaken low-resource challengers by fostering a volunteer, part-time politician syndrome. Above all, this syndrome features disinterest among elected officials in long-range political careers.[14]. Oakland's mayor and councilmen generally do not behave as pluralist politicians eager to keep their posts by making appropriate concessions to various groups. Jeffrey Pressman has observed, for instance, that Oakland's mayor judges a course of action less in terms of whether it satisfies a number of constituencies than whether it squares with the principles he has long applied to his private conduct.[15] Since elected officials do not value their political careers highly, minority challengers have more difficulty taking significant hostages and entering into a bargaining process.

Settings like Oakland's do, then, pose serious tactical quandaries for low-resource groups. To the extent that responsiveness efforts do occur in such cities, other explanatory factors generally become important. Two such factors are the presence of sympathetic bureaucrats and the existence of responsiveness scorecards.

Sympathetic officials help. Officials with power resources who sympathize with the minority cause help spur bureaucratic responsiveness efforts.[16] Oakland bureaucrats changed procedures in part because some felt that minority employment in city hall was too low. The economic thrust of the minority

---

[14] Kenneth Prewitt, "Political Ambitions, Volunteerism, and Electoral Accountability," *American Political Science Review* 64 (March 1970): 5-17, discusses the importance of ambition for keeping elected officials accountable.

[15] Jeffrey L. Pressman, "Preconditions of Mayoral Leadership," *American Political Science Review* 66 (June 1972): 518.

[16] Norman I. and Susan S. Fainstein, "Innovation in Urban Bureaucracies: Clients and Change," *American Behavioral Scientist* 15 (March/April 1972): 529-530.

argument in particular had appeal. Officials dimly perceived, and would have labeled as illegitimate, minority aspirations to use employment as a means of gaining more substantive representation through the bureaucracy. The mayor and certain bureaucrats did, however, see the demands for more jobs as a justifiable effort by minority groups to pull themselves up by the bootstraps. In addition, some officials, like the personnel director and the police chief, believed that an affirmative action program indicated professional enlightenment. Personnel and police trade journals stressed the importance of removing bias from selection procedures and taking steps to hire more minorities. Overall, then, the professional identities of certain bureaucrats plus the economic argument facilitated efforts at responsiveness.

Responsiveness scorecards encourage change. In addition to sympathy, responsiveness scorecards generally stimulate concessions to challengers. A responsiveness scorecard indicates whether officials are making progress in solving a problem posed by a constituency. When indicators of responsiveness become performance scorecards for an agency, officials who wish to avoid concessions face more tactical difficulties. A responsiveness scorecard makes it harder for recalcitrant officials to buy off opponents with symbolic rewards or their handling of special atrocity cases (for example, punishing the one policeman whose brutality was particularly conspicuous).[17]

Such scorecards also tend to facilitate responsiveness in situations, like Oakland's, where some bureaucrats want to help. Performance indicators work against officials deceiving themselves about the success of well-intentioned programs. Failure to show improvement will often spur renewed effort.

In addition to thwarting complacent self-deception, scorecards increase the salience of an objective for officials. Speaking more generally, Hawley has noted: "When under pressure from their environment to demonstrate their effectiveness, organizations tend to emphasize those activities that appear to be most readily measured whether or not those activities are central to the function of the enterprise."[18] Thus, the introduction of

[17] Lipsky, "Protest as a Political Resource," 1968, p. 1156, notes the use of this tactic.
[18] Willis D. Hawley, "Dealing with Organizational Rigidity in Public Schools A Theoretical Perspective." (Paper delivered at the American Political Science Association Convention, Chicago, Ill., 1971), p. 13.

responsiveness scorecards encourages officials to improve performance in areas which concern challengers.

The responsiveness effort engendered by such a scorecard varies. The responsiveness scorecard's impact will, for instance, usually be greater in the absence of other indicators which show that concessions to challengers come at a cost to various agency objectives. Consider personnel agencies which introduce responsiveness scorecards in the form of minority employment indicators. The degree of responsiveness precipitated by such an indicator in part depends on whether a skill scorecard is also present. Typically, personnel staffs lack measures of the skills level present in the bureaucracy. Assume, however, that officials developed and introduced a skill scorecard. Such an indicator would encourage minority hiring if it showed that recruiting minorities and fostering merit went hand in hand; but if the summary indicator of skill showed that affirmative action led to the recruitment of the less adroit, it would counteract the impact of the minority employment indicator. While responsiveness scorecards generally stimulate concessions, then, other scorecards can have the opposite effect. For challengers uncertainty can be bliss.

In fact, even responsiveness scorecards may at times inhibit efforts to aid challengers. I suspect that this occurrence is the exception rather than the rule. Nonetheless, where opponents of challengers are strong and a responsiveness indicator shows that attempts to help challengers have produced minimal results, the indicator may inhibit change. To be sure, sympathetic officials would often respond to an unimpressive showing on a responsiveness scorecard by calling for new programs and more effort. Unsympathetic officials might, however, use the scorecard to justify abandonment of responsiveness attempts. (Thus, certain conservatives excused their decision to do less for the poor on grounds that responsiveness scorecards demonstrated how little existing programs helped poverty victims.) Where challengers face powerful opponents, therefore, they may win more benefits if there are no responsiveness indicators.

In Oakland the introduction of a responsiveness scorecard tended to stimulate concessions. The scorecard was too new and the opposition was too weak for the indicator to function as decisive proof that responsiveness attempts would fail. Oakland officials established a responsiveness scorecard shortly after the U.S. Civil Rights Commission report of late summer 1969. At that time, the mayor asked the personnel director to submit monthly reports on the percentage of city employees who were minority. Throughout the struggle, then, both minority leaders and officials had access to numbers which revealed whether they were winning or losing.

This is not to say that the scorecard told actors all they wanted to know. Oakland's minority spokesmen were, after all, interested in more than the economic benefits of securing additional jobs for blacks and Chicanos. They also wanted to increase the extent to which the bureaucracy represented their interests. In this respect, minority leaders confronted the usual problems of those who seek representation through bureaucracies.[19] Even if the percentage of minority employees climbs sharply, troublesome questions remain. Will minority cops or museum officials once employed lose their sympathy with ghetto residents?[20] Even if minority employees have the right values, will these attitudes lead to action? Will the power structure of the department permit minority bureaucats to be responsive to the community? The proportion of employees who are minority is, then, a far better indicator of economic gain than of whether the minority community is acquiring substantive representation through the bureaucracy.

Whatever its limitations, the racial employment scorecard at least roughly indicated economic progress or setbacks to minority advocates. Furthermore, the indicator told city officials all they wanted to know about outcomes; officials were, after all, primarily interested in finding more jobs for minorities rather than fostering ghetto interest representation via the bureaucracy.

Sympathy with minority advocates, plus the presence of a responsiveness scorecard, helped push Oakland officials to

[19] For a lucid discussion of representative bureaucracy see Anthony Downs, *Inside Bureaucracy* (Boston: Little, Brown, 1967), pp. 231-233.

[20] For a pessimistic view of the likely orientations of black officers, see Nicholas Alex, *Black in Blue* New York: Appleton-Century-Crofts, 1969); for more optimistic data, see W. Eugene Groves, "Police in the Ghetto," *Perspectives on Urban Politics*, ed. Jay S. Goodman, (Boston: Allyn and Bacon, 1970), pp. 169-198.

search for alternatives which would facilitate minority hiring. In searching for options, the personnel staff confronted the strategic problems of where to apply pressure within the bureaucracy and how to modify both publicity and selection practices. How, then, did officials grapple with these problems? By examining a fire department recruitment drive and by drawing on more general observations, some answers emerge.

Find a vulnerable agency. Minority pressure for jobs tends to heighten intrabureaucratic conflict. Faced with demands from a segment of its job-hunting constituency, a central personnel office becomes more willing to risk prestige loss with employee leaders and department heads in order to attract more minority applicants. In bolstering minority hiring, a key problem of choice for an urban personnel director is to select a focus for pressure. Since a personnel agency typically lacks the resources to prod all departments, where should it focus its attention?

A personnel director who perceives the need to increase minority recruitment will generally put more pressure on departments which: (a) have hired few minorities, (b) have made little effort to recruit them, (c) have jobs which require simple skills, (d) restrict opportunity for serious abuse of authority by employees, and (e) have a substantial number of slots.

Thus, the Oakland fire department was a natural target for the personnel director. For one thing, fire officials were notorious for their lack of interest in "equal employment" opportunity. The agency had the lowest percentage of minorities of any department in the city (under 5 percent). Furthermore, unlike the police chief, fire officials made little effort to attract blacks, Chicanos, and Orientals. While police officials backed minority recruitment drives, firemen did not; while the police department participated in federally subsidized programs to help disadvantaged youth, the fire department refused.

From the perspective of civil service officials, the fire department's lack of commitment to minority hiring seemed particularly unjustified. They believed that the minority community did not find fire activities, unlike police work, onerous. Moreover, personnel analysts believed that more minorities had the ability to be hosemen than patrolmen. Analysts had few doubts that a cop's work was difficult and required exceptional ability. By comparison the tasks of a hoseman seemed simple to perform. At one point, even the most pro-employee civil service commissioner commented that he could "teach his wife in one afternoon" how to hook up a hose and put a ladder against the wall. Thus, while it was difficult to imagine a police department with skills slack, fire seemed to have excessive requirements given the lack of difficulty of the work.

The civil service staff's belief that lowering standards for hosemen posed few risks that employees would seriously abuse their authority also encouraged intervention against fire officials. The personnel director thought that reduced standards in the police department might lead to corruption and abuse. By contrast, the damage that a few incompetent firemen could do seemed much less. After all, hosemen were easy to supervise and not subject to the temptations which patrolmen face.

These considerations, along with the recognition that fire, as the second largest agency in the city, had enough jobs to make a major contribution to the minority hiring effort, led the personnel director to take action. With a hoseman test coming up in early 1971, he and an assistant suggested a variety of changes.

Change publicity tactics. One of the personnel analyst's first steps was to modify the publicity process. Whenever city officials encounter a recruitment problem the publicity phase of the hiring process generally undergoes more change more rapidly than the selection phase. Such behavior in large part stems from the belief that adjustments in the publicity process involve less immediate risk to the organization's supply of skills than do alternations in selection. The widely held belief that publicity adjustments involve less risk makes this the path of least resistance for any bureaucrat seeking change. Personnel staffs know that selection modifications tend to provoke more opposition from other bureaucrats than do publicity changes.

By the time the need arose to recruit more firemen, Oakland's personnel staff had had enough experience with affirmative action to conclude that publicity alterations alone would not solve the minority hiring problem. Staff members nonetheless thought that creative advertisement of jobs in the minority community was important. Consequently, the personnel analyst working on the problem took a number of steps. He began by ordering the picture on the announcement redesigned. For the first time, a black appeared on it, holding a hose with a white fireman. He also persuaded fire officials to cooperate in an effort to reach the minority community. Attempting to make community organizations conveyors of information, the analyst asked 25 group leaders to attend a special meeting on December 9, 1970. (To his disappointment only 10 came.) Going beyond ordinary civil service methods, the personnel analyst also placed ads in the *Montclarion, Oakland Tribune,* and the *Oakland Post* (the last in a give-away newspaper aimed at the minority community in the East Bay). A black recruitment team from the fire department visited Merritt and Laney Junior Colleges, where most students were minority.

In addition, the civil service office urged fire officials to transmit information which would not only encourage minority applicants but which would improve their chances of passing subsequent tests. For this purpose, the fire department agreed to hold open houses at stations in areas with large minority populations in East and West Oakland. Prospective applicants could visit the houses, become acquainted with fire activities, and climb the ladders used in the physical agility portion of the civil service test. The civil service office also persuaded several black firemen to conduct special classes every Tuesday from August 4, 1970, to February 9, 1971.

Many fire officials viewed the civil service publicity plans with little enthusiasm. They did not, however, fight these changes as vigorously as those directed at selection criteria.

Problem source and manipulability shape selection changes. Adjustments in the selection process will typically be small, primarily because officials wish to reduce the risk to skill, minimize the prospect that other city employees will mobilize against reform, and reduce the burdens of calculation. Apart from keeping adjustments incremental, officials altering selection procedures will focus on those criteria which seem to be the most direct source of a problem and those which they can most readily control.

Among the many selection criteria utilized, the personnel

director suspected that credential requirements, written tests, and the lack of a residence requirement worked to the disadvantage of minority applicants. Consequently, he attempted to modify each criterion.

With respect to credentials, Oakland's personnel director was well aware that the vast majority of city positions required a high-school diploma. He knew that minorities in all age categories were less likely than whites to have such a qualification.[21] Suspicious of agency education and experience demands the personnel director had acted to reduce requirements prior to the fire department campaign. The director had, for example, encouraged city participation in the federally subsidized New Careers Program. Under the auspices of this program, individuals with less than the normally required education were permitted to work in the parks and recreation department, the police department and other agencies. The director hoped that the program would help convince agency officials that their credential demands were excessive. However, administrators involved with New Careers denied that it set a precedent for lowering educational standards. At one point, for instance, a consultant claimed that the program showed how little a college diploma contributed to effective performance by recreation leaders. Parks and recreation officials quickly denied this and asserted that New Careers proved the opposite. Trainees without the degree did worse than regular employees and needed much more supervision. While the department could risk skills deficit in a few positions, officials argued that it could not do so more generally.[22] Thus, it had to maintain present background requirements.

Despite department sentiments against lower standards, the personnel director did engineer some reduction in background requirements.[23] A brief survey of examination announcements

[21] Oakland City Planning Department, *Options For Oakland,* 1969, p. 30. "Less than 20 percent of black residents in their sixties were high school graduates but the proportion increases as age level goes down: 26 percent in their fifties; 38 percent, forties; 55 percent, thirties; and 71 percent, twenties."

[22] The reaction of parks and recreation is comparable to that of 131 Cleveland firms. See John L. Iacobelli, "A Survey of Employer Attitudes Toward Training the Disadvantaged," *Monthly Labor Review* 93 (June 1970): 51-55.

[23] Some impetus for lowering education and experience requirements came from the consulting firm of Griffenhagen-Kroeger which conducted a classification study in 1969 see chapter 2).

from 1966 to January, 1971, indicates the results of this policy shift. For this period, there were 88 entry level examinations where a comparison with the previous announcement was possible. In 17 cases, or about 20 percent, the commission lowered the requirements from one time the civil service office gave the test to the next. Only twice did it raise standards.

Although the reductions in standards sought by the personnel staff were usually slight, line officials often opposed the changes. Consider, for instance, the resistance which the staff encountered when it attempted to modify hiring practices in the fire department. A personnel analyst suggested to fire officials that they accept a General Education Development (GED) test score in lieu of a high-school diploma. Up to this time, the fire chief had insisted that all applicants possess a twelfth-grade education. The analyst felt that this credential demand was needlessly stringent. After all, the police department, a key reference group on many matters for fire officials, permitted use of the test (though it insisted that a score of 262 was essential if an applicant lacked a diploma; most high-school graduates cannot do this well). But when the analyst made the GED proposal, the fire chief resisted. The latter felt that a high-school diploma predicted self-discipline, maturity, and the ability to get along with others.

Faced with this resistance, the analyst invested time building a case for change. One typical tactic he used was the "follow the leader" approach. When personnel analysts wish to justify a move and are unable to show precisely what the impact will be, they often attempt to make their case by showing that the new procedure is standard practice among respectable departments. Thus, Oakland's analysts contacted a number of other city fire departments to determine whether they permitted use of the GED. Of the agencies contacted, about half did. But these data did not convince Oakland's fire chief. For one thing, a substantial minority of the sampled fire units did not accept the GED. For another, the chief was unimpressed with the "follow the leader" approach. Where an agency head perceives his department to be in the forefront professionally, (as was true of the Oakland fire chief) data from other jurisdictions are less likely to persuade him to change.

Consequently, the analyst attempted to persuade the chief by looking for historical precedent within Oakland's fire department. To this end, the analyst went through civil service files and discovered that high ranking fire officials, hired many years ago, lacked diplomas. Confronted with this evidence and persistent pressure by the civil service office, the fire chief grudgingly accepted the GED. He insisted, however, that the passing score on it be the same as for patrolmen, even though the civil service staff felt that the score could be lower.

Of course, the personnel director and his analyst could have avoided negotiations with the fire chief simply by taking their case to the Civil Service Commission. But besides creating ill will between him and the department head, the personnel director would have risked reversal by the commission. In one instance, the personnel director unilaterally had tried to make vision requirements for hosemen less stringent, only to have the fire chief appeal and the commission overrule him.

The personnel director also met resistance when he tried to impose new residence requirements on applicants. Originally, the director attempted to impose a strict requirement that all applicants had to be residents of Oakland. Since the city had a substantial minority population, he assumed that this would increase the percentage of minority job applicants. The fire chief and firefighters association, however opposed such a requirement (the latter threatening to sue). They believed that the residence stipulation would eliminate quality applicants from consideration; they knew that it would undermine the department's friends and relatives recruitment strategy, whereby present employees solicited applications from acquaintances whom they believed would make "good firemen." Resistance from the association and fire chief, coupled with the city attorney's opinion that the legal status of the stipulation was uncertain led the Civil Service Commission to another compromise. It authorized two lists—one for Oakland residents and another for nonresidents. The city would hire job hunters on the latter list only after it had offered work to successful Oakland applicants.

In addition to taking these steps, personnel analysts adopted a strategy which they had utilized in previous recruitment

drives: they attempted to make the written test more "relevant" by removing questions that did not directly relate to
the job. Through such action they hoped not only to make
their examinations more valid but also to hire more minorities.

Other things being equal, black is beautiful. Well before
anyone launched an affirmative action program for the fire
department, some officials had also changed their oral examination techniques. Certain personnel analysts and department
officials came to believe that where the interview performance
of a black or Chicano was about the same as that of a white,
the minority should receive a higher ranking. By adopting this
decision rule, many interviewers thought that they could avoid
any major "sacrifice" in skill, yet still hire more minorities.

Officials changed their decision rules in the oral test even
though they had little evidence that minorities suffered disproportionately at this stage of the selection process. The manipulability of the oral helps account for the attention that it has
received. Examiners can directly give minority applicants the
benefit of a doubt in the interview; they do not, as in the case
of written tests, have to proceed indirectly by first construc⁺ing
a criterion sympathetic to minorities and then subjecting the
criterion to a color blind scoring process. Instead, orals make
favoritism feasible both in structuring the mechanism and
scoring applicant responses. Furthermore racial preference in
an oral is not as visible within the bureaucracy as other
adjustments aimed at helping minorities (for example, lowering
credential requirements). Consequently, manipulation of the
oral is less likely to precipitate organized opposition.

Civil service efforts have little payoff. The strategies that
personnel officials used vis-à-vis the fire department are typical
of those they generally employ in their efforts to attract more
minorities. In the case of the fire department, however, personnel analysts took special pains to gather information which
would help them evaluate their efforts. Staff members soon
found that their publicity tactics had borne results. The 220
minority applicants taking the examination represented an
increase of more than ten times the number who had taken
it the previous time the staff gave it in April 1969. More than
one third of those entering the examination process were
minorities. But if the new publicity tactics succeeded, the slight

change in selection criteria did not, as Table 13 shows.

TABLE 13: SELECTION PROCESSES SCREENED OUT PROPORTIONATELY MORE
MINORITY THAN CAUCASIAN HOSEMAN APPLICANTS (1971)

	Blacks	Chicano	Oriental	Minorities combined	Caucasian
Number taking written test	174	41	5	220	411
Number left after written test	11 (6.3%)	6 (14.6%)	1 (20%)	18 (8.2%)	165 (40.1%)
Number left after physical agility	11 (6.3%)	4 (9.8%)	1 (20%)	16 (7.3%)	110 (26.8%)
Number left after oral	8 (4.6%)	4 (9.8%)	1 (20%)	13 (5.9%)	94 (22.9%)

Source: Oakland Civil Service Office.

The table indicates that while 23 percent of the Caucasians passed the three basic test phases, only 6 percent of the minorities did.[24] The written examination, in particular, exacted a disproportionate toll among minority applicants. With the passing score equal to 70 percent correct, more than 90 percent of the minorities failed while roughly 60 percent of the Caucasians did.

What implications do these data have for the recruitment pool from which the fire department will draw individuals to fill vacancies? Table 14 offers some answers. With more than 85 percent of the eligible list white, the personnel director and Civil Service Commission knew that the racial composition of the fire department would not change much. The results would do little to improve their status in the minority community.

Viewed broadly, the personnel director responded to inadequate minority representation in the fire department by promoting small changes in a wide range of recruitment procedures. From the start, he was uncertain whether these moves would produce the desired increase in minority employees. Many of the adjustments he made in fact bore no fruit. For instance, permitting use of the GED test did not result in any more blacks, Chicanos, or Orientals making the eligible list. In fact,

[24] As of April 1971, one cannot tell how many the city will hire.

TABLE 14: A SMALL PERCENTAGE OF THE ELIGIBLE LIST IS MINORITY

	Resident eligible list (Receives hiring preference)	*Non-resident eligible list*	*Total*
	(Percentages)		
Minority	14.0	10.0	12.2
White	86.0	90.0	87.8
	(n=57)		(n=107)

Source: Oakland Civil Service Office.

the step permitted two Caucasians to get through the process who would have faced rejection otherwise. Nor did the residence requirements greatly benefit minorities, though the local list had a slightly higher percentage of minorities than the nonresident one.

As the case of the fire department illustrates, minority hiring gains do not come easily. Nonetheless, the percentage of minorities in the bureaucracy has crept upward slowly. In 1967, 18.7 percent of the city's employees were minority while in June 1970, 20.8 percent were. Given that turnover rates during this time ranged from 5 to 15 percent per year, the gain is not as tiny as it may seem at first glance.

As is generally true, the public safety agencies are the main drag on city hall's efforts to boost its percentage of minorities.[25] Police and fire departments contain about half of the bureaucracy's full-time man-years. Yet just over 5 percent of the employees in these departments are minority. The building and housing department also has less than 10 percent minority representation, in large part because the agency relies on craft unions as a source of applicants. Such unions have, of course, been difficult for minorities to enter.

CONCLUSION

The recent thrust by minority advocates has dispersed recruitment leverage more than ever. Even prior to minority activism, hiring processes featured a more decentralized leverage pattern than was evident in either manpower or pay arenas.

[25] Oakland's experience is similar to that of other cities; see Robert G. Bryan, "Minority Employment in State and Local Government," *Monthly Labor Review* 92 (November 1969): 68.

In the hiring sphere, the civil service staff, the rank-and-file, and top department officials help disseminate information about job vacancies. As for selection, a veto group pluralist structure prevails whereby actors have "attained a power to stop things conceivably inimical to [their] interests and within far narrower limits to start things."[26] Personnel analysts, various department representatives, professionals from other jursidictions, and medical doctors all have the authority to slam the gate shut on job hunters at some point.[27] None has the ability to appoint an applicant over the objection of others. The veto group pluralist pattern is also evident with respect to more basic structural issues. While some, for instance, would like to promote higher educational requirements, their anticipation of civil service office opposition has discouraged them from trying.

Greater leverage dispersion and the absence of skill scorecards create greater barriers to understanding in the hiring sphere than exist in either manpower or pay arenas. Since more actors participate in recruitment choices, top officials cannot so readily grasp the decision rules in use and how various policy alternatives would affect choice processes and recruitment outcomes. The lack of quality indicators of skill also increases uncertainty about the most suitable tactics. There is no firm consensus concerning how to define skill, let alone measure it. The game score is not, therefore, as clear as in manpower and pay arenas. Gauging progress with respect to minority hiring goals is, of course, easier. Yet even with regard to this objective, uncertainty persists. Attempts to hire more minorities have often failed, leaving officials to ponder what other methods to try.

Many of the ingredients creating uncertainty for decision makers in the recruitment arena are also present in removal politics.

[26] David Riesman with Nathan Glazer and Reuel Denny, *The Lonely Crowd* (New Haven: Yale University Press, 1963), p. 213.

[27] I have contended that the many participants in the recruitment process lead to a pattern of dispersed control. One might argue that the numerous actors involved create only the illusion of decentralized power; that in fact all bureaucrats see matters in about the same way, so that, for example, who sits on the oral examination board is irrelevant for outcomes. While there is some similarity of outlook among municipal employees, I believe that there is also significant variation. An agency head cannot specifically tell a subordinate how to make judgments in an oral examination. Personnel analysts bring a different perspective to decision sites than department representatives.

7

The Politics of Removal

It is more difficult to get an employee transferred
from one department to another than it is to exchange prisoners of war.

Fiorello LaGuardia[1]

Removal, as well as recruitment politics, affects government
capability. Blessed with good information and the capacity to
control demotions, transfers, firings, and resignations, an administrator could build city hall's reservoir of skills: a police
chief could keep a competent patrolman at that position; a
head librarian could shift a disgruntled, incompetent book
cataloguer into reference work where she was more adroit; or
a finance director could dump a blatantly inept computer
programmer. Assuming that this executive was not losing badly
in other personnel arenas, his strength in removal politics would
help him improve service and enhance his reputation.

No one in Oakland has this much power over removal.
Rather, many individuals with varying amounts of resources
shape removal outcomes.[2] This chapter considers why players
choose certain tactics and the implications of their behavior
for the game's leverage pattern. In this vein, it deals first with

[1] In William C. Thomas, Jr., "Generalist vs. Specialist: Careers in a Municipal
Bureaucracy," *Public Administration Review* 21 Winter 1961): 9.
[2] Oakland is not unique. Removal for a top executive is often an uncertain and
risky business. Two authors who capture some of the problems involved are Edward
Greer, "The Liberation of Gary, Indiana," *Trans-action* 8 (January 1971): 37, and
Alan A. Altshuler, *Community Control: The Black Demand for Participation in Large
American Cities* (New York: Pegasus, 1970), pp. 152-155.

problems officials face in gathering and evaluating performance information. Then it focuses on the politics of involuntary removal, whereby officials attempt to transfer, demote, or fire someone against his will. A third section briefly analyzes voluntary removal, whereby the employee, on his own initiative, seeks to leave a position.

WHO KNOWS ABOUT PERFORMANCE?

Knowledge facilitates control. If an agency head presumes to make intelligent removal choices, he must grasp how well employees are behaving. Such information is often hard to acquire. In evaluating employee performance, high-level bureaucrats face two fundamental questions: First, what are the appropriate criteria and standards for judging occupational behavior? Second, in light of these norms, how can one tell whether the subordinate is living up to them? Department heads are uncertain about the answers to both these queries in a substantial number of situations. Rarely can anyone precisely specify what makes a good employee; nor is it easy to find out what he does with his time.

Employees, themselves, often strive to foster ambiguity concerning these matters by keeping potentially damaging information from superiors. As Goode notes:

> Almost every inquiry into the productivity of workers has shown that the informal work group protects its members by setting a standard which everyone can meet, and [that] they develop techniques for preventing a supervisor from measuring accurately the output of each man.[3]

In essence, subordinates sense the value of knowledge in personnel politics and strive to keep certain things from management's eyes. For observers like Goode, this ability is so great that "Once the person enters the work group ... the social arrangements do not permit much overt discrimination between the less able and the rest."[4]

[3] William J. Goode, "The Protection of the Inept," *American Sociological Review* 32 (February 1967): 6.
[4] *Ibid.,* p. 8.

Though securing meaningful performance information almost always poses problems, some top bureaucrats have it easier than others. In order to provide an overview of this variation, I present Chart 8. The matrix classifies jobs first according to whether performance criteria and standards are crystallized in the minds of top officials. In short, do officials

CHART 8: UNDERSTANDING OF PERFORMANCE QUALITY VARIES BY POSITION

		Superficially Ambiguous	*Relatively Clear*
	Clear	Building and Housing Inspectors	Secretaries Janitors Hosemen Parks Maintenance
Criteria and Standards of Performance Evaluation			
	Unclear	*Ambiguous* Patrolmen Recreation Directors	*Superficially Clear* Curators City Planners
		Low	High

Visibility of Subordinate Behavior or
Performance Results to the Upper Echelons

feel confident that they know precisely what incompetence is? The second dimension of the matrix refers to whether high-level executives can readily acquire information concerning subordinate behavior (apart from whether they can then evaluate it). The types of situations that emerge from the matrix are relatively clear, superficially clear, superficially ambiguous, and ambiguous. In each cell, I present examples of positions which fall into the category.

Employees charged with maintaining the grass and trees in city parks and landscaped areas exemplify those whose performance is relatively clear. These men do not work in isolation; usually a supervisor can easily tell if they have done a good job. He can, for instance, discern whether the grass is too long or weeds are choking park gardens. The supervisor also has some understanding of how much work employee should do,

for example how long it should take a crew to mow a lawn.
Thus, criteria and standards of performance are relatively easy
to establish.

An example of a superficially clear job is museum curator.
Since such employees work in close proximity to the agency
head, the latter can, without too much effort, observe how the
staff spends its time. Moreover, by strolling through the museum's corridors periodically and keeping up with the programs
the staff offers, he gets some idea of their historical, artistic,
and scientific outputs. But by what scorecard should the
displays or programs be judged? Though much of a curator's
output is visible, how do you evaluate it? Is an art show good
if it draws praise from an art history professor at the University
of California, pleases the museum auxiliary, or is of great
interest to ghetto residents? Assessing an exhibit is a far cry
from deciding whether the grass in the parks looks a well-wa-
tered green.

It is difficult to find superficially ambiguous jobs but building
and housing inspectors come close.[5] These personnel conduct
a wide range of inspection activities using rather specifically
stated decision rules to evaluate the physical structure of
buildings. These rules limit the discretion of the inspector.
What is problematic for a control-oriented administrator is that
the men work alone throughout the city. Rarely does anyone
doublecheck their judgments. Nor do citizens usually complain
if inspectors apply the rules inappropriately. Hence, even
though job criteria and standards are fairly apparent, a supervisor is often unsure if employees are meeting them.

Among Oakland agency heads, the police chief has the worst
information deficit of all. The chief, himself, has remarked that
the qualities of a "good cop" are far from apparent.[6] What,

[5] Ermer perceptively argues that housing inspectors face considerable uncertainty
in Baltimore. In the case of Oakland, however, I found considerable consensus concern-
ing the criteria and standards of job performance associated with the role. Virginia
B. Ermer, "Housing Inspection in Baltimore: Vermin, Mannequins, and Beer Bottles,"
Blacks and Bureaucracy, ed. Virginia B. Ermer and John H. Strange (New York:
Thomas Y. Crowell, 1972, pp. 82-93.

[6] James Q. Wilson, "The Police in the Ghetto," *The Police and the Community*,
ed. Robert F. Steadman (Baltimore: Johns Hopkins University Press, 1972), p. 72; see
also The San Francisco Committee on Crime, *A Report on the San Francisco Police
Department* (San Francisco: Western Star Press, 1971), p. 48. This report appropriately
notes that "no city to the best or our knowledge has assembled its collective wisdom
to determine what it really wants its police to do or not to do."

for instance, is the community relations aspect of an officer's performance and how important is it? To what extent is merit indicated by the ability of an officer to meet informal ticket quotas or establish a high clearance rate?[7] Beyond this basic difficulty, the chief faces problems because his men often work alone and are geographically dispersed. Even if he assigns two men to a patrol car, he cannot count on one officer to inform on the other. Often, he cannot tell whether his men are shirking enforcement of the law (the most persistent police tendency generally) or mishandling a case. Since as Goode points out "the less able are protected more in those types of performance that are difficult to evaluate," the chief confronts serious difficulties.[8]

Of the four types of positions discussed here, what is the distribution of city hall employees among them? To offer a rough estimate, the performance of about half the work force is relatively clear and about a quarter, ambiguous; the rest, except for a small fraction, are superficially clear.

The fact that performance in one-half the positions is relatively clear does not mean, however, that top bureaucrats are absolutely confident when they evaluate behavior in such slots. Though they know from experience what, on the average, they can expect, officials do not understand precisely what they should demand. If parks personnel mow a lawn in an hour, the question remains: Should they do it in half that time? City hall has no modern day F. W. Taylors in its ranks specifying scientifically how much work employees can do.[9] Thus, problems of defining skill deficit linger under the best of circumstances.

THE POLITICS OF INVOLUNTARY REMOVAL

Oakland's top executives, then, face the problem of discovering if and where skills deficit exists. In addition they confront

[7] For a discussion of these indicators see James Q. Wilson, *Varieties of Police Behavior* (Cambridge: Harvard University Press, 1968), pp. 95-99, Jerome H. Skolnick, *Justice Without Trial* (New York: John Wiley, 1967), pp. 164-181.

[8] Goode, "The Protection of the Inept," p. 12.

[9] See Frederick Winslow Taylor, *The Principles of Scientific Management* (New York: W. W. Norton, 1967).

issues regarding what to do about inept performance once they locate it. We will consider their tactical response to both these problems below.

THE STRATEGY FOR LOCATING SKILLS DEFICIT

How do officials locate skills deficit within their ranks? Ostensibly, they seem to conduct a considerable amount of surveillance. They have underlings write out performance evaluations regardless of whether the employee is performing poorly. In part this is because agency heads accept the legitimacy of Civil Service Commission authority. The commission requires supervisors at every level to write out ratings for regular employees annually and probationary ones four times per year. The employee, his immediate supervisor, and the department head must eventually sign the evaluation; the civil service office then stores this information in its files.

High-risk agencies use more complex forms. The forms that bureaucrats use to accumulate and code performance information vary. The standard rating sheet, which the commission authorizes, calls for the supervisor to assess an employee on ten attributes (quality of work, quantity of work, dependability, work habits, cooperation and relationships with people, initiative and ingenuity, analytical abililty, ability as supervisor, administrative ability, and "factors not listed above"). With respect to each attribute, an individual can receive one of five grades ranging from "unacceptable" to "outstanding."

To increase the specificity and relevance of the data on these forms, some departments, such as fire, police, and general services, have their own rating systems. A glance at such forms indicates that "high risk" agencies, that is, those where skills deficit often has direct implications for the safety of life and property, strive for more elaborate assessment of performance. Hence, both police and fire departments evaluate employees on more attributes than the civil service office prescribes. Fire supervisors rate subordinates on 33 factors which fall into 6 major categories—station work, drills, emergency work, fire prevention, public relations, and supervisory ability.

Going further, the police department requires its supervisors to assess more than one hundred characteristics. They must score employees from 1 to 100 on such items as "felony arrest record," "attitude toward department goals and objectives," and "team member." Dealing with these five-page reports requires a calculating machine. The supervisor finds an average score for items in five basic categories (work quality, quantity, dependability, personnel relations, and attendance), and then derives an overall figure which he rounds to two decimal places. In the case of city hall, then, one finds the paradoxical circumstance that the department where employee evaluation is most difficult—where good information is hardest to secure and interpret—calls for the most precise assessment on the largest number of variables. Elaborateness of the rating, then, correlates with the perceived risk involved in subordinate performance rather than with the availability of information.

Record but do not read. Though the commission promises that such performance evaluations will improve removal decisions and agency personnel consume considerable time filling them out, top bureaucrats rarely look at them. In part this is because they lack time. The police chief, for example, would have more than a thousand forms to scrutinize. Beyond this, many believe that the reports transmit little useful data and are loaded with platitudes. For instance, the direct of general services found that the evaluation elicited meaningless "stereotypes" while the city auditor bemoaned the "cliches" that they contained. Although the police department uses quantified evaluations, many top officials do not believe that such scoring yields much useful information. Different supervisors vary in the way they rate performance. Even so simple an issue as assessing the absenteeism of an officer has produced different numerical interpretations. One sergeant assigns a score of 100 to an officer who invariably comes to work. Another scores a patrolman well below this for being on the job every day.

Function need not follow form. Given the tiny amount of information that performance evaluation forms yield to department heads, it is surprising that top officials overwhelmingly comply with requirements to keep them up. On the surface it appears that Oakland bureaucrats ritualistically spend their time filling out useless pieces of paper. This is not the case. The mistake is to judge the practice simply on the basis of how much data it yields to high echelon officials, when in fact performance evaluation provides different benefits.

Downs has noted that the use of employee rating forms can inculcate "the fear of punishment" into subordinates for failure to meet standards. He goes on to suggest that such "compliance-inducing functions explain why bureaus normally require so many more reports than higher level officials can possibly read. Even if 90 per cent of all such reports are never looked at, they may still have a potent effect in causing compliance with the bureau's standards."[10]

Agency heads, then, seldom use evaluation forms to locate a problem. Rather, they use the ratings to prevent problems from arising and to justify a disciplinary or removal decision to outsiders.[11]

Wait and see. For a top official to spend hours poring over performance evaluations would, then, be a costly exercise which might create animosity among subordinates.[12] Rather than do this, agency heads adopt a wait and see strategy; they assume matters are progressing smoothly until a subordinate or citizen informs them that something is wrong. Not that department heads are passive. They will attempt to inform subordinates concerning what misbehavior to report and when. The police chief, for instance, has sponsored a violent-officer program under which supervisors single out and bring to the chief's attention policemen who persistently elicit violent responses from those they arrest. But once an agency head has laid down guidelines, he essentially waits for a supervisor to notify him of a problem.

Better to discover your own dirty linen. High-ranking bureaucrats strongly prefer one of their underlings to discover skills deficit rather than an outsider. Then, if the time comes to fire a subordinate, the department head initiates the action and can take credit for keeping his own house in order. When

[10] Anthony Downs, *Inside Bureaucracy* (Boston: Little, Brown, 1967), pp. 145-146.
[11] Herbert Kaufman, *The Forest Ranger* (Baltimore, The Johns Hopkins University Press, 1960), p. 158, notes a similar phenomenon.
[12] Downs, *Inside Bureaucracy*, p. 146, notes that some agency heads survey performance by randomly focusing on certain employees. In Oakland, most department heads believe that a performance problem will come to their attention and do not do this. For examples of problems caused by close supervision see Alvin W. Gouldner, *Patterns of Industrial Bureaucracy* (New York: Free Press, 1964), pp. 159-161.

a citizen complains, a top bureaucrat runs the risk that the grievance will flow first to the city manager or councilmen, possibly damaging his prestige with them. Worse, the outsider may take his lament to the press. Since the more who learn of the criticism the greater tends to be the status cost to the agency, newspaper coverage is a threat to high officials.

Among Oakland's department heads, the police chief is far and away the most besieged with public outcries against the behavior of his subordinates.[13] Throughout the sixties minority spokesmen frequently accused the police of abuse. In responding to such charges, the chief senses that regardless of what he does the incident hurts. Those inclined to doubt the police will find their opinions reinforced whether he zealously investigates the case or not. His final judgment about the complaint is unlikely to receive as much publicity as the initial attack.

In sum, the chief well understands the problems posed by client complaints. He and other department heads are, therefore, reluctant to solicit them. The desire to discover and deal with one's own dirty linen helps explain the antipathy of officials toward citizen review boards. When in 1965 minority advocates mounted a drive for a police review board, the chief resisted the idea. He feared that bad publicity and unfair treatment of his men would result; he also feared that the board would undermine his authority over removal and thereby weaken his general control over the police department. The city manager and elected politicians supported the chief and have consistently resisted proposals for review structures.

THE TACTICAL RESPONSE TO SKILLS DEFICIT

Once officials learn of a problem they engage in a standardized search for a solution. Chart 9 summarizes the removal process for a classified employee. It shows how officials document a case and often seek a solution which falls short of firing the subordinate. To this end, they may demote the employee, transfer him, wait for him to retire, or attempt to reform his behavior. The reasons why Oakland officials go to some length to avoid a firing include a sense of loyalty to the subordinate,

[13] While not necessarily precipitated by citizen complaints from fiscal 1966 to 1970, the internal affairs section handled an average of 527 cases per year.

a belief that they have sunk costs in the employee, and an awareness that the subordinate can appeal for outside help.

Nobody likes to fire. A key factor inhibiting firings is the mental dissonance they produce. Though committed to weeding out those who produce skills deficit, top bureaucrats find the

CHART 9: THE REMOVAL CALCULATIONS OF AN AGENCY HEAD
FOR A NONPROBATIONARY EMPLOYEE

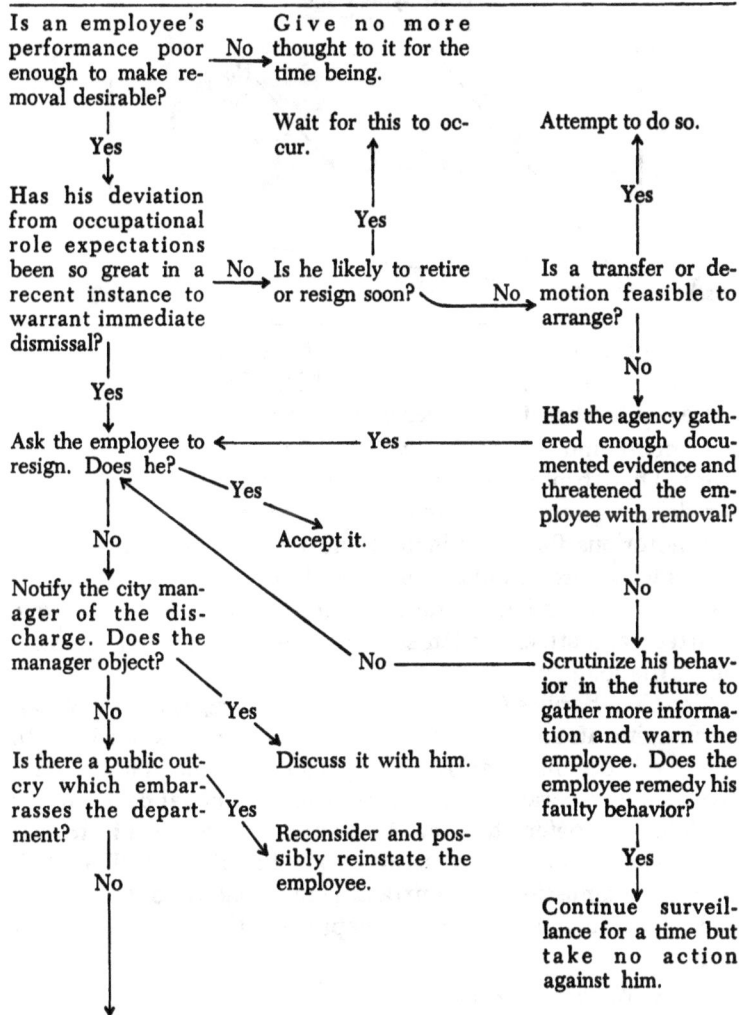

Is an employee's performance poor enough to make removal desirable? — No → Give no more thought to it for the time being.

↓ Yes

Has his deviation from occupational role expectations been so great in a recent instance to warrant immediate dismissal? — No → Is he likely to retire or resign soon? — Yes → Wait for this to occur.

Is he likely to retire or resign soon? — No → Is a transfer or demotion feasible to arrange? — Yes → Attempt to do so.

Is a transfer or demotion feasible to arrange? — No → Has the agency gathered enough documented evidence and threatened the employee with removal?

↓ Yes

Ask the employee to resign. Does he? ← Yes ← Has the agency gathered enough documented evidence and threatened the employee with removal?

Ask the employee to resign. Does he? — Yes → Accept it.

↓ No

Notify the city manager of the discharge. Does the manager object?

Has the agency gathered enough documented evidence and threatened the employee with removal? — No → Scrutinize his behavior in the future to gather more information and warn the employee. Does the employee remedy his faulty behavior? — No

Notify the city manager of the discharge. Does the manager object? — Yes → Discuss it with him.

↓ No

Is there a public outcry which embarrasses the department? — Yes → Reconsider and possibly reinstate the employee.

Does the employee remedy his faulty behavior? ↓ Yes → Continue surveillance for a time but take no action against him.

↓ No

CHART 9—*Continued*

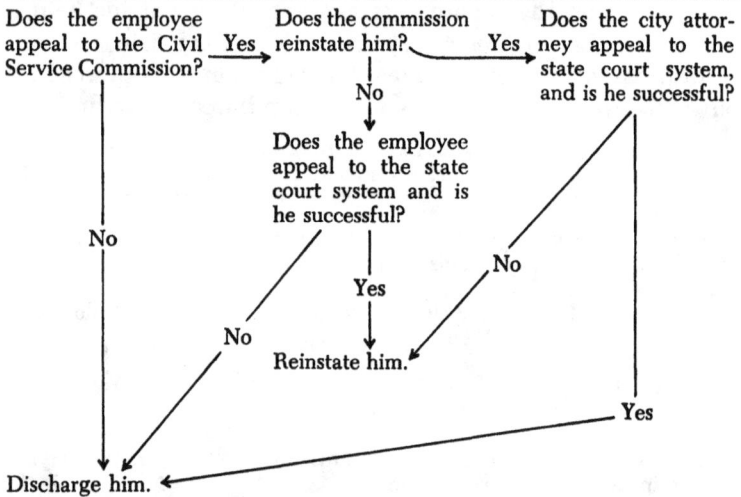

Does the employee appeal to the Civil Service Commission? —Yes→ Does the commission reinstate him? —Yes→ Does the city attorney appeal to the state court system, and is he successful?

No (from commission reinstate him?)

Does the employee appeal to the state court system and is he successful?

No

Yes

Reinstate him.

No

Yes

Discharge him.

task unpleasant, particularly if the subordinate has earned a reputation for being a "nice guy."[14] Psychological discomfort increases further if the supervisor knows the man has a family to support and will probably have a hard time finding other work. Though present in all agency officials, these sentiments run deeper in some than others. A former librarian, for example, was notorious for being lenient; he kept women on full-time status who were too disabled to work more than two or three days a week. Similarly, the city auditor admitted being "soft hearted" and sticking with subordinates who did not measure up in the long run.

The Civil Service Commission also discourages firings. When discharging an employee, the decision maker does not have to fret about the manager overriding his choice. The chief executive virtually always backs a department removal decision. By so doing, he defers to their first-hand knowledge of circumstances and shows faith in his "right-hand" men. The Civil Service Commission, by contrast, is more likely to demand an elaborate explanation from the department and reject its decision.

[14] Goode, "The Protection of the Inept," p. 12.

Most agency heads loathe having to appear before this body. Though relatively few of them have been involved in a disciplinary hearing, almost all view such proceedings with distaste. For example, the director of general services referred to the appeals system as a "stinking mess" where participants constantly dragged personalities into deliberations; one of his top aides called it a "brutal process." The police chief, who has had more experience with the commission than anyone else, believes that it hampers management. In his view, "The Civil Service Board is employee oriented where meetings become an emotional affair where sound judgment does not often win out."

Apart from the unpleasantness of the proceedings, per se, department heads dislike being overruled. When this occurs they sense that they have wasted many hours. They also believe that such rulings are a blow to their prestige and the legitimacy of their authority, and will ultimately encourage other employees to disobey.

The costs department heads have sunk in an employee also cause them to delay firings. Many have spent time and money recruiting and training a subordinate; training costs in agencies like police and fire are particularly high. Having invested resources in an underling, officials are reluctant to abandon him; instead they commit a little more time to reforming him in hopes that previous expenses were not incurred in vain.

Agency behavior during an employee's probationary period suggests the significance of sunk costs, personal loyalty, and the Civil Service Commission. Top officials disproportionately fire employees during this time, which lasts through a subordinate's first year on the job. When a bureaucrat is on probation, the commission has no authority to overrule a department head's dismissal decision. Furthermore, since the employee is new, he has had little time to develop bonds of friendship which might mute the inclination of supervisors to fire him; feelings of personal attachment and loyalty are weaker. Finally, the employee's recent arrival on the job means that officials have not spent as much time training him. By acting quickly, officials prevent sunk costs from becoming larger.

Avoid firing through transfer or demotion. Agency heads are, then, reluctant to fire regular employees. Two alternatives to dismissal that they at times explore are transfer and demotion. Through either of these actions, they may be able to shift an employee from a slot where he is inept to one where he will at least display skills congruence.

Position classes and formal department boundary lines are the key constraints standing in the way of a successful transfer. The Civil Service Commission lumps the more than 3500 city hall employees into roughly 300 classes which vary greaty in size. There are over 500 patrolmen, for example, but fewer than 5 junior administrative analysts. Civil service regulations require that a transfer cannot be made out of class (such as removing a junior typist from one slot and making her a secretary stenographer elsewhere). Therefore, the more slots in a class and the greater variation among positions within it, the more feasible is the transfer. Consider the police chief. The 120 sergeants under the chief perform diverse functions ranging from criminal investigation to supervising animal control. If an officer is inept at one kind of work, there is good chance that the chief can transfer him to a different kind of job. But the museum director is not so fortunate. If the associate curator of history performs badly, where can he transfer him? There are no other slots in this class where the subordinate will fit in.

Department boundaries are also barriers to transfers. For some agency heads, interdepartmental transfers are simply out of the question because a class is unique to a unit. A hoseman works for the fire department and cannot be moved out because no other city department has such a class. Beyond this, shifting personnel to another agency is difficult because it requires a consensus. The finance director can unilaterally transfer a secretary from one position to another in his department so long as it is in the same class. In order to ship her off to parks and recreation, however, he must persuade the head of this agency to agree to the move. Often, fear of harming relations with his colleagues will inhibit the agency head. In the words of one division chief, palming off mediocre personnel on other departments would "stir friction." On the rare occasion when an official does try to move an employee to another agency, it consumes time. For example, the mayor spent eighteen months trying to transfer a secretary with undesirable racial attitudes to the park and recreation department.

Demotions, like transfers, are difficult to arrange. Under civil-service rules, promoted employees can be demoted (not fired) without appeal during the first six months of their appointment. Consequently, top bureaucrats know that it is wise to come to a quick conclusion on the performance of a promoted employee. In August 1969, for example, the head of the parks division moved rapidly when he noted that a recently advanced tree trimmer was having problems with heights. Subsequently, he demoted the man back to a gardener position. Like transfers, demotions are easier for the official if classes are large. If there are only five slots in the class immediately below the subordinate, they may all be filled. If turnover occurred at the average rate of 10 percent, he would have the option of demoting the employee once every two years.[15]

Transfers and demotions are means by which an agency head can reduce or avoid open conflict with a subordinate. Even more satisfactory from a department head's perspective is employee reform or resignation. To increase prospects that one of these events will transpire, top bureaucrats use a tactic which will also yield benefits if they have to fire the employee.

Gather evidence and threaten. Faced with poor performance, high officials accumulate evidence while simultaneously threatening the employee. An inept bureaucrat whets their appetite for paper work. Supervisors conscientiously note misbehavior on performance evaluations, writing as many as one per week, if they can find reason to do so. While fattening the subordinate's personnel file, they notify him of their dissatisfaction and at least tacitly threaten him with removal. Often they gear threats to increments.[16] They move from admonitions to increasingly severe penalties. The practices of fire officials are

[15] A final organizational alternative to firing a bureaucrat is the "kick upstairs" whereby executives remove a man by giving him a face-saving sinecure. But in organizations like Oakland City Hall, where officials believe there is acute fiscal scarcity, such practices are absent. The manager will not fund a new high-level position unless there is a clear need for more help.

[16] See Thomas C. Schelling, *The Strategy of Conflict* (New York: Oxford University Press, 1963), p. 41.

illustrative. They believe in letting things "simmer," slowly escalating the penalty for misbehavior. Consequently, the first time a firefighter is late for an 8:00 A.M. shift, a supervisor warns him; the second time he receives something like a nine-day suspension; the third time within a year would probably cause discharge or prolonged suspension.

Officials wish to avoid any impression that they are building a case against an employee for reasons other than purely professional ones. As a result, some top bureaucrats prefer to have a minority supervisor deal with disciplinary problems posed by black or Chicano employees. The head of the municipal buildings divison, for example, felt that black janitors in his unit were particularly sensitive to criticism, often taking it personally. He believed that using black supervisors to deal with these employees made it apparent that racism was not involved in a disciplinary decision.

Once department heads have warned the employee, they hope that he will reform or resign of his own volition. When improved performance fails to materialize, a resignation is generally preferable to a discharge if for no other reason than that it is less time consuming and minimizes prospects of Civil Service Commission intervention. Employees who believe that agency heads have the removal deck stacked against them often seize this option. In this way, they get out without a bad mark on their employment record. An inspector in the housing division, for example, increasingly believed that he had to defend the nation against a communist conspiracy. As his interest shifted to this cause, the inspector's work deteriorated and soon the housing division director called him in for a conference. Since the man had four children, the director wanted to warn him explicitly that his future employment hinged on improved performance. But the man could not adjust. After several warnings, the employee decided resignation was preferable to discharge, and took to the circuit espousing his political viewpoint.

Fire as a last resort. Sometimes, data gathering and threats produce neither reform nor resignation. At such moments, an agency head often attempts the problem solution he has tried to avoid—dismissal. When this happens, his patient accumulation of data may pay off. A case from the Office of Public Works is illustrative.

In October 1969, a semi-skilled laborer in the street and engineering division was with a paving crew and was having difficulties changing a cutting tool on a pavement breaker. Exasperated with the obstinate equipment, the laborer began hitting the tool. Though other members of his work group urged him to stop, he persisted until the metal shattered and a fragment of it struck another man in the face. The supervisor consequently reprimanded the petulant laborer and noted the incident on a performance evaluation.

Less than a year later, in August 1970, the supervisor had his second run-in with the worker. Spot checking a street crew he noted that the man was absent. Glancing about he saw the employee sitting in a truck, whereupon the supervisor approached and inquired what the employee was doing. The laborer replied that he was figuring the footage which the crew required, a statement which the supervisor immediately checked and found to be untrue. Walking back to the cab of the truck, the supervisor discovered the sports page of the *San Francisco Chronicle* and a copy of the underground newspaper, the *Berkeley Barb,* beneath the front seat. When the supervisor then confronted the worker with this "evidence," the man became angry and accused the foreman of "picking on him." The supervisor asked the man to return to the corporation yard to discuss the incident with a higher official. The worker refused and the supervisor suspended him on the spot. Further problems arose. When the supervisor later gave the semi-skilled laborer the formal letter of suspension, the latter told him to "shove it," complaining that he had a family to support and needed to keep on working.

By this time supervisors were paying careful attention to any signs of misperformance on the part of the laborer. Soon other irritations emerged. Though required to keep his driver's license up-to-date, the laborer let it lapse. Finally, in 1970, an irate citizen caught the worker stealing the windshield wipers from a "junk" car sitting in the former's yard. When the resident complained, streets and engineering officials felt confident that they had accumulated enough evidence to discharge him. Though the employee appealed the firing to the Civil Service Commission, the latter sustained management's decision. Thus, the ultimate return on patient, careful documentation can be a successful discharge.

SUBORDINATE RESISTANCE TACTICS

Department heads do not always succeed, however. At times, lower echelon employees utilize due process rules and expand the scope of conflict to thwart removal.[17]

Expand the scope of conflict through commission appeals. While employees may fight early threats, the most obvious conflict emerges when subordinates seek Civil Service Commission help after the manager has formally fired them. In city hall the number of dismissals ranges from 15 to 30 per year—less than 1 percent of the full-time work force. Roughly two-thirds of those fired are on probation and, therefore, have no right to appeal to the commission. Chances are about one in three that a nonprobationary employee will seek commission aid if he receives his walking papers.

Different types of employees vary in their tendencies to appeal. An employee is more likely to do so if he belongs to an occupational group which feels under outside attack, works in relative isolation, believes that rules inhibit his ability to perform effectively, or is a member of a union or association which encourages resistance.

These factors are more manifest in the police department than in any other agency.[18] Not surprisingly, police officers make a disproportionate number of appeals. Though less than one-third of city hall's man-years are in this department, two-thirds of the discharge hearings involve personnel from this agency.[19] Policemen perceive that they periodically come under

[17] By expanding the scope of conflict I mean increasing the number of actors who are involved.

[18] John H. McNamara, "Uncertainties in Police Work: The Relevance of Police Recruits' Backgrounds and Training," *The Police: Six Sociological Essays,* ed., David J. Bordua (New York: John Wiley, 1967), p. 81, among others, finds considerable police suspicion of disciplinary procedures. See also Wilson, *Varieties of Police Behavior,* pp. 186-187.

[19] For a better understanding of the propensity to appeal, one should know the number of appeals compared to the total number of agency discharges. These data were unavailable to me.

unjust attack from certain community groups and that discharges are at times perverse efforts to appease these outsiders. Officers also believe that laws aimed at protecting the civil rights of people accused of crimes inhibit policemen from doing a good job.[20] This engenders a conviction that some rule breaking is necessary in the line of duty and often does not warrant severe punishment. The fact that officers frequently work alone or with one other policeman also heightens suspicion of a firing. Under such circumstances large numbers of eye witnesses are unavailable and the guilt of the accused officer easy to doubt.

The willingness of the police officers' association to support an appeal also encourages resistance. When fired, an officer can ask the three-man grievance committee of the Oakland Police Officers Association for legal assistance in presenting his case to the Civil Service Commission. Most of the time the committee agrees to back the officer. The president of the association justifies this practice on grounds that the policeman has a right to be heard; the president believes that without a lawyer it is difficult to get fair treatment from the Civil Service Commission since the prosecution frequently "lies." Consequently, only in instances when the action of an officer is blatantly illegal (for example, a drunken patrolman going on a shooting rampage) or where the police association committee members believe the officer is lying to them will they deny him support.

The civilian sector furnishes further evidence of the significance of employee group support. United Public Employees Union #1 handled about one-fourth of the appeals from 1967 to 1970 and more than one-half in the last year of that period. The leadership of this group has sought to present itself as a militant defender of employee interests. By building this reputation they hope to compete with the larger Oakland Municipal Civil Service Employees Association. For union officials, disciplinary appeals are difficult to lose. If the Civil Service Commission rules in their favor, union officials point to it as a reason why workers should join their group. If the commission denies the appeal, union leaders claim it is yet

---

[20] See Skolnick, *Justice Without Trial*.

another indication of "management's insensitivity to employee interests." (In this regard, the union's executive director noted that for organizing purposes, it is better to have city government "staffed by bad guys than good guys.") Other group leaders do not share these sentiments and do less to encourage appeals.

Appeals hearings before the Civil Service Commission often last for two meetings and resemble courtroom proceedings. The department, whom the deputy city attorney represents, calls for witnesses and prosecutes. The spokesman for the accused is usually a lawyer, employee leader, or friend.

Commissioners, of course, view these hearings through different lenses than department heads. Unlike top bureaucrats, they have had no long irritating association with the employee and will have none if he returns to work. Commissioners worry less about department productivity, than whether the subordinate has received due process and an appropriate penalty. Thus, the commission is likely to alter a department decision if it believes that the employee has not received proper preliminary notice of his faults,[21] the department has presented little documented evidence against the accused, or mitigating circumstances exist (for example, the subordinate went to school on the side or blundered in an honest effort to perform his duties).[22] With these considerations in mind, the commission reinstated about two-fifths of the nineteen discharged employees who appealed during the period from 1967 to 1970.

Some expand the scope of conflict to the courts or public. The judgment of the Civil Service Commission is not invariably final. If the employee or city attorney feels strongly about an adverse decision and perceives that it has more general legal implications, he may take the case to the state court system. For instance, in late November 1968, the commission reinstated a patrolman who claimed that police investigators had forced him to resign. The city attorney, however, convinced the Alameda County Superior Court to overturn the commission's

[21] In October 1969, for example, the Civil Service Commission ruled that the head of the streets and engineering division could not demote a semi-skilled laborer to custodian because the employee had not received an adequate number of performance evaluations.

[22] Morris Stone, "Why Arbitrators Reinstate Discharged Employees," *Monthly Labor Review* 92 (October 1969): 47-50, lists factors which guide other arbitrators in assessing discharge appeals.

decision. But the patrolman, in turn, appealed this reversal
to a higher court. Finally, in September 1970, almost two years
after his removal, the State Court of Appeals reversed the lower
judge, deciding that police officials had coerced the officer into
quitting. The Court noted that the patrolman had gone without
sleep for twenty-four hours and was emotionally upset at the
time of the incident.

Public outcry may also enable an employee to win back his
position without seeking help from the Civil Service Commission. Generally, public intervention is more likely to occur if
an employee has developed a close, friendly relationship with
an outside clientele.

Recreation center personnel get to know children and their
parents on a personal basis and provide a service which almost
everyone feels is useful. At times this client relationship comes
in handy. In early 1971, for example, the parks and recreation
director learned that a part-time employee at the Montclair
recreation center (located in a prosperous neighborhood deep
in the Oakland hills) had an arrest record. The worker, while
in the Navy, had begun to take drugs, at first marijuana, then
"speed" and LSD. On two separate occasions, once in San Diego
and another time in the Bay Area, he had, while on LSD trips,
doffed his clothes and subsequently been incarcerated for
indecent exposure.

When the director learned of his subordinate's record, he
asked the employee to resign; if the latter failed to do so by
March 31, the department head vowed to fire him. In the agency
head's mind the employee's past record had made his future
performance too unpredictable. Keeping the subordinate on
would unnecessarily risk the status of the parks and recreation
department.

Upset with this, but as a part-time employee having no rights
of appeal, the worker took his case to the local *Montclarion*,
a community newspaper On April 4, 1971, the paper featured
a story on the employee's plight which ran to four columns
and sympathetically portrayed how the worker had performed
his duties. At one point the column read: "Like a good shepherd
he had tried to bring the stray sheep into the fold. That's a
tough assignment given the alienation of youth toward organi-

zational institutions. But he's managed well." The article increased public interest in the firing. Supporters of the dismissed recreation worker met with the parks and recreation director. Others wrote him letters. Wishing to appear responsive, the director promised further investigation into the dismissal. Two months later, with the *Montclarion* featuring an approving article, the department head reinstated the employee.

The politics of involuntary removal boils down, then, to a fundamental conflict between department head and subordinate. For the employee, an extremely important option is expanding the scope of conflict to include more actors in the decision arena. Schattschneider has observed about politics that "If a fight starts watch the crowd, because the crowd plays the decisive role."[23] Since there is no natural audience to view and step into a skirmish between an employee and his boss, the former must work to develop one. Once fired, only the employee benefits from whetting the interest of others in his case.

IT'S HARD TO KEEP A GOOD MAN

If high officials often have trouble removing an employee, they have even fewer resources to keep him once he indicates that he wants to resign. The proportion who leave city hall varies. Economic prosperity causes the rate to rise as alternative employment becomes more plentiful.[24] At times mandatory retirement may cause a higher outflow than usual.[25] By and large, however, those departing range from between 5 and 15 percent of the work force, with considerable variation among classes.

[23] E. E. Schattschneider, *The Semi-Sovereign People* (New York: Holt, Rinehart and Winston, 1964), p. 3.
[24] In July 1971, when the national recession was in progress and the labor market slack, the assistant personnel director noted that the office had given half the tests it usually gave.
[25] Mandatory retirement comes late in Oakland. Uniformed police and firemen must retire at 65 and everyone else at 70. Note, however, that firefighters and policemen can retire at half pay either (a) after 25 years of service, or (b) after 20 years on the job at age 55.

Turnover is greater for those employees who are likely to have satisfactory alternative means of support or who do boring, unpleasant work for the city. Young "professionals," for example, often find better options elsewhere and leave. Hence in 1968 assistant planners had a turnover rate of 55 percent; junior administrative analysts, 200 percent; junior accountant auditors, 19 percent; and recreation directors, 22 percent. These types of personnel have not attained the benefits which come with seniority and can often find lucrative job alternatives. Other factors also lure employees from city hall's ranks. The fact that many secretarial classes have more than a 25 percent turnover rate in part stems from the tendency of women to fill those roles and leave when they get married or wish to devote time to a family. Tedium may also produce resignations. Roughly 20 percent of the police communication dispatchers, for example, left during fiscal 1968 and 1969, respectively. Police supervisors attribute this to the monotony of the job, which consists of answering the phone and routinely dispatching patrolmen to trouble spots.

Whatever the reasons for turnover, the department heads feel they can do little to curtail it. Desirable promotions or transfers are not easy to arrange on the spur of the moment. In fact, the main, albeit remote, hope for the official is to persuade the outstanding employee to stay by giving him a special pay increase. Chart 10 suggests the calculations implicit in getting an employee more money. The diagram indicates that many factors inhibit the agency from seeking a pay boost for a subordinate. One is that the employee may not be good enough to fight for. Another is that the departing employee usually has a markedly better job elsewhere. In mid-1971, for example, an administrative analyst in the office of finance informed his superiors that he had an option to become executive director of OCCUR, a local citizens group which advises city hall on such matters as housing and employment. At $15,000 per year, the post carried a salary at least $2,000 higher than that which the analyst presently received. Furthermore, the analyst felt that the new job would be far more interesting and relevant than his present one, which involved reviewing the police department budget yearly and undertaking such

CHART 10: REACTION TO A RESIGNATION

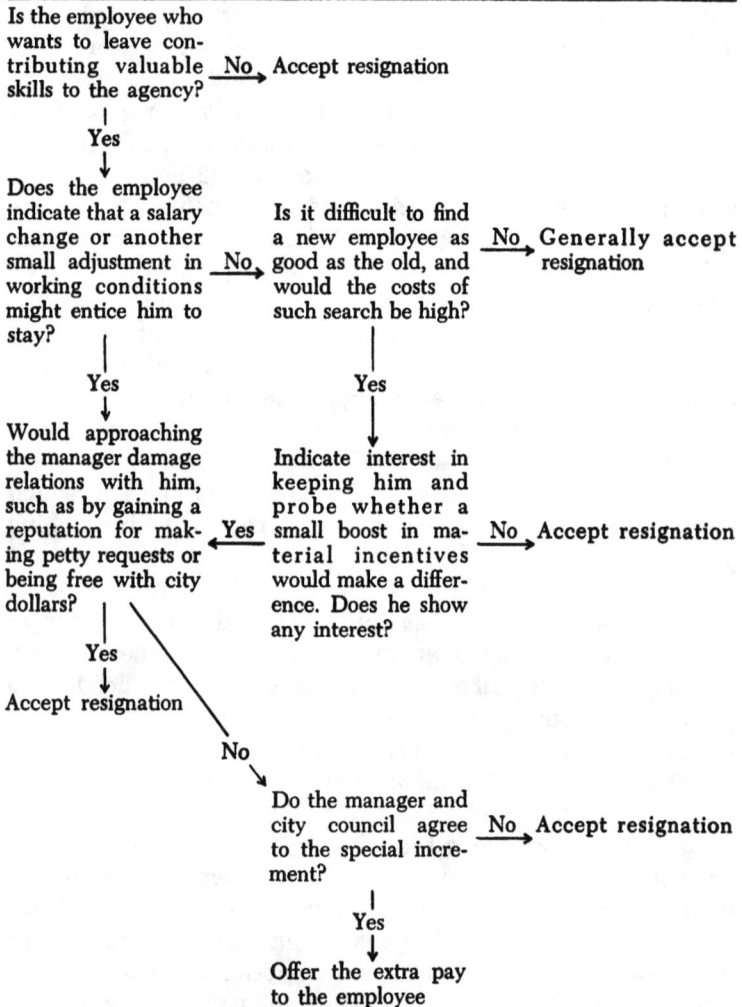

Is the employee who wants to leave contributing valuable skills to the agency? ___No→ Accept resignation

|
Yes
↓

Does the employee indicate that a salary change or another small adjustment in working conditions might entice him to stay? ___No→ Is it difficult to find a new employee as good as the old, and would the costs of such search be high? ___No→ Generally accept resignation

| |
Yes   Yes
↓   ↓

Would approaching the manager damage relations with him, such as by gaining a reputation for making petty requests or being free with city dollars? ←_Yes_ Indicate interest in keeping him and probe whether a small boost in material incentives would make a difference. Does he show any interest? ___No→ Accept resignation

|
Yes
↓
Accept resignation

No↘

Do the manager and city council agree to the special increment? ___No→ Accept resignation

|
Yes
↓
Offer the extra pay to the employee

---

assignments as deciding whether a new state law permitted the city animal pound to sell cats without first spaying or neutering them.

In cases like these, the agency head has virtually no chance of convincing a subordinate to change his mind. Even if the department head could, he might not want to. Special pay increases must receive council approval and require the agency head to win the support of the manager. This is time consuming and risks annoying those who hold authority. For these and other reasons, top bureaucrats almost never make an effort to keep a quality employee. Like the head of the streets and engineering division, high officials feel there is little they can do to keep good a man.

CONCLUSION

Like recruitment, the removal arena features a widely dispersed leverage pattern—one that involves personnel in all agencies at all hierarchical levels. In terms of the supervisor-subordinate relationship, the lowly are often mighty. When a subordinate wants to leave no one can stop him; when he wants to stay, department heads have a hard time getting rid of him.

As in the recruitment sphere, the dispersed leverage pattern and the lack of a skill scorecard create decision uncertainties. With so many involved, who can be sure of the decision criteria and standards generally in use? Without a quality scorecard who can be positive about the level of skills deficit prevalent in the organization? Assessing one's tactics and determining whether better alternatives exist is complex. It is primarily after supervisors have located and defined a certain employee's behavior as a problem that they gain confidence about the most appropriate course of action. Then too, high-level bureaucrats nurture a fatalistic certainty about their options when dealing with an outstanding subordinate who wants to quit.

8

Politics, Policy, and City Jobs

> ... he who neglects what is being done for what
> should be done will learn his destruction rather than
> his preservation.
>
> Machiavelli [1]

From Oakland to Boston city officials must cope with manpower, pay, recruitment, and removal issues. Undoubtedly the
politics of jobs varies from one city to the next.[2] Yet Oakland's
experience points to some basic properties of personnel processes. In this chapter we will explore some of these properties
and consider circumstances which would produce behavior
different from that found in Oakland. We will also return to
a fundamental thesis of this volume: that the prescriptive
literature must openly acknowledge the politics of the personnel process if it is to generate a more perceptive analysis of
options for policy makers.

LEVERAGE, SCORECARDS, AND CHOICE

Decision makers live in a world where good information is
often conspicuous by its absence. In many instances officials
cannot specify the precise consequences of using one tactic

[1] Niccolò Machiavelli, *The Prince*, ed. Mark Musa (New York: St. Martin's Press,
1964), p. 127.
[2] I operationalize larger cities as those with 200,000 population or more.

rather than another; doubts persist whether they fully understand the array of options available to them, and whether they have discovered the most satisfactory means for achieving their objectives.

All personnel arenas pose some uncertainties for top officials. Some, however, present greater obstacles than others. In general, policy arenas with more dispersed leverage patterns and fewer meaningful scorecards present the greatest amount of uncertainty for the decision maker.

LEVERAGE

Different personnel arenas have characteristic leverage patterns. Where a dispersed pattern exists, a high official has more variables to assess and anticipate; he is less likely to grasp the values and tactics of all decision makers and less likely to understand the dynamics of the process. Selecting the best means to an end becomes more difficult.

Concentration: manpower and pay. A relative concentration of control generally exists in manpower and pay arenas. Mayor and city managers are particularly likely to wield substantial leverage over manpower processes. By comparison they exert less clout over pay decisions. Several factors account for the leverage differences between the two arenas.

Control in part depends on who cares. Department heads believe that they have a substantial stake in manpower choices but few others do. Interest groups at the local level seldom lobby persistently for more service and hence for more manpower. Furthermore, employee leaders are often indifferent to the budgeting of positions and to reorganizations, so long as such processes do not directly undermine their resources. It is primarily when manpower proposals raise the spectre of layoffs or threaten the authority of those who protect employee groups (for example, a civil service commission) that employee representatives start to care. By contrast, employee leaders nurture a much more intense and persistent interest in matters pertaining to compensation.

Opposition from employee unions and associations is particularly crucial for the city's chief executive since the scope and legitimacy of his authority over them is severely limited. While a chief executive can at times order department heads to submit budget requests exclusively to him, he does not have the authority to tell employee leaders to do the same. Moreover when the manager or mayor rejects departmental budget requests and hints that agency heads are not to endorse employee demands for higher salaries, department officials may be peeved, but they usually acknowledge his right to rule. Employee leaders are far more likely to deny the legitimacy of the chief executive's authority. When management announces that subordinates have no legal right to strike or to disrupt work, the labor unions are going to dispute it. In the absence of legitimate hierarchical authority there are apt to be open conflicts over pay. The chief executive is less likely to emerge as an omniscient expert when he deals with such issues.

Then too, when rank-and-file employees refuse to cooperate with the chief executive, the consequences are usually far more ominous for him than when department officials refuse to obey. An agency head might rebel but if he does so, the city manager or mayor can often fire him without a great impact on the organization. Some publicity may result, but city hall will continue to function and the chief executive will eventually find a replacement. If on the other hand, employee spokesmen successfully lead a strike, they may drastically curtail government's ability to provide important services. Such a service withdrawal is particularly serious in areas involving public health and safety. (In part because workers in these areas are so important, their employee leaders, if at all assertive, will often be major catalysts for basic structural changes in procedures for setting salaries.) When employees do walk out, a chief executive typically does not have many attractive options. A tough-minded policy of dismissal is hard to pursue. If the chief executive fires strikers he will still be without workers. New recruits may be hard to find and expensive to train. With his subordinates off the job, the chief executive becomes a controversial figure and risks loss of prestige. Appealing to the authority of the courts is futile since most of the time unions and associations ignore injunctions. Union action, then, can fling open Pandora's box.

Leverage patterns within pay and manpower arenas vary

somewhat among cities. Unreformed political systems (that is, those with a full-time mayor, and partisan, ward elections) would, for instance, tend toward greater leverage dispersion in the manpower arena than reformed settings like Oakland's. The assertiveness of elected officials would in part account for this. Elected office holders in unreformed contexts tend to see themselves more as politicians; they are aware of opportunities to exert leverage and are more open to bargaining. Consequently they more readily view manpower choices as having implications for their electoral constituencies; in some instances they overtly consider personnel decisions as opportunities for patronage. This awareness impels councilmen toward more involvement in manpower budgeting. With elected officials more interested, department heads become more tempted to make end-runs around budget officials in an effort to appeal directly to councilmen.

So too, unreformed structures tend to have an impact on the pay arena. While no government is immune from payoffs and bribes, such activity may well occur more often in unreformed settings. Where such corruption emerges, leverage over pay becomes more dispersed. Various citizens seeking special favors from government join city officials and union leaders in allocating material rewards.

Unreformed structures might on the other hand be more likely to encourage a collective bargaining structure that centralizes leverage more exclusively with the chief executive or employee groups. In this respect much would depend on the role of unions and associations in elections. Where a mayor can mobilize a party organization at election time, he becomes less dependent on the support of employee organizations and can resist their bread-and-butter demands with greater impunity. Furthermore, where members of public unions or associations are also members of his party, he may be able to draw on party allegiance to keep these workers from embarrassing him with militant tactics. On the other hand, where parties are absent or weak, mayors would feel more pressure to yield large pay boosts either to win union election support or to avoid a strike which would be unpopular with the public. Or the mayor might attempt to give up authority to professional

negotiators rather than assume responsibility for such decisions.[3] City managers are less likely to confront these same
pressures or to have the same political advantages as mayors.

Dispersion: recruitment and removal. Recruitment and removal processes feature more dispersed leverage patterns than
manpower and pay arenas. City managers or mayors who are
hungry for power over salary and position decisions often make
little effort to mold hiring and firing practices. While the formal
authority possessed by a civil service commission accounts for
some of the chief executive's inactivity, other explanatory
factors also play a part.

Lack of time contributes to the hands-off policy of a mayor
or manager. With hours relentlessly slipping away and many
issues before them, these individuals tend to focus on questions
which seem to pose the clearest immediate risk to their priorities.

For a chief executive, this often means concentrating the
most attention on fiscal matters. While the cumulative effect
of hiring and firing on financial costs and organizational productivity can, over a period of time, be substantial, the impact
of a few such decisions, particularly at the lower echelons, seems
small. By contrast, when a city manager or mayor figures out
how many men to budget and how much to pay them, two
or three choices can have a great impact on his cost-cutting
goals. A few salary and fringe benefit concessions granted to
an employee group in one afternoon can add a million dollars
to the budget; likewise, a decision to add ten new patrolmen
to the force can drain city coffers of well over $100,000 per
year.

Another reason why the chief executive does not participate
much in recruiting or removing personnel is that he knows
both these arenas have other watchdogs. When matters of
economy are at stake, who will guard the purse if he fails to
do so? Department heads and employee representatives articulate goals that would increase expenses—more service and better
pay. Consequently, if the mayor or city manager fails to defend

[3] For an example of the use of this strategy see Raymond D. Horton, *Municipal
Labor Relations in New York City: Lessons of the Lindsay-Wagner Years.* (New York:
Praeger Publishers, 1973).

the city's cash-drawer, someone else must pick up the cudgel or tax rates will soar. On the other hand, the chief executive is often much less at odds with the other personnel aspirations of his department heads. Like them, he wants to attract good employees and rid the city of inept ones at minimal cost. When differences of viewpoint are slight, the chief executive lets his department heads do the work.

Even if the mayor or manager wanted to control these other decisions he would run up against his own inexpertise. It is one thing to tackle position and pay issues where he can easily translate outcomes into dollar costs. It is another to assess the potential contribution of a computer programmer or an engineering applicant, or to estimate whether a job hunter will (or should) get along with existing work groups. Nor is a top official likely to know much more than his underlings about which subordinates are inept.

When there is little central direction, a wide array of actors move to center stage. In this regard, hiring processes usually elicit more specific and intentional efforts by outsiders to acquire control than do other personnel arenas. Job applicants, for instance, constantly manipulate information in an effort to create a favorable impression with recruiters. Then, too, minority groups often become particularly active in the hiring arena.

Why is recruitment, as opposed to other personnel arenas, particularly likely to attract the attention of minority groups? One does not have to look far for the reasons: this is the arena where their efforts bear the most fruit. Consider first the relatively barren arenas. The impact of city salary and fringe benefit levels on minority interests is often obscure.[4] When firemen win substantial pay raises, the consequences for the minority community are extremely difficult to assess. Nor do minority leaders see much reason to become involved in manpower choices. Sensing that the city has less money and controls fewer social services than other government levels, minority spokesmen seldom press for more benefits through an expanded bureaucracy. What intrigues them is controlling the one that

---

[4] There are some exceptions to this. Civil rights groups have at times used union issues in the city as a rallying point for protest.

exists. This perspective need not push minority leaders towards recruitment activism. They could instead focus on removal processes and urge the creation of police review boards or similar bodies. The sixties, however, saw the notion of a review board and other comparable proposals meet defeat in a number of cities. Given the intense opposition of employee unions to such plans and the desire of local officials to deal with their own dirty linen, this rejection is easy to understand.

Challenges in the recruitment arena are by comparison much less likely to provoke intense opposition. To be sure, since hiring decisions affect the flow of power resources into the bureaucracy, officials seek to sustain their prerogatives. Unless cooptation seems feasible, bureaucrats in the recruitment sphere will generally reject proposals for citizen participation. Opposition will be especially strong where officials adhere to a localized version of the domino theory. Yet the same city officials who shy away from citizen participation often remain open to hiring more minorities. They believe that greater numbers of minority employees will pose no serious threat to their control; that such employees will behave much like white ones. Minority advocates on the other hand sense that black officials will do more to represent minority interests. The fact that little hard evidence exists concerning which side is correct permits both to persist in their views. This makes it easier for minority advocates to acquire leverage over hiring than over other personnel decisions.

Not all cities would feature the degree of leverage dispersion found in Oakland. In unreformed settings, for instance, the mayor would be more likely to counteract some of the dispersion, particularly if he wanted the party faithful to win and retain jobs. By one account, Mayor Daley pores over the qualifications of applicants for low-level positions.[5] Moreover, even if a highly partisan mayor did not spend time reviewing applicants he would still gain some leverage simply by insisting that lower echelon officials consider party labels in hiring and removal judgments. Chief executives can more easily control the discretion of lower-level decision makers when the point of the game is to reward the party faithful rather than to attract

[5] Mike Royko, *Boss* (New York: Signet, 1971), pp. 22-23.

and retain the competent. Nonetheless, even in unreformed settings, officials cannot ignore the importance of competence; further, forces such as time shortages and limited executive expertise tend to push the city toward dispersed leverage.

SCORECARDS

Scorecards as well as leverage patterns affect the confidence of officials. Good indicators of productivity can do much to reduce uncertainty for top bureaucrats when they are involved in making decisions. Such indicators give an official feedback concerning the results of his behavior. They help him gauge whether he is winning or losing in efforts to accomplish his goals. Without scorecards, deciding whether better alternatives exist becomes all the more difficult.

Just as certain leverage patterns characterize different personnel arenas, so too, some arenas have better scorecards than others. From the perspective of top officials, better indicators exist in manpower and pay spheres than in recruitment and removal arenas.

In the manpower game the chief executive and top department officials use dollars, the number of slots, and the location of positions in the hierarchy as the primary counters for keeping score. These markers give officials a sense of where they stand in the game. Thus, a mayor or manager can tell whether his budget procedure helps him hold down the number of personnel. He can tell whether the formal organization is coming to look more like the one he pictures as the ideal. So too, agency heads know whether they are succeeding in their efforts to acquire more desirable positions. Often they are fatalistic about the outcomes of the manpower game. Faced with an economizing mayor or city manager who has many more power resources than they do, tactics become irrelevant. Agency heads sense that they will win no additional slots regardless of what they do.

In the pay and fringe benefits arena, once again financial indicators provide a handy counter for keeping track of the situation. The chief executive has a good idea of what different types of personnel cost him, and the price tag attached to bargaining settlements; he also is reasonably sure whether his salaries are competitive with those paid elsewhere. Employee groups look to similar indicators to get their bearings. Both sets of players can tell where they stand in the game and how much progress they are making. Players do of course experience some uncertainty when making decisions. Since a clear-cut conflict situation exists between opponents with comparable amounts of resources, participants are not sure which tactics are likely to be the most productive at a particular point. The manager or mayor's representatives and employee leaders jockey for advantage, and to a degree, try to confuse one another. Still further uncertainty stems from any recent changes in the decision-making structure. Officials have constantly been called upon to develop new procedures for dealing with employees, without being sure how such changes would eventually affect pay allocations. Nonetheless, data on personnel expenditures provide useful feedback as to whether various strategies have paid off.

Shifting to removal and recruitment, financial indicators no longer function as a means of getting one's bearings. Officials engaged in removal face considerable complexity in marrying choices to objectives. How can high-echelon bureaucrats tell whether they are reducing ineptitude in the removal arena as well as they might? There are no convenient numerical counters of skills deficit, or of overall skills level; officials cannot look to some ledger or budget document to learn how well they are doing. To be sure, administrators receive some reports about employee performance from the public and the lower echelons. But they cannot be sure that the information they are receiving is very accurate or provides a good general picture; nor does it help them to define precisely what skilled performance is.

Only when confronted with a specific employee problem (for example, blatant incompetence, the resignation of a star bureaucrat) do top administrators develop a firm sense of what winning or losing amounts to (in the particular case) and how they can best pursue their objectives.

A similar situation exists with respect to recruitment. Without good measures of skill, officials are seldom sure that they are living up to the formal goal of recruiting the most competent workers available. Of course, there are some clues which permit them to gauge how well they are doing. If large numbers apply for positions, staff members feel satisfied with their publicity techniques; if the percentage of minority bureaucrats increases, city officials know that they are making progress on the affirmative action front; if department heads complain about the low quality of recruits, personnel officials sense that their hiring techniques produce bad results. Yet these indicators of the game score only partially satisfy decision makers. How can personnel officials be sure that they are consistently directing announcements of job openings toward those potential applicants with the most talent? How do personnel staff members know whether they might not be consistently screening out applicants who are more competent than those who get the jobs?

Goals and scorecards. The adequacy of scorecards in a personnel arena is, of course, in part a function of the goals of the officials.[6] In cities, for instance, where winning in the manpower arena is defined less in terms of holding down costs and more in terms of promoting efficiency, uncertainty regarding decision making would increase. The benefit side of the efficiency ratio is, after all, more difficult to compute than the cost portion. Who knows the precise impact of manpower choices on how much service, or benefit, a department will yield? Good scorecards of productivity seldom exist in the government sector.

While there is undoubtedly a difference in goals among officials, many basic objectives are uniform from one city to the next. Convinced of revenue scarcity and wishing to keep tax rates down, most chief executives define the point of the manpower game as holding the line on costs;[7] they shun greater efficiency if it means spending more money. In the pay arena, officials typically worry about keeping salary levels from soaring while simultaneously keeping pay rates competitive. Fostering competence looms as an almost universal concern with respect to recruitment and removal decisions.

Each personnel arena, then, tends to feature a characteristic

---

[6] The reverse is also true. The availability of scorecards often shapes goals.

[7] New York may be a major exception. See James Q. Wilson, *Political Organizations* (New York: Basic Books, 1973), pp. 88-89.

leverage and scorecard configuration. Other things being equal, recruitment and removal create more decision uncertainties for top officials than do manpower and pay.

SIMPLIFICATION AND SEARCH[8]

Just because office holders face uncertainty in a personnel arena does not mean that it is an egregious source of anxiety for them. Administrators find ways to reduce the complexities of choice; often they rely on a set of simple rules or a standard operating procedure to help them cope with decisions. Such rules allow them to make choices in a minimal amount of time without prolonged calculation. Thus, officials rely on salary formulae, on rules to construct written tests, on rules that orient budget analysts toward manpower requests, and so on. Once they establish decision rules personnel players are reluctant to abandon them, in part because they must then confront more of the complexities inherent in a choice.

Officials will, however, consider new alternatives when a performance scorecard indicates deterioration, when relevant constituencies introduce new scorecards, when a reference group applies new standards of excellence to performance indicators, or when a major constituency begins to complain. A genuine search for new methods is particularly likely if officials believe that their critics have too many resources (or hostages) to be defeated, or that the grievances of critics are morally valid.

In considering change, officials tend to prefer low-risk alternatives—those that would inflict the least amount of pain if they should backfire. Distaste for risk leads officials to opt for small adjustments in procedures rather than large ones. A personnel director will, therefore, permit the substitution of a GED test for a high-school diploma rather than reduce the education requirement to eight years of schooling. Risk avoidance also leads officials to focus on one particular set of procedures rather than others. When confronted with a recruitment problem, for instance, personnel staffs usually modify the publicity process first because they believe that such modifications involve less risk to skills level than tinkering with selection procedures.

In coping with a special problem, or practicing administration as usual, bureaucrats are at least intuitively aware of the politics of the personnel process. They realize the importance of such factors as the interests who seek representation in personnel decisions, the distribution of power resources, and the prevailing leverage patterns.

POLICY OPTIONS

If prescriptive personnel writings are to analyze proposals for change with greater acumen they must become more sensitive to administrative politics. The consequences of paying insufficient attention to the politics of jobs become more apparent if we consider two principles which receive broad endorsement in the prescriptive literature: merit validation and equal pay for equal work. My analysis will suggest that recommendations derived from these principles are often politically infeasible;[9] that the recommendations, if adopted, would impose costs which local officials (and many other students of urban affairs) would find excessive.

THE MERIT-VALIDATION PRINCIPLE

The merit-validation principle rests at the core of much prescriptive personnel literature.[10] This principle urges policy makers to design a recruitment system which will enable them to gather and evaluate data about a number of applicants and then predict which job hunter will be the most competent.[11]

[9] A politically feasible recommendation is one likely to attract enough support from those with power resources to be adopted.

[10] For a major exception see David Rosenbloom, "Equal Employment Opportunity: Another Strategy," *Personnel Administration/Public Personnel Review* (July/August 1972): 38-41.

[11] See J. J. Donovan, "Introduction," *Recruitment and Selection in the Public Service,* ed. J. J. Donovan (Chicago: Public Personnel Association, 1968); O. Glenn Stahl, *Public Personnel Administration* (New York: Harper and Row, 1971), p. 117; A. C. Germann, *Recruitment, Selection, Promotion and Civil Service,* President's Commission on Law Enforcement and the Administration of Justice (Washington, D.C.: U.S. Government Printing Office, 1967), p. 61; Alan R. Bass, "Personnel Selection and Evaluation," *Management of the Urban Crisis: Government and the Behavioral Sciences,* ed. Stanley E. Seashore and Robert J. McNeill (New York: Free Press, 1971), p. 301.

To live up to the ideal is, then, to eliminate uncertainty concerning who will do the best job—to predict the future. But the principle argues for more than this; it also exhorts officials to demonstrate their ability to forecast skilled behavior by conducting validation studies. A recent publication of the Urban Institute suggests, for instance, that "presentation of validity evidence must be available to test users, and to the public. Under no circumstances should the general reputation of a test, its authors, or casual reports of test utility or other non-empirical or anecdotal accounts of testing practices or testing outcomes be accepted in lieu of evidence of validity."[12] Others have argued that a city should use written tests "only where their validity can be demonstrated."[13] The commitment to validation expressed in these statements may seem extreme; the fact remains, however, that much of the prescriptive literature touts validation as a high-priority activity for personnel staffs.[14]

The commitment to validation runs strong even among some who heavily emphasize the need for expanded minority hiring. For example, the U.S. Commission on Civil Disorders in its concern for minority job hunters urged that "local testing procedures be revalidated."[15] Advocates for removing cultural bias from existing selection processes often make de facto cases for validation. They suggest that once officials alter the substance and language of tests, higher percentages of minorities will pass and the selection process will be a better predictor of skill.[16] Thus, attracting more minorities and attracting the competent go hand in hand.

[12] Robert Sadacca, *The Validity and Discriminatory Impact of the Federal Service Entrance Examination* (Washington, D.C.: Urban Institute, 1971), p. 9.

[13] E. S. Savas and Sigmund Ginsburg, "The Civil Service—A Meritless System?" *The Public Interest* 32 (Summer 1973): 70-72.

[14] See Stahl, *Public Personnel Administration,* p. 120; Kenneth L. Wentworth, "Development and Use of Written Tests," in *Recruitment and Selection,* ed. J. J. Donovan, p. 115; Norman R. Sharpless, Jr., "Public Personnel Selection—An Overview," *Ibid.,* p. 20; Bass, "Personnel Selection," p. 306.

[15] *Report of the National Advisory Commission on Civil Disorders* (New York: Bantam Books, 1968), p. 417.

[16] See, for instance, David Rogers, *The Management of Big Cities: Interest Groups and Social Change Strategies* (Beverly Hills, Calif.: Sage Publications, 1971), pp. 37-38; Richard Margolis, *Who Will Wear The Badge?*, U.S. Commission on Civil Rights (Washington, D.C.: U.S. Government Printing Office, 1970), p. 32; Ollie A. Jensen, "Cultural Bias in Selection," *Public Personnel Review* 27 (April 1966): 125-130; Bennett Harrison, *Education, Training, and the Urban Ghetto* (Baltimore: Johns Hopkins

While prescriptive personnel writers often agree on the desirability of validation, they differ on the form it should take. There are two basic types of validation: strict experimental and compromised. In the name of feasibility, the personnel literature usually endorses the latter type. Prior to assessing compromised strategies, however, it is important to understand strict validation and why city officials find it unappealing. For strict validation is in essence the ideal type against which we can usefully compare compromised measures.

The complexities of strict validation. Strict experimental validation requires officials: (a) to score a statistically adequate group of job hunters on selection criteria;[17] (b) to employ all job applicants (or a representative sample) in comparable job settings over the same period of time; (c) to develop high-quality job performance measures which are uniformly applied to the behavior of all employees; and (d) to correlate selection scores with performance ratings. Obviously, if those with higher selection scores consistently perform better on the job than those with lower selection ratings, analysts infer that the hiring process is valid.

Strict validation is complex. Consider, for instance the problem of developing job performance measures. City administrators are not as fortunate as baseball managers who can use batting averages and a host of other statistics to assess the quality of their personnel. For many positions, a firm consensus concerning how to define and measure skill does not exist. With criteria and standards of competence often ambiguous, different supervisors tend to vary in the way they rate performance.[18]

Validation experts would, then, eat up much time simply trying to define and operationalize their definition of skill. Furthermore they would face the problem of ensuring that all subjects worked under comparable conditions (for example, performed the same task, had the same kind of supervision). Otherwise uncontrolled variables could contaminate the experiment and produce misleading results. Difficulties like these,

University Press, 1972), p. 194; Vernon Taylor, *Employment of the Disadvantaged in the Public Service* (Chicago: Public Personnel Association, 1971).

[17] To avoid self-fulfilling prophecy, neither applicants nor supervisors who rate performances should have access to information concerning selection scores.

[18] Bass, "Personnel Selection," p. 322-324.

plus others such as finding a statistically adequate sample, make strict validation complex and expensive. The cost alone would be sufficient to deter most city halls from attempting such researh.[19]

Strict validation is a risky investment. Although its price would tend to discourage officials, let us assume that policy makers would be willing to invest in strict validation if it were to yield valuable returns. Under these circumstances, would personnel officials be able to make a convincing case for such research?

Personnel staff members would find the route to persuasion full of obstacles. For one thing strict validation dictates that an employer hire at least a representative sample of those who apply. This typically means employing some who failed to measure up to the selection criteria. Since there is some chance that existing processes are valid, a local government risks placing inept people in various jobs for the duration of the experiment; this would tend to reduce the quality of city services, an outcome which would have particularly serious implications in police and fire departments.

Another barrier to strict validation is the danger that policy makers would get nothing for something. For it is unclear that a substantial allocation would necessarily produce highly valid selection instruments. Then, too, the possibly ephemeral quality of validation findings would increase skepticism about funding such research. Officials might quickly come to feel like Sisyphus, who kept pushing a stone up the mountain only to have it fall back of its own weight. This is because selection instruments which predicted performance at one point might not in the future. A police examination, for example, which was valid when whites were the majority in a city's population might become invalid once blacks passed the 50 percent mark.

As if these factors were not enough to discourage city officials, additional problems lurk in the wings.[20] Even if strict validation

[19] Some have been sensitive to the economic costs of such research; see for example *ibid.,* p. 316.

[20] Officials might also face the problem of differential validity; for a discussion see "Employment Testing: The Aftermath of Griggs v. Duke Power Co.," *Columbia Law Review* 72 (May 1972), p. 922, and Hugh Steven Wilson, "A Second Look at Griggs v. Duke Power Company: Ruminations on Job Testing, Discrimination and the Role of the Federal Courts," *Virginia Law Review* 58 (1972), p. 869.

helped bureaucrats hire more competent people, the question
would remain: Does the increase in skill justify the expense?
Furthermore, strict validation could reduce government legitimacy in the minority community. Since white Americans have
inflicted numerous deprivations on blacks and other racial
groups, nonwhite job hunters may well possess fewer skills on
the average than their white counterparts. If this is the case,
validation would be unlikely to help greater proportions of
minorities win jobs. A tradeoff may, in short, exist between
attracting the most competent workers and fostering racial
representation.[21] While strict validation would stave off court
intervention on behalf of minorities, this would be a Pyrrhic
victory for city officials if such research precipitated greater
alienation from government within the minority community.

The probability that strict validation will produce undesirable consequences is, then, sufficient to make city officials chary
of investing in such research. If strict validation has limited
appeal, however, what about less expensive compromised strategies which receive widespread endorsement in the literature?

The limits of compromised validation. The old cliché that
"you get what you pay for" adequately characterizes much
of the difference between strict and compromised validation.
Compromised strategies are less expensive than the stricter
version but also do less to reduce uncertainty about the predictive powers of a selection process. Chart 11 briefly describes
three typically compromised strategies: concurrent, content,
and follow-up validation. All three research schemes aim at
devising tests which more accurately predict competence; yet,
as the chart indicates, all three stop short of the experimental
procedures endemic to strict validation. The findings of such
studies are therefore less trustworthy. Moreover, while compromised validation is relatively inexpensive, its price is high
enough to make officials question whether the information
gained is worth the cost.

To be sure, compromised validation could be a useful investment for personnel officials under some circumstances. Such
research might have symbolic value. A personnel director who

---

[21] Rosenbloom, "Equal Employment Opportunity," is among those making the same
point.

Title	Basic Method	Some Flaws
Concurrent Validation	Personnel officials administer the test to present employees in a specific class of positions; if employees who have received the highest performance evaluations do best on the test, personnel staffers assume that the instrument is valid; they then administer it to applicants.	Performance evaluations may be inaccurate and produce misleading findings; even if star employees do best on the tests, this does not prove that the tests *predict* performance; if star bureaucrats do no better than mediocre ones, the tests might nonetheless have predicted differences at the time mediocre and star bureaucrats first applied; or the tests might still function to weed out the inept (i.e., those who never got jobs).
Content Validation	Personnel officials consult with experts in a field and closely analyze selection criteria and standards to ascertain that all information sought of applicants relates to the job.	Never correlates selection ratings of applicants with their eventual job performances.
Follow-Up Validation	Analysts check the eventual performance of those who passed tests and took jobs in city hall; if those who passed with high scores receive better performance evaluations than those who passed with low scores, analysts assume tests are valid.	Self-fulfilling prophecy may affect outcomes (i.e., employees with top scores may feel more confident and therefore perform better); or supervisors' evaluations may be inaccurate for some or all thereby producing misleading results; the sample analyzed does not include those who failed in the selection process and consequently never got city jobs; therefore analysts can assess the predictive power of the test only among a small group of top scorers.

has sponsored a compromised strategy could respond to community critics or to the courts by claiming that he had validated his selection process. While such a claim might stave off court intervention, however, it would usually not impress minority advocates unless blacks and other members of disadvantaged groups subsequently obtained more jobs. In this respect there is no convincing evidence that compromised validation would help nonwhite job hunters very much, particularly if written tests remain part of the selection process.[22]

The abolitionist movement. Some would challenge this pessimistic conclusion concerning compromised validation and minority hiring. They suggest that one result of validation research would be to convince personnel officials to do away with those very written tests that frequently damage minority job prospects. Many suggest that officials could instead use role-playing tests (analogous to secretarial typing examinations), particularly when a job does not require much capacity to read, write, or engage in abstract reasoning.[23]

Abolishing written tests would tend to increase the percentage of successful minority applicants. With pencil and paper examinations no longer as important, more minorities would move on to the oral interview. Given the inclination of some department officials to hire more blacks and Chicanos, minority applicants would tend to pass the oral at higher rates than they do the written.

But while abandoning the written test has some appeal from the standpoint of promoting racial representation, the proposal nonetheless poses problems for personnel directors. Pencil and paper tests are an economical way of whittling down the number of applicants. It takes much less time to reject job hunters through written examinations than most other screening devices, including role-playing tests.[24] Unless a personnel

[22] My pessimistic conclusion concerning the impact of written tests comes not only from my Oakland observations but from a number of other publications as well. See, for instance, Christopher Jencks et. al., *Inequality* (New York: Basic Books, 1972) pp. 81-82; Sadacca, *Validity and Discriminatory Impact*, p. 22; Margolis, *Who Will Wear the Badge?* p. 23; Clay L. Moore, Jr., John F. MacNaughton, Hobart G. Osburn, "Ethnic Differences Within an Industrial Selection Battery," *Personnel Psychology* 22 (Winter 1969): 481-482; Richard L. Garlatti, "Police Recruiting: Success Story in Philadelphia," *Public Personnel Review* 32 (April 1971): 104.

[23] See for instance William Scheuer, "Performance Testing in New Jersey," *Good Government* (Spring 1970): 5-15; Nesta M. Gallas, "Toward a Theory of Selection," in *Recruitment and Selection*, ed. J. J. Donovan, pp. 40-41.

[24] See David T. Stanley, *Managing Local Government Under Union Pressure* (Washington, D.C.: Brookings Institution, 1971), p. 34.

director were dealing with positions for which there were few applicants or could find a low-cost work-load reducing mechanism to replace the written test, he would usually oppose an abolitionist strategy on economic grounds alone.

Finding an economical substitute for written examinations is far from simple: from the standpoint of increasing racial representation, many cures are as bad as the disease. Consider, for instance, the obvious step of limiting the number of applictions to the first fifty or so submitted. Under such a system, those with the quickest access to job vacancy information have the best chance of being among the job hunters considered. Since friends and relatives of city employees learn rapidly about vacancies, they would be disproportionately represented among the applicants. Bureaucracies that were white would therefore tend to remain so.

Apart from economic considerations, concern with skill also diminishes the attractiveness of written test abolition. Many officials believe that examinations do, to some extent, predict competence. (While bureaucrats lack evidence that tests forecast performance they also have little data to the contrary.) Some also look favorably on the tendency of tests to shift leverage away from elected politicians, whom they see as the natural enemy of skilled professional performance.[25] Such sentiments mean that a personnel director who advocated test abolition would risk loss of status with such constituencies as department heads and employee representatives. Leaders of public safety departments, where minority hiring problems are generally the most acute and controversial, would be particularly reluctant to endorse written test abolition. Such leaders could make a plausible case that positions in their department demand those analytic abilities measured by written examinations. They could also argue that role-playing tests are most appropriate for bureaucracies which seek to recruit people who already possess specific skills (for example, typists, carpenters). Where the point of a hiring process is to find individuals with aptitude and then to teach them precise skills (as with public

[25] The interest of party officials in patronage is far from dead. See Raymond Wolfinger, "Why Political Machines Have Not Withered Away and Other Revisionist Thoughts," *Journal of Politics* 34 (May 1972): 365-398.

safety units), developing adequate role-playing tests becomes difficult.

Overall, then, excessive concern with merit validation helps produce advice which has limited appeal to those who make choices. Among other things, the principle fails to take the concept of optimal ignorance sufficiently into account. It champions uncertainty reduction without adequately stressing the need to assess whether the information gained is worth the cost. Even if the federal government removes some fiscal pressure from city officials by picking up the tab for validation (a very substantial outlay) difficulties would persist. Validation may, for instance, do little to ease minority hiring problems.

In a more fundamental sense, the emphasis on merit validation reflects the tendency of the prescriptive literature to ignore personnel politics. If prescriptive theorists devoted more attention to such factors as the power resources available to players, prevailing leverage patterns, and the various social interests seeking representation in personnel decision making, they would enhance their understanding of the process which they hope to improve. Theorists would be more able to gauge the feasibility and likely impact of proposals for change. Furthermore, if personnel specialists more openly acknowledge that a number of social interests have a right to representation in personnel decision making, these specialists would generate a wider array of insightful policy options. Thus, rather than reiterating the need to hire the most competent available, the prescriptive literature would readily accept that personnel staffs worry not only about attracting competence but holding down costs, recruiting members of disadvantaged groups, and generally preserving agency status.[26] Taking multiple values into account, prescriptive theorists would be more careful to analyze interrelationships and possible tradeoffs among objectives. They would become more suspicious of proposals which narrowly focused on maximizing one goal. Instead they would gravitate toward policy options that would improve performance on one or several dimensions while fostering the satisfac-

---

[26] One can hardly expect actors to ignore the implications of action for their reputations. Moreover, concern with status may motivate officials toward greater competence and responsiveness.

tory attainment of other objectives. Or minimally prescriptive theorists would be aware when proposals they favor contain grave risks for certain values.

Once prescriptive writers more fully probe and accept the politics of the recruitment process they will acquire a new perspective on policy alternatives. Consider, for instance, one recommendation generally ignored by proponents of merit validation which would be useful to many personnel directors: test scoring modification.

Modify test scoring. Many have commented on test scoring from the perspective of enhancing validity. The ideal is to pick a cutting point, or a pass-fail mark, which differentiates those who can do competent work from those who cannot. In fact, few urban personnel officials take this ideal seriously. Instead they set a cutting point in order to diminish the recruitment work load and reduce substantially the risk that they will hire someone who is inept (even if it means screening out many who are capable of doing the job). Consequently, personnel agencies typically set high pass marks (for example, answering 70 percent of the multiple choice questions correctly). In addition to establishing high cutting points, personnel agencies generally rank applicants who pass with top scores higher than those who pass with low scores.

Without abandoning a concern with skill or economy a personnel director could modify these scoring rules and foster more racial representation. He could do this by: (a) lowering the number of correct answers needed to pass the test; and (b) grading written tests on a pass-fail basis.[27] The first step would permit more applicants, including minorities, to take the oral examination. In cities where some officials give blacks and Chicanos the benefit of a doubt in an oral, this step would increase the number of minority applicants who eventually win placement on the eligible list. Grading written tests on a pass-fail basis would also help minorities; no longer would a minimal passing score on the written test relegate the individual to a low position on the eligible list. The oral exam, where

[27] At the federal level Rosenbloom, "Equal Employment Opportunity," has suggested a similar step.

minorities have a better chance of doing well, would receive more weight in the final ranking of applicants.

While fostering racial representation, this modification would not seriously risk other pertinent values. Even if a personnel agency's tests are valid, the reform would not significantly increase the risk of decline in skills because it would not abolish examinations completely. Pencil and paper tests would still weed out many. Modifying scoring standards would be some- what uneconomical; more applicants would take the time-con- suming oral test. But the increase in job hunters admitted to the interview need not be so great as to make the costs of the change absolutely prohibitive. In part for these reasons department heads are unlikely to fight the reform. Nor would unions or employee associations have much incentive to resist. (To reduce further the probability of conflict and status loss with employee group leaders, personnel officials could exempt promotional tests from the proposed change.) Thus, test scoring alterations need not pose unacceptable disadvantages for per- sonnel staffs.

Greater insight into the politics of personnel will, then, help prescriptive theorists gain new perspective. To illustrate this point more graphically, I will examine still another principle deeply rooted in the personnel literature: equal pay for equal work. While the validity and equity principles are substantively different, their utility to officials is similar.

EQUAL PAY FOR EQUAL WORK

A number of principles pertaining to pay emerge from the prescriptive literature. One of the most fundamental ones is that there should be equal pay for equal work. This principle suggests first that employees doing the same work should receive roughly the same amount of money. Hence, a secretary stenographer in one office should receive roughly the same remuneration as a secretary stenographer in another. Second, the principle asserts that inequity of payment needs to be structured properly. Marxist notions of equal rewards for dif- fering amounts of work have no place in most prescriptive personnel writings. Instead, the literature assumes that employees doing more complex, "responsible" work deserve more remuneration. Thus, college educated accountants should receive more than janitors. High-ranking bureaucrats should garner more than those in the lower echelons. As one observer notes:

> Supervisors and department heads should usually earn substantially more than subordinates; professional specialists, in view of their extensive education and specialized experience, should be paid at levels well above those of their less qualified associates; employees should have a real monetary incentive to seek advancement.[28]

In short, appropriately structured inequity is important. Often, analysts emphasize setting up and maintaining "proper" pay relationships among classes. These analysts assume that after careful study of different kinds of work, they can recommend appropriate pay ratios. Experts might, for instance, conclude that junior accountants should earn $3 for every $2 a janitor makes.

Once analysts have arrived at the ideal pay relationship among classes, they tend to worry about factors which upset the ordained ratios.[29] For instance, some prescriptive theorists are uneasy about how competition among organizations for personnel can undermine "proper" pay relationships.[30] Though personnel specialists might feel that job complexity entitles accountants and administrative analysts to equal pay, for instance, the going labor market rate for accountants may be rising much more rapidly than that for analysts. But paying competitive salaries to the accountants would undermine the equity principle. Thus, many prescriptive writers must acknowledge an uncomfortable conflict between values. As one observer notes, competing with other employers often "does violence to the equal pay for equal work principle."[31]

[28] David T. Stanley, *Managing Local Government*, pp. 72-73.

[29] Such theorizing is implicit in Keith Ocheltree, "Keeping the Pay Plan Current," in *Practical Guidelines to Public Pay Administration*, vol. II, ed. Kenneth O. Warner and J. J. Donovan (Chicago: Public Personnel Association, 1965), pp. 100-110.

[30] In fact, federal pay history reflects an effort to assure this competitiveness. See, for example, John W. Macy, Jr., *Public Service, The Human Side of Government* (New York: Harper and Row, 1972), pp. 195-214; see also, Donald Wagner, "Compensation Seen Through Management Eyes," in *Practical Guidelines*, ed. Warner and Donovan, p. 21.

[31] Stahl, *Public Personnel Administration*, p. 91.

Public employee organizations are another irritant to those concerned with the equity principle. Unions and associations can easily upset "proper" ratios. If certain employees have a stronger union representing them than others, the former may win a larger percentage salary increase. Prescriptive writings often define this as a problem. One analyst, for instance, writes that the equity principle "is as important to both management and employees under collective bargaining as under traditional classification and pay-setting methods, but potentially more difficult to attain." He goes on to say that "problems of equity become acute when occupations of strong and intimate concern to the public and to politicians are involved: policemen, firemen, garbage collectors, nurses."[32] Thus, concern with the equity principle continued to pervade thinking about pay setting in an era of more militant employee activity.

Many prescriptive writings have not been content simply to espouse the equity principle. Such literature has also derived a number of more specific prescriptions from "equal pay for equal work." Among these prescriptions, two are particularly central: keep the classification structure accurate; give standard percentage wage increases.

Do accurate classification. Prescriptive theorists point out that achieving the equity principle requires commitment to an accurate classification plan. After all, properly putting positions in the same class is tantamount to saying that the roles are similar in the demands they make on workers and, therefore, that employees in these roles deserve equal pay.[33]

Personnel writings have laid down certain caveats in support of precise classification. Personnel offices are supposed to specify what the duties, responsibilities, and complexities of a position are; they are to review the role in relationship to other slots in the organization. With respect to this second point, one student of personnel advises:

> It is not enough to study the work of various positions in isolation. No adequate picture of authority and responsibility can be secured without an analysis of the work of the particular organization units

[32] Stanley, *Managing Local Government,* pp. 67-68.
[33] See Merrill J. Collett, "Building the Framework of the Pay Plan," in *Practical Guidelines,* ed. Warner and Donovan, p. 32.

in which the positions under review are located, or without comprehension of the relationship of the individual position to other positions and to the whole hierarchy of authority.[34]

The personnel analyst in charge of classification, then, must have an exhaustive understanding of the organization if he is to do a good job.

Prescriptive theorists also emphasize that classification is a full-time activity. This arises from the fact that the formal classification structure tends to describe inaccurately what employees do over a period of time. From month to month workers shape their roles in different ways; informally, employees come to do more or less than the class specifications prescribe. Individual personality in part accounts for this; changing demands on an agency and consequent adaptation by bureaucrats also promote inaccuracy. Whatever the precise reason, bureaucrats do modify their roles which in turn leads to them being mislabeled. Because of this tendency, prescriptive writings emphasize that personnel officials must be zealous information gatherers. Only if a personnel agency regularly checks to ascertain that employees are doing what their class specifications prescribe and appropriately relabels bureaucrats, will the formal class label be descriptive of behavior. Unless the formal class labels remain accurate, officials will find it impossible to realize "equal pay for equal work."

Percentage counts more than amount. In addition to prescribing up-to-date classification, the equity principle leads to an emphasis on uniform rate increases for employees. In this way, officials can preserve proper ratios among classes. (The assumption is, of course, that officials know what these ratios are and have established them.) One analyst expresses a typical commitment to this prescription when he argues:

> The pay plan administrator must, at all costs, resist the tendency to grant salary increases in terms of flat dollar amounts, or to grant increases only to the lower part of the salary range. As we pointed out earlier, this approach tends to compress salary ranges at the top and penalizes the upper level of administrative and professional employees, who are the key people in assuring the success of the jurisdiction's

[34] Stahl, *Public Personnel Administration*, p. 167.

objectives. Never permit yourself to think in terms of anything but percentage increases. The other may be forced upon you, but by all means go down with all flags flying.[35]

The message, then, is clear: avoid dollar increases because they upset existing pay relationships. Equal percentage increases for everyone will maintain existing salary ratios.

This concern with uniform rate increases has also marked some of the prescriptive literature dealing with collective bargaining. One Brookings Institution study, for instance, suggests that if "bargaining units are numerous and compete for employees in closely related occupations, differences in pay settlements may reflect differences in the strength of unions more than differences in work performed. Each union is perfectly willing to accept higher settlements for its own members but outraged if other unions get more." Going further, the study notes that "the problem of equity . . . is reduced if a large union bargains on behalf of its locals. . . ."[36] From the standpoint of the equity principle, then, dealing with many employee groups who are competing with one another is undesirable. Better to deal with a larger union which is more secure. In this way, rate increases will be more uniform and the equity principle will be served.

"Equal pay for equal work," is then, central to much of the writing concerning pay allocation in government. In terms of more precise prescriptions, the equal pay commitment leads prescriptive writers to support accurate classification and rate increases which maintain proper pay ratios.

The limits to equal pay. Many of the recommendations derived from "equal pay for equal work" have little appeal to city officials. Consider, for instance, the admonition to keep all positions accurately classified. If officials took this dictum seriously they would consume inordinate amounts of time. Classification structures, after all, tend toward inaccuracy. Moreover, few players in the classification game have much incentive to counteract the tendency toward imprecision especially when it would result in downgrading. Department heads

[35] Ocheltree, "Keeping the Pay Plan Current," p. 109.
[36] Stanley, *Managing Local Government,* pp. 167-168.

and their subordinates see little reason to suggest that a slot be pushed down to a lower class. When downgrading occurs, the agency head forfeits a higher level position that has more skill associated with it and faces the prospect of dealing with unhappy subordinates. Then too, the bureaucrat who would be (or is being) downgraded dislikes the idea because it costs him status, money, and perhaps, authority. Nor is a personnel director highly motivated to fight for accurate labeling through constant inspection of department activities. Even if the director had the staff necessary to undertake such surveillance, he would not do so. Constantly checking up on employee behavior could cost him prestige with departments as he earned a reputation for being a meddler. Overall, then, accurate classification, the keystone of "equal pay for equal work," has few friends. To be sure, a chief executive has some interest in precise labeling because it contributes to his supply of information and can reduce payment of "excessive" salaries. These benefits are, however, usually insufficient to justify the effort required to keep the classification structure constantly up to date.

Like the exhortation to maintain an accurate class structure, the recommendation to increase salaries by the same rate has limited appeal to officials. A mayor or city manager sees little point in worrying about whether all classes receive the same percentage increase. Whether patrolmen win a 10 percent increment while electricians receive 5 percent is far less important than the overall cost of the increase. If the chief executive can save money and still stay competitive in the labor market, it matters little to him whether some employees received a greater percentage pay boost than others.

For similar reasons a mayor or city manager will often reject the prescription to negotiate with a few employee leaders who represent clearly defined segments of the rank and file. Although many prescriptive theorists point to the importance of this strategy in fostering uniform rate increases, a chief executive frequently prefers to encourage competition among a number of employee groups instead. Rather than immediately holding employee elections to clarify which leaders are to represent certain classes of bureaucrats, a mayor or city manager finds it beneficial to procrastinate. By postponing the elections, he can encourage competition among groups trying hard to organize the same employees. While this untidy competitive situation repels some supporters of equal pay for equal work, a chief executive tends to see the situation in another light: such competition will on occasion permit him to divide and rule. With comparable bureaucrats split in their allegiances to two or more employee groups, each group tends to be weaker in dealing with the mayor or manager. During bargaining, no one union or association can claim to represent all the organized employees in a class (for example, all janitors). As a result, employee leaders cannot as easily impress the chief executive when they threaten to strike. Since the competing groups are unlikely to cooperate in a walk-out, top officials become more confident that a withdrawal of service will involve only a portion of the employees in a given class.

A divide and rule strategy can, then, save a manager or mayor money. Often city officials fare less well when they bargain with the police and fire leaderships which are not usually in competition with other employee groups and which can honestly claim to represent all bureaucrats in certain classes. Thus, negotiating with one big union or working to eliminate competition among employee organizations may promote more uniform rate increases, but it may also be the more expensive strategy to follow.

Some of the key recommendations derived from the equal pay principle are, then, unappealing to officials. This is not to discount the value of the principle entirely. Many city officials would agree that all gardeners should have a similar pay schedule. Such a practice benefits a mayor or manager by reducing the complexity of the salary structure; it eliminates the need to calculate a new salary for each gardener who joins the city staff; it also forestalls complaints by unhappy employees and impedes salary discrimination on the basis of race, sex, or other criteria.[37] While paying employees in the same occupational roles roughly the same amount (a more limited objective than "equal pay for equal work") may have a firm rationale,

---

[37] I in no way intend that my critique of "equal pay for equal work" justify discrimination against women or racial minorities. My point is that there are other more direct and succinct principles which we can use to fight race and sex bias.

it is nonetheless difficult to understand why a chief executive should worry about the ratio of gardener salaries to those of semi-skilled laborers. Nor is it clear that a mayor or manager should spend time thinking about pay ratios in a career line. Perhaps a supervisor should make more than those directly beneath him in the hierarchy in order to motivate lower echelon employees to seek advancement; but why should the manager worry about sustaining a precise ratio?

In fact there are good reasons for a chief executive not to pay much attention to ratios. To do so would create additional uncertainty for him. Salary calculations would become more complex; not only would the manager or mayor have to worry about keeping down the cost of a settlement; he would also have to ascertain whether the package he negotiated would foster "proper" pay relationships among classes. Compounding the calculation problem would be the absence of a ready scorecard which would tell the chief executive whether existing pay ratios were appropriate and class specifications accurate.

In espousing the equal pay principle, then, prescriptive writers have paid insufficient attention to the concerns which the politics of pay generates. Such concerns frequently include a desire to economize, to stay competitive in the labor market, to keep vital city services flowing without disruption and, less importantly, to pay workers in the same class roughly the same amount of money. When they assess policy proposals and offer recommendations prescriptive theorists would be wise to take this mix of objectives into account. In cities where unions are strong, for instance, theorists could fruitfully focus on measures likely to make the executive an effective defender of economy. In the few places where unions and associations are weak, prescriptive theorists could orient themselves toward the problem of how a city manager or mayor can keep salaries of his employees competitive with those paid elsewhere. Nor can the prescriptive literature safely ignore those cases where employee groups are a force in electoral politics. When focusing on such systems, condemnation is less appropriate than the analysis of feasible strategies that a chief executive can use to cope with the situation.

As with merit validation, then, recommendations derived

from the equal pay principle are generally not attractive to city officials. These two principles are not isolated examples. The literature is replete with prescriptions like them.[38]

Serious analysts of personnel policy cannot, then, afford to ignore the politics of jobs. Recommendations for change are after all, hypotheses.[39] They assert that if we do X there will be certain modifications in Y, and perhaps some other variables as well. Unless one understands the politics of personnel, however, such hypothesizing is an extremely precarious venture. Policy changes are more likely than ever to produce costs and ramifications which no one anticipates. Moreover, many proposals will be infeasible.

Analysis of personnel policy which is sensitive to political costs and benefits is important not only for a few specialists in an arcane field. Our capacity to deal intelligently with the most basic problems of city government hangs in the balance. The challenge to city hall which mushroomed during the turbulent sixties heightened interest in urban bureaucracies. Some saw city agencies as prime culprits, perpetuating conditions which foster deprivation and alienation from local institutions. Recommendations for making local agencies more "responsive" or "effective" soon became a dime a dozen. Ultimately our capacity to assess these recommendations and generate creative options depends on many things. One critical prerequisite to success is, however, an understanding of why city governments presently behave as they do. Insight into the politics of jobs is indispensable for such understanding. Thus, questions concerning the creation and implementation of personnel policy intersect with basic questions of governance.

[38] Consider, for instance, some of the following prescriptions found in Stahl, *Public Personnel Administration* (New York: Harper and Row, 1962); be deliberate about objectives in the use of human resources (p. 13); avoid residence requirements in recruitment (pp. 58-59); extend merit recruitment systems (p. 27); keep down the number of provisional appointments (p. 103); do not use performance evaluations as instruments of discipline (p. 274); focus on staff training and development (p. 279).

[39] See Martin Landau, "On the Concept of a Self-Correcting Organization," *Public Administration Review* 33 (November/December 1973): 539.

Appendix

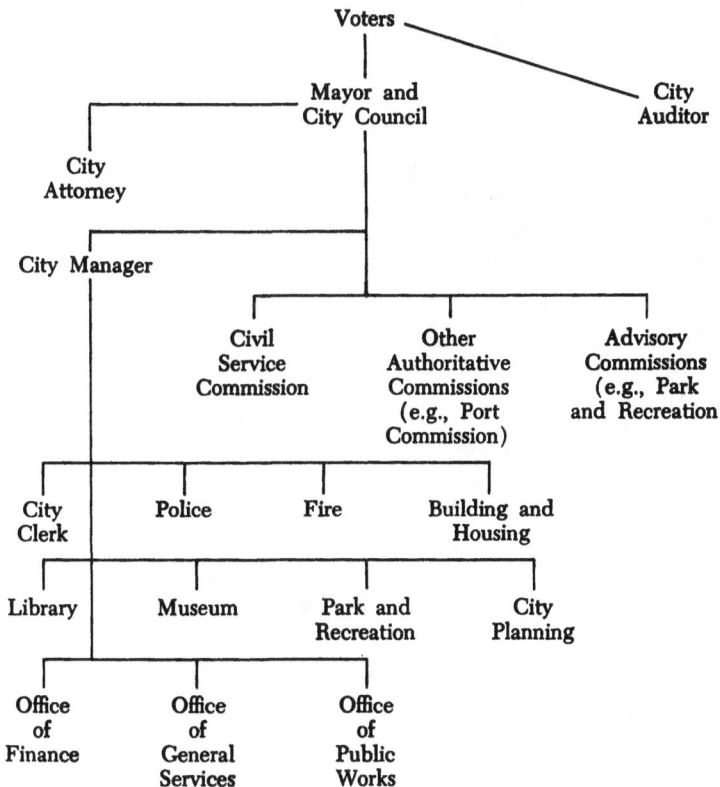

Bibliography

BOOKS AND MONOGRAPHS

Alex, Nicholas. *Black in Blue*. New York: Appleton-Century Crofts, 1969.

Altshuler, Alan. *The City Planning Process: A Political Analysis*. Ithaca, N.Y.: Cornell University Press, 1970.

———. *Community Control: The Black Demand for Participation in Large American Cities*. New York: Pegasus, 1970.

Banfield, Edward C. *The Unheavenly City*. Boston: Little, Brown, 1970.

———, and Wilson, James Q. *City Politics*. New York: Vintage Press, 1963.

Barnard, Chester F. *The Functions of the Executive*. Cambridge: Harvard University Press, 1966.

Baum, Bernard H. *Decentralization of Authority in a Bureaucracy*. Englewood Cliffs N.J.: Prentice-Hall, 1961.

Berg, Ivar. *Education and Jobs: The Great Training Robbery*. Boston: Beacon Press, 1971.

Braybrooke, David, and Lindblom, Charles. *A Strategy of Decision*. New York: Free Press, 1970.

Churchman, C. West. *The Systems Approach*. New York: Dell Publishing, 1968.

Cyert, Richard, and March, James G. *A Behavioral Theory of the Firm*. Englewood Cliffs, N.J.: Prentice-Hall, 1963.

Donovan, J. J. *Recruitment and Selection in the Public Service*. Chicago: Public Personnel Association, 1968.

Downs, Anthony. *Inside Bureaucracy*. Boston: Little, Brown, 1967.

Etzioni, Amitai. *Modern Organizations*. Englewood Cliffs, N.J.: Prentice Hall, 1964.

Fenno, Richard F. *The Power of the Purse: Appropriations Politics in Congress*. Boston: Little, Brown, 1966.

———. *The President's Cabinet*. New York: Random House, 1959.

Glaser, Barney G., and Strauss, Anselm L. *The Discovery of Grounded Theory.* Chicago: Aldine Publishing, 1967.

Goodwin, Leonard. *Do The Poor Want To Work?* Washington, D.C.: Brookings Institution, 1972.

Gosnell, Harold F. *Machine Politics: Chicago Model.* Chicago: University of Chicago Press, 1968.

Gouldner, Alvin W. *Patterns of Industrial Bureaucracy.* New York: Free Press, 1964.

Harrison, Bennett. *Education, Training, and the Urban Ghetto.* Baltimore: Johns Hopkins University Press, 1972.

Hawkins, Brett W. *Politics and Urban Policies.* New York and Indianapolis: Bobbs-Merrill, 1971.

Horton, Raymond. *Municipal Labor Relations in New York City: Lessons of the Lindsay-Wagner Years.* New York: Praeger Publishers, 1973.

Ilchman, Warren F., and Uphoff, Norman Thomas. *The Political Economy of Change.* Berkeley: University of California Press, 1969.

International City Managers Association. *Municipal Yearbook, 1970.* Chicago: International City Managers Association, 1970.

Irish, Richard K. *Go Hire Yourself An Employer.* Garden City, N.Y.: Anchor Books, 1973.

Jencks, Christopher, et al. *Inequality.* New York: Basic Books, 1972.

Kaufman, Herbert. *The Forest Ranger.* Baltimore: Johns Hopkins University Press, 1960.

Liebow, Elliot. *Tally's Corner.* Boston: Little, Brown, 1967.

Lowi, Theodore J. *At the Pleasure of the Mayor: Patronage and Power in New York City 1898-1958.* Glencoe, Ill.: Free Press, 1964.

McFarland, Andrew. *Power and Leadership in Pluralist Systems.* Stanford: Stanford University Press, 1969.

Machiavelli, Niccolò. *The Prince.* Edited by Mark Musa. New York: St. Martin's Press, 1964.

Macy, Jr., John W. *Public Service, The Human Side of Government.* New York: Harper and Row, 1972.

Meltsner, Arnold J. *The Politics of City Revenue.* Berkeley: University of California Press, 1971.

Mosher, Fredrick C. *Democracy and the Public Service.* New York: Oxford University Press, 1968.

Nigro, Felix A. *Public Personnel Administration.* New York: Holt, Rinehart and Winston, 1959.

Parkinson, C. Northcoate. *Parkinson's Law.* New York: Ballantine Books, 1964 edition.

Pressman, Jeffrey L., and Wildavsky, Aaron B. *Implementation.* Berkeley: University of California Press, 1973.

Riesman, David, with Nathan Glazer and Reuel Denney. *The Lonely Crowd.* New Haven: Yale University Press, 1963.

Riordon, William L. *Plunkitt of Tammany Hall.* New York: E. P. Dutton, 1963.

Rogers, David. *The Management of Big Cities: Interest Groups and Social Change.* Beverly Hills, Cal.: Sage Publications, 1971.

Royko, Mike. *Boss.* New York: New American Library, 1971.

Sadacca, Robert. *The Validity and Discriminatory Impact of The Federal

Service Entrance Examination. Washington, D.C.: Urban Institute, 1971.

Sayre, Wallace S., and Kaufman, Herbert. *Governing New York City.* New York: W. W. Norton, 1965.

Schattschneider, E. E. *The Semi-Sovereign People.* New York: Holt, Rinehart and Winston, 1964.

Schelling, Thomas C. *The Strategy of Conflict.* New York: Oxford University Press, 1963.

Seidman, Harold. *Politics, Position and Power: The Dynamics of Federal Organization.* New York: Oxford University Press, 1970.

Shafritz, Jay M. *Position Classification: A Behavioral Analysis for the Public Service.* New York: Praeger Publishers, 1973.

Sheppard, Harold L., and Belitsky, A. Harvey. *The Job Hunt.* Baltimore: Johns Hopkins University Press, 1966.

Sherwood, Frank P. *A City Manager Tried to Fire His Police Chief.* Indianapolis: Bobbs-Merrill, 1963.

———, and Markey, Beatrice. *The Mayor and the Fire Chief: The Fight Over Integrating the Los Angeles Fire Department.* Birmingham: University of Alabama, 1959.

Simon, Herbert A. *Administrative Behavior.* New York: Free Press, 1957 edition.

Skolnick, Jerome H. *Justice Without Trial.* New York: John Wiley, 1967.

Stahl, O. Glenn. *Public Personnel Administration.* New York: Harper and Row, 1962.

———. *Public Personnel Administration.* New York: Harper and Row, 1971.

Stanley, David T. *Managing Local Government Under Union Pressure.* Washington, D.C.: Brookings Institution, 1971.

Taylor, Frederick Winslow. *The Principles of Scientific Management.* New York: W. W. Norton, 1967.

Taylor, Vernon. *Employment of the Disadvantaged in the Public Service.* Chicago: Public Personnel Association, 1971.

Thompson, James D. *Organizations in Action.* New York: McGraw Hill, 1967.

Tolchin, Martin, and Tolchin, Susan. *To the Victor: Political Patronage from the Clubhouse to the White House.* New York: Random House, 1971.

Waldo, Dwight. *The Administrative State.* New York: Ronald Press, 1948.

Wilcock, Richard, and Franke, Walter H. *Unwanted Workers.* New York: Free Press, 1963.

Wildavsky, Aaron. *The Politics of the Budgetary Process.* Boston: Little, Brown, 1964.

Wilensky, Harold L. *Organizational Intelligence.* New York: Basic Books Inc., 1967.

Wilson, James Q. *Political Organizations.* New York: Basic Books, 1973.

———. *Varieties of Police Behavior.* Cambridge: Harvard University Press, 1968.

ARTICLES

Abbot, Frank C. "The Cambridge City Manager." In *Public Administration and Policy Development: A Case Book,* edited by Harold Stein. New York: Harcourt, Brace, 1952, pp. 580-617.

Adrian, Charles R., and Press, Charles. "Decision Costs in Coalition Formation." *American Political Science Review* 62 (June 1968): 556-563.

Bass, Alan R. "Personnel Selection and Evaluation." In *Management of the Urban Crisis: Government and the Behavioral Sciences,* edited by Stanley E. Seashore and Robert J. McNeill. New York: The Free Press, 1971, pp. 299-341.

Bowen, David; Feuille, Peter; and Strauss, George. "The California Experience." In *Unionization of Municipal Employees,* edited by Robert H. Connery and William V. Farr. New York: Columbia University Press, 1970, pp. 107-123.

Clark, Peter B., and Wilson, James Q. "Incentive Systems: A Theory of Organizations." In *The National Administrative System: Selected Readings,* edited by Dean L. Yarwood. New York: John Wiley, 1971, pp. 274-296.

Coates, Charles H., and Pellegrin, Ronald J. "Executives and Supervisors: Informal Factors in Differential Bureaucratic Promotion." *Administrative Science Quarterly* 2 (September 1957): 200-215.

Collett, Merrill J. "Building the Framework of the Pay Play." In *Practical Guidelines to Public Pay Administration,* edited by Kenneth O. Warner and J. J. Donovan. Chicago: Public Personnel Association, II, 1965, pp. 30-40.

Downs, Anthony. "Why the Government Budget Is Too Small in a Democracy." *World Politics* 12 (June 1960): 541-563.

"Employment Testing: The Aftermath of Griggs v. Duke Power Co." *Columbia Law Review* 72 (May 1972): 900-925.

Ermer, Virginia B. "Housing Inspection in Baltimore: Vermin, Mannequins, and Beer Bottles." In *Blacks and Bureaucracy,* edited by Virginia B. Ermer and John H. Strange. New York: Thomas Y. Crowell, 1972, pp. 82-93.

Eulau, Heinz, and Eyestone, Robert. "Policy Maps of City Councils and Policy Outcomes: A Developmental Analysis." *American Political Science Review* 62 (March 1968): 124-143.

Fainstein, Norman I., and Fainstein, Susan S. "Innovation in Urban Bureaucracies: Clients and Change." *American Behavioral Scientist* 15 (March/April 1972): 511-532.

Gallas, Nesta M. "Toward a Theory of Selection." In *Recruitment and Selection in the Public Service,* edited by J. J. Donovan. Chicago: Public Personnel Association, 1968, pp. 22-44.

Garlatti, Richard L. "Police Recruiting: Success Story Written in Philadelphia." *Public Personnel Review* 32 (April 1971): 101-105.

Gergen, Kenneth J. "Assessing the Leverage Points in the Process of Policy Formation." In *The Study of Policy Formation,* edited by Raymond A. Bauer and Kenneth J. Gergen. New York: Free Press, 1968, pp. 181-203.

Goode, William J. "The Protection of the Inept." *American Sociological Review* 32 (February 1967): 5-19.

Greer, Edward. "The Liberation of Gary, Indiana." *Trans-action* 8 (January 1971): 30-39.

Groves, W. Eugene. "Police in the Ghetto." In *Perspectives on Urban Politics,* edited by Jay S. Goodman. Boston: Allyn and Bacon, 1970, pp. 169-198.

Halperin, Morton H. "Why Bureaucrats Play Games." *Foreign Policy* 2 (Spring 1971): 70-90.

Harmon, Michael M. "Normative Theory and Public Administration: Some Suggestions for a Redefinition of Administrative Responsibility." In *Toward a New Public Administration,* edited by Frank Marini. Scranton, Pa.: Chandler Publishing, 1971, pp. 172-185.

Herson, Lawrence. "The Lost Word of Municipal Government." *American Political Science Review* 51 (June 1957): 330-345.

Holden, Matthew Jr. "Imperialism in Bureaucracy." *American Political Science Review* 55 (December 1966): 943-951.

Jensen, Ollie. "Cultural Bias in Selection." *Public Personnel Review* 27 (April 1966): 125-130.

Jones, Roger W. "The Merit System, Politics, and Political Maturity." *Public Personnel Review* 25 (January 1964): 28-34.

Landau, Martin. "Redundancy, Rationality and the Problem of Duplication and Overlap." *Public Administration Review* 29 (July-August 1969): 346-358.

———. "On the Concept of a Self-Correcting Organization." *Public Administration Review* 33 (November/December 1973): 533-542.

Levine, Jerome M., and Murphy, Gardner. "The Learning and Forgetting of Controversial Material." In *Readings in Social Psychology,* edited by Eleanor E. Maccoby, Theodore M. Newcomb, Eugene L. Hartley. New York: Holt, Rinehart and Winston, 1958, pp. 94-101.

Lijphart, Arend. "Comparative Politics and the Comparative Method." *American Political Science Review* 65 (September 1971): 682-693.

Lipsky, Michael. "Protest as a Political Resource." *American Political Science Review* 62 (December 1968): 1144-1158.

———. "Street-Level Bureaucracy and the Analysis of Urban Reform." In *Blacks and Bureaucracy,* edited by Virginia B. Ermer and John H. Strange. New York: Thomas Y. Crowell, 1972, pp. 171-184.

Long, Norton. "Power and Administration." In *Bureaucratic Power in National Politics,* edited by Francis E. Rourke. Boston: Little, Brown, 1965, pp. 14-23.

Lowi, Theodore J. "Forward." In *Machine Politics: Chicago Model,* by Harold F. Gosnell. Chicago: University of Chicago Press, 1968, pp. v-xviii.

McNamara, John H. "Uncertainties in Police Work: The Relevance of Police Recruits' Backgrounds and Training." In *The Police: Six Sociological Essays,* edited by David J. Bordua. New York: John Wiley, 1967, pp. 163-250.

Mann, Dean. "The Selection of Federal Political Executives." *American Political Science Review* 57 (March 1964): 81-99.

Miewald, Robert D. "On Teaching Public Personnel Administration: A Weberian Perspective." *Western Political Quarterly* 36 (March 1973): 97-108.

———. "Political Science and Public Personnel Administration." *Public Personnel Review* 30 (July 1969): 178-180.

Moore, Clay L. Jr.; MacNaughton, John F.; Osburn, Hobart G. "Ethnic Differences Within an Industrial Selection Battery." *Personnel Psychology* 22 (Winter 1969): 473-482.

Ocheltree, Keith. "Keeping the Pay Plan Current." In *Practical Guidelines to Public Pay Administration,* edited by Kenneth O. Warner and J. J. Donovan. Chicago: Public Personnel Association, II, 1965, pp. 100-110.

Pressman, Jeffrey L. "Preconditions of Mayoral Leadership." *American Political Science Review* 66 (June 1972): 511-524.

Prewitt, Kenneth. "Political Ambitions, Volunteerism, and Electoral Accountability.' *American Political Science Review* 64 (March 1970): 5-17.

Rosenbloom, David H. "Equal Employment Opportunity: Another Strategy." *Personnel Administration/Public Personnel Review* (July/August 1972): 38-41.

Savas, E. S., and Ginsburg, Sigmund S. "The Civil Service—A Meritless System?" *The Public Interest* 32 (Summer 1973): 70-85.

Scheuer, William. "Performance Testing in New Jersey." *Good Government* (Spring 1970): 5-15.

Sharpless, Jr., Norman R. "Public Personnel Selection—An Overview." In *Recruitment and Selection in the Public Service,* edited by J. J. Donovan. Chicago: Public Personnel Association, 1968, pp. 1-21.

Simon, Herbert; Kozmetsky, George; Guetzkow, Harold; Tyndall, Gordon. "Management Uses of Figures." In *Public Budgeting and Finance,* edited by Robert T. Golembiewski. Itasca, Ill.: F. E. Peacock Publishers, 1970, pp. 15-23.

Thomas, William C. Jr. "Generalist vs. Specialist: Careers in a Municipal Bureaucracy." *Public Administration Review* 21 (Winter 1961): 8-15.

Wagner, Donald. "Compensation Seen Through Management Eyes." In *Practical Guidelines to Public Pay Administration,* edited by Kenneth O. Warner and J. J. Donovan. Chicago: Public Personnel Association, II, 1965, pp. 14-29.

Wentworth, Kenneth L. "Development and Use of Written Tests." In *Recruitment and Selection in the Public Service,* edited by J. J. Donovan. Chicago: Public Personnel Association, 1968, pp. 112-122.

Wildavsky, Aaron, with Singer, Max. "A Third World Averaging Strategy." In *The Revolt Against the Masses and Other Essays on Politics and Public Policy,* edited by Aaron Wildavsky. New York: Basic Books, 1971, pp. 463-482.

Wilson, Hugh Steven. "A Second Look at Griggs v. Duke Power Company: Ruminations on Job Testing, Discrimination and the Role of the Federal Courts." *Virginia Law Review* 58 (1972): 844-874.

Wilson, James Q. "The Police in the Ghetto." In *The Police and the Community,* edited by Robert F. Steadman. Baltimore: Johns Hopkins University Press, pp. 51-90.

Wilson, Woodrow. "The Study of Administration." *Political Science Quarterly* 56 (December 1941): 481-506.

Wolfinger, Raymond. "Why Political Machines Have Not Withered Away and Other Revisionist Thoughts." *Journal of Politics* 34 (May 1972): 365-398.

PUBLIC DOCUMENTS

Bryan, Robert G. "Minority Employment in State and Local Governments." *Monthly Labor Review,* Bureau of Labor Statistics 92 (November 1969): 67-70.

Germann, A. C. "Recruitment, Selection, Promotion and Civil Service." United States President's Commission on Law Enforcement and the Administration of Justice, Washington, D.C.: U.S. Government Printing Office, 1967.

Iacobelli, John L. "A Survey of Employer Attitudes Toward Training the Disadvantaged." *Monthly Labor Review,* Bureau of Labor Statistics 93 (June 1970): 51-55.

Margolis, Richard. *Who Will Wear The Badge?* U.S. Commission on Civil Rights. Washington, D.C.: U.S. Government Printing Office, 1970.

Oakland City Charter. *The Charter of the City of Oakland In Effect July 1, 1911, prepared and proposed by the Board of Freeholders Elected July 6, 1910, as Amended To and Including June 8, 1953.*

Oakland City Charter. *Proposed New Charter of the City of Oakland and Alternative Propositions to be Voted on at the Special Municipal Election Consolidated With the General Election to be Held November 5, 1968.*

Oakland City Planning Department. *Options For Oakland,* December, 1969, written on grant from HUD.

Oakland Finance Department. *City of Oakland Tentative Budget, 1967-68.*

————. *City of Oakland Revised Preliminary Budget, 1966-67.*

————. *City of Oakland Tentative Budget, Fiscal Year 1968-69.*

————. *City of Oakland Preliminary Budget, Fiscal Year 1969-70.*

————. *City of Oakland Preliminary Budget, 1970-71.*

————. *City of Oakland Preliminary Budget, Fiscal Year 1971-72.*

San Francisco Committee on Crime. *A Report on the San Francisco Police Department,* Parts I and II. San Francisco: Western Star Press, 1971.

Stone, Morris. "Why Arbitrators Reinstate Discharged Employees." *Monthly Labor Review,* Bureau of Labor Statistics, 92 (October 1969): 47-50.

U.S. Advisory Commission on Civil Disorders. *Report of the National Advisory Commission on Civil Disorders.* New York: Bantam, 1968.

U.S. Commission on Civil Rights. *The Federal Civil Rights Enforcement Effort: One Year Later.* Washington, D.C.: U.S. Government Printing Office, 1971.

U.S. Department of Commerce. *Pocket Data Book USA, 1971.* Washington, D.C.: U.S. Government Printing Office, 1971.

————. *Statistical Abstract of the United States.* Washington, D.C.: U.S. Government Printing Office, 1971.

U.S. Supreme Court. "Griggs v. Duke Power Co." *U.S. Supreme Court Reports,* Lawyers' Edition, Vol. 28 L Ed 2d #1, April 1971, pp. 158-167. 158-167.

UNPUBLISHED MATERIALS

Ahart, Alan M. "An Economic and Demographic Study of Oakland, California, 1960-1966, With Comparisons to Other Cities" (student paper for Wildavsky, 1970).

Collins, Randall Alfred. "Education and Employment: A Study in the Dynamics of Stratification." Unpublished Ph. D. dissertation, University of California, Berkeley, 1969.

Harrison, Bennett. "Ghetto Employment and the Model Cities Program." Paper presented at the American Political Science Association Convention, Washington, D.C., 1972.

Hawley, Willis D. "Dealing With Organizational Rigidity in Public Schools: A Theoretical Perspective." Paper presented at the American Political Science Association Convention, Chicago, Ill. 1971.

Lockard, Duane. "Value, Theory and Research in State and Local Politics." Paper presented at the American Political Science Association Convention, Los Angeles, 1970.

May, Judith. "Budgeting in the Street and Engineering Department." Unpublished paper, University of California, Berkeley, 1968.

———. "Progressives and the Poor: An Analytic History of Oakland." Unpublished paper, University of California, Berkeley, 1970.

Meltsner, Arnold, and Wildavsky, Aaron. "Leave City Budgeting Alone! A Survey, Case History and Recommendation for Reform." Unpublished paper, University of California, Berkeley, 1969.

Muir, William K., Jr. "The Development of Policemen." Paper presented at the American Political Science Association Convention, Los Angeles, 1970.

Seidler, Murray. "Manpower Training and the Conquest of Poverty: A Detroit Case Study." Paper presented at the American Political Science Association Convention, Los Angeles, 1970.

Index

Alameda County as employer, 114

Alameda County Central Labor Council, 62

Alameda County Legal Aid Society: sues city over hiring, 116; deals with city officials, 119, 123

Alameda County Superior Court, 158

Association of Bay Area Governments, 116

Averaging strategy, 65–66

Background requirements: role, 92; differences among departments, 93–95; efforts of department heads to raise, 95–97; impact of manpower scarcity on, 97–98; resistance to increased requirements, 99–100; background investigations, 100–101; lowered, 133–135

Berkeley Barb, 155

Black Panther headquarters, 98

Brookings Institution, 189

California Council on Criminal Justice, 123

California Institute of Technology, 87

California State College, Fresno, 89

Case analyses, uses of, 9–11

City council. *See* Elected officials

City manager, Oakland: authority, 16; concern with fiscal matters, 21–22, 41, 43; reluctance to add manpower, 22, 25, 43; reliance on Finance Office, 23; leverage over budget, 24, 43; induces self-inflicted reductions, 28–31; concern with position classification, 31–33; philosophy of organization, 33–34; role in manpower imperialism, 37; factors shaping manpower concessions, 41–43; attempts holding action, 47–48; establishes Meet and Confer Committee, 52; resists compulsory arbitration, 53; concedes little time to employees, 54; divides and rules, 54–55; keeps issue scope narrow, 55–56; reduces uncertainty over pay, 63; hoards pay information, 64–65; concedes merit pay increase, 65–66; grants pay boosts, 69–71; limited role in recruitment, 71; favors exempt positions, 76; in removal arena, 148

Civil Rights Act of 1964, 112

Civil Service Commission: handles employee appeals, 31, 156–159; authority, 16–17, 145; role in classification, 32, 152; resists exempt positions, 77; approves publicity plan, 82; dependence on personnel director, 85; postpones decision on background requirements, 98; supports written tests, 102; deals with minority leaders, 111, 116–121; view of fire department, 131, 135; disappointment over minority hiring, 137; discourages firing, 150–151, 154

www.ingramcontent.com/pod-product-compliance
Lightning Source LLC
Chambersburg PA
CBHW052004270326
41929CB00015B/2780